Inuit TakugatsaliuKatiget
On Inuit Cinema

Inuit TakugatsaliuKatiget

On Inuit Cinema

EDITED BY MARK DAVID TURNER

MEMORIAL UNIVERSITY PRESS

Copyright of the collective work Mark David Turner © 2022

Copyright of each individual chapter contained herein belongs to the respective author(s) of such work © 2022. All such works are reproduced herein with permission.

All rights reserved. No part of this publication may be reproduced, stored in a retrieval system, or transmitted in any form or by any means, without the prior written consent of the publisher.

A CIP record for this book is available from Library and Archives Canada.

Cover artwork, illustration of Inuit Territories: Jessica Winters
Copy editing: Sandy Newton
Cover design, page design, and layout: Graham Blair

Published by Memorial University Press
Memorial University of Newfoundland and Labrador
P.O. Box 4200
St. John's, NL A1C 5S7
www.memorialuniversitypress.ca

Printed in Canada

28 27 26 25 24 23 22 22   1 2 3 4 5 6 7 8

For my parents, David Turner and Patricia Sullivan.

Contents

Nakummesuak	ix
A Note About Inuit Languages	xiii
Inuit Territories: Lands, Ice, and Waters	xvi
1. INTRODUCTION	1
Interview Process and Structure	6
Inuit/Cinema	9
2. INTERVIEWS	
Arnait Ikajuqtigiit | Arnait Video Productions	14
Stephen Agluvak Puskas	58
A Checklist for Making Film	
In and With Inuit Communities	79
asinnajaq	84
Inuk Silis Høegh	109
OKâlaKatiget Society	132
Fran Williams	133
Sarah Abel	152
3. MOMENTS IN INUIT CINEMA	167
4. FILMOGRAPHY	181
Image Credits	225
Bibliography	227
Index	237

Nakummesuak

The idea for this book came from the film programs offered during the 2016 Inuit Studies Conference in St. John's, Newfoundland and Labrador, Canada, and its two associated events, iNuit Blanche and the katingavik inuit arts festival. I am grateful to the following film artists, producers, advocates, and interlocutors:

Sarah Abel
Alethea Arnaquq-Baril
Lucassie Arragutainiaq
asinnajaq (Isabella Rose Weetaluktuk)
Susan Avingaq
Gary Baikie
Helen Balanoff
Kat Baulu
Kathleen Blanchard
Guy Bordin
Jamie Brake
Amélie Breton
Marie-Hélène Cousineau
Ashlee Cunsolo
Randy Edmunds
Echo Henoche
Amy Hudson
Patricia Johnston

Sheila Katsak
Arn Keeling
Simone Kohlmeister
Emily Kudlak
Johnny Kudluaro
Tanya Lukin Linklter
Mikisoq Lynge
Joar Nango
Malve Petersmann
Derrick Pottle
Stephen Agluvak Puskas
Sophie Quevillon
France Rivet
Hans Rollmann
Inez Shiwak
Jamie Snook
Frank Tester
Nancy Wachowich

....
Labrador Inuttitut/Inuttut for "thank-you very much."

Through the events they created and the conversations that followed them, these people helped me to broaden my understanding of what cinema is and how it might work. I owe particular debts to Heather Igloliorte and Britt Gallpen, my iNuit Blanche co-curators, as well as to Carolyn Chong, who was the Manager of the katingavik inuit arts festival.

I am grateful to Tom Gordon for his support and mentorship. When he first encouraged me to develop this book, he was serving as the inaugural Principal Investigator for *Tradition and Transition Among the Labrador Inuit*, a research partnership funded by the Social Sciences and Humanities Research Council of Canada (SSHRC), the Nunatsiavut Government, and Memorial University. This book has benefited from financial and administrative support provided by *Tradition and Transition* and I am grateful to Lisa Rankin, the partnership's second and final Principal Investigator, as well as to Andrea Quigley, the Special Project Coordinator. *Tradition and Transition* also secured a meticulous transcriber in Catherine Mitsuk. All of the interviews in this book (with the exception of the interviews with Arnait Video Productions) were first rendered by her. I am also grateful for supports from the SSHRC-funded project *Gatherings: Archival and Oral Histories of Canadian Performance*, led by another colleague and friend, Stephen Johnson.

In preparing these interviews, all contributors shared their time and their wisdom freely. And while their work reveals itself in the eloquence of their printed words, there is more to acknowledge. The interviews with the members of Arnait Video Productions would not have been possible without the tireless efforts of Blandina Makkik. Her work as interviewer, transcriber, and translator is peerless and I am grateful to Marie-Hélène Cousineau for suggesting Blandina to serve in these roles. Marie-Hélène was essential in coordinating edits to the interview after the peer-review process. And I am grateful to Elizabeth Qulaut for proofing the Inuktut in the final edited manuscript.

The interview with asinnajaq would not have been possible without Kat Baulu at the National Film Board of Canada, who also produced asinnajaq's 2017 film *Three Thousand*. Kat provided indispensable assistance at every phase of this interview, from running the "New Voices in Inuit Cinema" workshop during the 2016 Inuit Studies Conference that laid its groundwork through securing Jobie Weetaluktuk as interviewer, as well as coordinating the recording at the National Film Board's Montreal studio and even jumping in to help out in the interview with asinnajaq.

I owe a great debt to my friends at the OKâlaKatiget Society. Long before my professional relationship with them, they hosted me on numerous research trips, provided me with access to their archive, graciously answered all my questions, gave me space to work in, and, on one trip, provided me with a place to stay. In particular, I would like to thank former Executive Directors Sarah Leo and Morris Prokop, the current Executive Director Arlene Ikkusek, Bookkeeper/Administrator Bonnie Lyall, and President of the Board Carol Gear. Sarah Abel, Senior Television Producer and contributor to this book, has been beyond generous with her time and knowledge. For her, I am still learning to speak Nain. To Fran Williams, who worked as a Program Director and Executive Director with the OKâlaKatiget Society and is also a contributor here, I am grateful that I can call you a friend. Your table in Nain was one of my favourite places in the world. I look forward to visiting your table in Hopedale.

On issues regarding language, I benefited greatly from the wisdom of Douglas Wharram. On many occasions, he has helped me work through the nuance of Labrador Inuttitut/Inuttut. Because of him and the generosity of our mutual friend Joan Dicker, we were able to develop a title for this book that, I hope, is deferential to the nuance of Inuttitut/Inuttut.

At Memorial University, the Institute of Social and Economic Research (ISER) and Memorial University Press (MUP) have encouraged this project from its beginnings. I am grateful to Diane Tye, Director of ISER, for key supports during the COVID-19 pandemic. Fiona Polack, the Academic Editor at MUP, provided vital direction during a unique review process. Alison Carr, the Managing Editor at MUP, went well beyond the call in the administration of this project. Angela Power, Editorial Intern, assisted in proofing the Filmography. Sandy Newton's editing work was essential. The book has also benefited from a Publications Subvention grant from Memorial University's Research Grant and Contract Services.

I am deeply fortunate to have worked with several talented designers and artists on this book. Mark Bennett helped me develop a clear concept for the book's components. The concept was given life by Jessica Winters, who created the cover art and the illustration of Inuit territories, Graham Blair, who designed the final pages, and Alison Carr who provided guidance and support. The work of these people gives shape, structure, and texture to this book. I am in their debt.

Any errors that remain on these pages are mine.

I am grateful to the lands which have sustained me during this work and to stewards of those lands. Most of my work was completed in Toronto, the traditional territory of many nations including the Mississaugas of the Credit, the Anishnabeg, the Chippewa, the Haudenosaunee, and the Wendat Peoples. These lands are covered by Treaty 13 with the Mississaugas of the Credit. Some work I completed in Montreal, the traditional territory of the Kanien'kehá:ka Nation and a place that has long served as a site of meeting and exchange for many First Nations. Other work was conducted in my home, the island of Newfoundland, which is the ancestral homeland of the Beothuk and Mi'kmaq, as well as in Labrador, the ancestral homeland of the Inuit of Nunatsiavut and NunatuKavut, and the Innu of Nitassinan. Earlier, both Newfoundland and Labrador were the traditional territory of the Maritime Archaic and Dorset Peoples.

I am grateful to the Inuit, the stewards of vast amounts of land, water, and ice in the northern hemisphere of our planet. As we are learning, their stewardship has kept our planet safe. I am among those who live outside these lands, and I believe we must do better and follow their example.

Finally, I am grateful for Henry and Theodore, who challenge me to move beyond the limits of my thinking every day. And none of this would have been possible without Gillian, the greatest gift of all.

A Note About Inuit Languages

I am neither a linguist nor a speaker of an Inuit language. However, as Inuit voices are the focus of this book, a few words on Inuit languages are necessary.

Inuit languages are a family of related languages and dialects that developed in the northern part of the American state of Alaska, northern Canada (Inuit Nunangat[1]) and Greenland (Kalaallit Nunaat[2]). Broadly, these languages include Inupiaq (Alaska, Inuvialuit Nunangat), Inuvialuktun (Inuvialuit Nunangat, Yukon, and Northwest Territories), Inuinnaqtun (Nunavut), Inuktitut (Nunavut), Nunavimmiutut (Nunavik, Quebec), Nunatsiavummiutut (Nunatsiavut, Newfoundland and Labrador), and Kalaallisut (Kalaallit Nunaat). They are distinct from Yupik languages (Russia, Alaska) and the Chukchi language, spoken in Chukotka (Russia).

These languages and dialects are not always mutually intelligible, something naming conventions can make a little unclear. Inuit Tapiriit Kanatami, the national advocacy organization for Inuit in Canada, has resolved that "Inuktut" is "the most appropriate term to describe the Inuit language as a whole in Canada,"[3] moving away from the long-standing colloquial word for the Inuit language: Inuktitut. Inuktut encompasses Inuvialuktun, Inuinnaqtun, Inuktitut, Nunavimmiutut, and Nunatsiavummiutut, many of which can be subdivided further. For example, the word Nunatsiavummiutut means "in the manner of people

....

1. Inuit Nunangat (Canada) is subdivided into four regions, east to west: Nunatsiavut, Nunavik, Nunavut, and Inuvialuit Settlement Region (which is referred to hereafter as Inuvialuit Nunangat).

2. Hereafter, Kalaallit Nunaat is used.

3. "Approval of Inuktut Resolution."

from Nunatsiavut," so it applies to all Inuit languages and dialects spoken in that region. The dominant form of Inuktut in Nunatsiavut is currently Inuttitut (also known as Inuttut). Until recently, a separate dialect—Inuktut (distinct from Inuit Tapiriit Kanatami's term) and also known as Chorale—was spoken by Inuit in the area of the community of Rigolet.

To the east, it is common to refer to Kalaallisut as the "dialect" of Kalaallit Nunaat. But this word more accurately refers to the dialect of West Greenlandic, which is spoken by the majority of people in Kalaallit Nunaat. Inuktun, a separate dialect of Inuktut, is spoken in the northwest of Kalaallit Nunaat, and the Tunumiit oraasiat "dialect" is spoken in the east. A speaker of Tunumiit oraasiat would likely have a difficult time understanding a speaker of North Slope Iñupiaq (Inupiaq). And for many of the so-called regional dialects, a case could be made that they are separate languages.[4]

The approaches for how to represent words from Indigenous languages in English text are evolving. In this book, I've followed an established convention: non-English words are set in italicized type. For words that repeat frequently, the italics have been applied only at the first appearance. I have also chosen to use Inuit language placenames for some regions; I've used the main Inuit language or dialect spoken in that region—Kalaallit Nunaat, for example—and foregone italics in these instances.

My approach to the Arnait interview (which took place in Inuktut) is to present it in both the roman orthographic rendering of the original language (but in this case *not* italicized) and in an English translation. While my original idea was to present all contents of this book in both English and an Inuit language translation, the logistics and cost of such a task were, relative to the resources available for this project, prohibitive. The result is not a perfect solution. But it is one that, I think, will allow a large number of people to learn about Inuit cinema from Inuit themselves.

There are, of course, certain words that ring better in Inuit languages. From time to time, interviewees use these words, and they are presented here in their original language in italics with a translation in a footnote. One of the

....

4. Dorais, *The Language of the Inuit*, 46–49.

more frequently used Inuit language terms you will see in these pages is *Qallunaat* (plural *Qallunaaq*). In a number of Inuit languages, this word roughly translates as "a non-Inuit, generally of White, European descent." For more context on the term, it is worth watching the 2006 film *Qallunaat! Why White People Are Funny*[5] (directed by Mark Sandiford, National Film Board of Canada).

The varieties of Inuit language made titling this book challenging. In the conversations I had with colleagues and contributors, there did not appear to be a concise translation in any Inuit language for the word "cinema" in the sense that I use it in this book—which encompasses various media, the people that make that media, the spaces in which the media are screened, and discussion of all the above. In this instance, my solution was not to use a term or phrase that attempted to include all languages/dialects/regions, but to focus on the precision of one language or dialect, Inuttitut/Inuttut, a branch of Nunatsiavummiutut and the language of my colleagues and friends in Nunatsiavut. One of them—Joan Dicker, a *Nainimiuk*[6]—suggested "On Inuit Cinema" could be represented as *Inuit taggajâgatsalianik takugatsalianillu suliagijaujut isumagillugit*, which means roughly "appreciating/keeping in mind the work that is put into filmmaking of/with Inuit and that are worth watching." Refining the idea with our colleague and friend Douglas Wharram (a linguist), a more title-friendly rendering resulted—*Inuit TakugatsaliuKatiget* or "people, together, making something to be seen."

....

5. All films mentioned in the text appear in the Filmography.

6. A person from Nain in Nunatsiavut (northern Labrador).

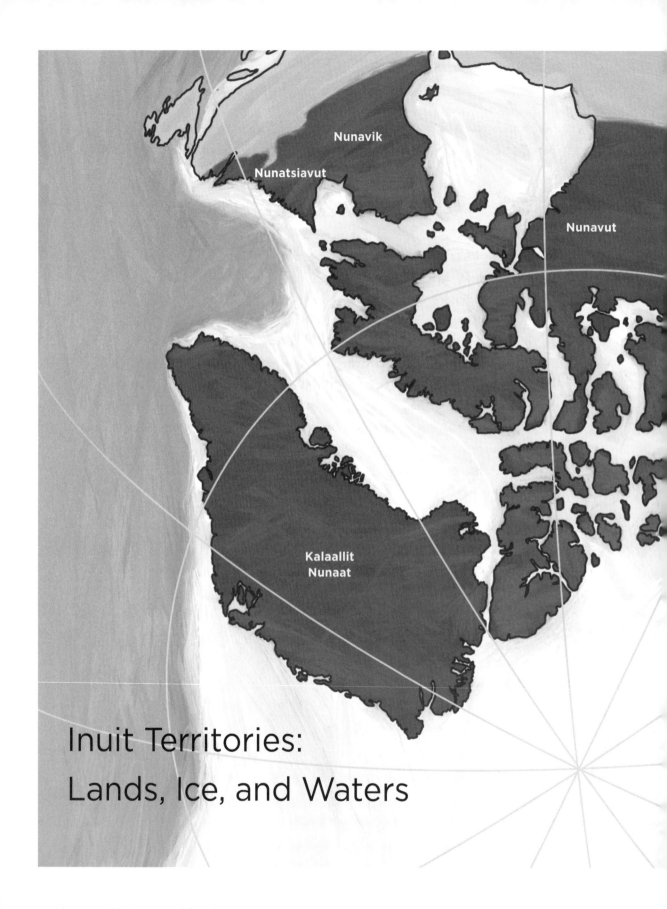

Inuit Territories:
Lands, Ice, and Waters

1. Introduction

This book tells a story about Inuit cinema. It is not a story for me to tell alone. Rather, it needs to be told by and with Inuit filmmakers, media advocates, and producers, as well as with their collaborators, colleagues, and families. Together, all these people are involved in the making of Inuit cinema.

This book is an experiment in re-positioning those voices. While plenty of academic literature about Inuit *media* exists, much of which is listed in this book's bibliography, I am unaware of anything within that body of work that provides space for sustained Inuit-directed thought on any media *practices*. Historically, academic writing produced in the Western humanities tradition has preferred author-directed interpretation. Only since the publication of Linda Tuhiwai Smith's *Decolonizing Methodologies: Research and Indigenous Peoples* (1999), and its broader application across the social sciences, has it become more commonplace for non-Indigenous authors working on Indigenous subjects in the humanities to create space for Indigenous perspectives and objectives.

Beyond the academy, the Inuit-helmed Inuit Art Foundation (IAF) has developed a methodology that positions writing within a broader program of advocacy. Publications such as *Inuit Art Quarterly* and the web-based *IAQ Online* and *IAQ Profiles* serve the IAF's mandate to both "support Inuit artists working in all media and all geographic areas" and "empower and support Inuit artists' self-expression and self-determination, while increasing the public's access to and awareness of artists' work."[1] This book attempts to blend these academic humanities and advocacy approaches to explore a specific Inuit art

....
1. "About Us."

practice—cinema—that places the people involved in that practice in a more dominant position.

My fundamental motivation for this book has been and remains to find ways to include more Inuit voices in discussions of Inuit cinema, and to help create conditions for more Inuit-directed discussions of Inuit cinema. Originally, it was organized around the idea that by interviewing the people involved in the making of Inuit cinema and by keeping my contextual work to a minimum, I could minimize my voice in this story. I am grateful to the reviewers of the manuscript for pointing out the flaws in that line of thought and for encouraging me to think with greater precision about my role in developing this book. Less of my voice, less clarity about my motivations as an editor, and less contextual apparatus would not serve the interviewees, the interviewers, the broader audience interested in the subject, nor the subject itself.

I am a member of a settler culture trained in Western humanities and performing-arts traditions. For the past 10 years, I have also worked for and with the organizations in communities in—and government of—Nunatsiavut (a part of the Canadian province of Newfoundland and Labrador that is also a part of Inuit Nunangat) on projects relating to cultural and documentary heritage. I begin here by acknowledging these positions. They have provided me with a conceptual framework, with access to content, and with a range of relationships that have made this project possible. I understand my role as an interlocutor. My objective is to create a dialogue. The interviews are the foundation of that dialogue. My contextual work builds upon that foundation. Together, they do not lay out a unified case for the existence of Inuit cinema. Rather, they sketch a field and start a larger discussion.

The main catalyst for this book was the 2016 Inuit Studies Conference and its two associated festivals, iNuit Blanche and the katingavik inuit arts festival. Because I served on the organizing committee for the conference, was the artistic director for the katingavik inuit arts festival, and was a co-curator for iNuit Blanche, I was responsible for either overseeing or assisting in programming a range of film workshops, screenings, and other events. We were able to schedule a dozen or so events across the conference and festivals, but we did not have the capacity to accommodate at least another dozen. During those we did program, the discussions and interactions between facilitators and audiences were so robust, it seemed to me that they required some form of documentation and expansion. The most direct way to start to do that was through further dialogue.

A second catalyst for this book was my continuing work on the history of media in Newfoundland and Labrador and, particularly, Nunatsiavut. *Nunatsiavummiut*[2] have a long history of working with moving imagery. It began at the Pan-American Exposition in Buffalo in 1901 and continues today with the work of my colleagues at the OKâlaKatiget Society in Nunatsiavut, animator Echo Henoche, and many others. But as rich as the history of media work in Nunatsiavut is, its outward appearance of occurring in fits and starts, its nuance, and the lack of accessible primary sources make it difficult to see a continuous story. I attempt to develop that account here through interviews with former and current employees of the OKâlaKatiget Society and by including more contributions by Labrador Inuit in the other sections.

This book is presented in four parts. The Introduction describes my motivations and working process and gives general context. Reading it first is helpful, as it sets the stage for what follows. The remaining three sections can be read in any order. Section 2 contains the interviews. Section 3, "Moments in Inuit Cinema," lists and describes significant events mentioned by the contributors in their interviews, as well as several I have encountered in my own work. These "moments" are presented chronologically. Section 4, "Filmography," provides a representative selection of film and television productions about and by Inuit. As I have learned from both the contributors and reviewers of this book, the criteria of what constitutes an Inuit film shifts depending on your viewpoint. The Filmography is presented as a visual essay. Rather than use representative frame enlargements throughout the book, I have included them all in Section 4 to document a visual through-line. The book's designer, Graham Blair (ON, BC, NL), has been instrumental in the rendering of this section.

One of the unique properties of books is that they can create communities of readers. It is my hope that this book might help strengthen a growing community of people working or interested in Inuit and circumpolar Indigenous

....
2. People from Nunatsiavut.

cinema. Outside of film festivals, international distribution of Inuit and circumpolar Indigenous films can be challenging. In some countries, including Canada, even domestic access to Inuit-produced television can be difficult, something Inuit broadcasters in Canada such as Uvagut TV and IsumaTV are addressing head on.

Greater awareness can lead to greater access. But as contributor Stephen Puskas—and others—also points out, it is important to develop communities that will support Inuit and circumpolar Indigenous cinema by Inuit and circumpolar Indigenous Peoples. With Stephen's words in mind, all proceeds from this book are being directed to a fund maintained by the Inuit Art Foundation that is used for further communication in, on, and about Inuit cinema.

One final note: in my contextual pieces that follow, I attempt to provide the contemporary name for the territory or region to which people are connected. An illustration of Inuit territories on page xvi.

Interview Process and Structure

After the 2016 Inuit Studies Conference, I immediately did two things. First, I contacted several facilitators of the film programs to request their involvement in this book. Early in those discussions, Marie-Hélène Cousineau (Quebec, Canada) suggested that many of the Inuit members of Arnait Video Productions might be more comfortable speaking with a long-time confidante, collaborator, and Inuktut speaker such as Blandina Makkik, rather than a stranger. The idea made a great deal of sense and, when possible, I attempted to extend that principle to other interviews. Kat Baulu (Quebec), asinnajaq's producer at the National Film Board of Canada (NFB), was able to recruit the filmmaker and author Jobie Weetaluktuk (asinnajaq's father, Nunavik) to conduct her interview. This general approach changed the nature of the interviews. Friends and family could ask better questions; their precision is evident in the final transcripts.

My work was to develop general areas that needed to be covered in order to yield transcripts that would be self-contextualizing. I also listened to interviews I had conducted earlier with Fran Williams (Nunatsiavut) and Sarah Abel (Nunatsiavut) for separate research on film policy and production in Newfoundland

and Labrador. I had known Fran and Sarah for five years at the time those interviews were conducted. Included in Section 2, they provided the basic parameters for all new interviews.

After these new parameters were developed, I shared them with Stephen Agluvak Puskas (Northwest Territories), asinnajaq (Nunavik), and Inuk Silis Høegh (Kalaallit Nunaat) for feedback. With their input in hand, I prepared final versions of the interview guidelines, which were then shared again with all three before the interviews took place.

Once the transcripts were developed (by Catherine Mitsuk, Nunatsiavut), I performed minimal editing (for content and clarity) and shared the interview transcripts with Stephen, asinnajaq, Inuk, Fran, and Sarah for feedback prior to sending out the entire book for peer review.

The process was similar for Arnait Video Productions, but it was directed by Blandina Makkik who conducted those interviews, translated them, and communicated with Madeline Ivalu (Nunavut), Marie-Hélène Cousineau, and Lucy Tulugarjuk (Nunavut). Conducted separately, the Arnait interviews were amalgamated into a single presentation for this book.

After the peer-review process was finished, all interviewees were given another opportunity to review the text for edits and revisions. In this phase, work with Arnait Video Productions was coordinated by Marie-Hélène. Elizabeth Qulaut (Nunavut) proofed the Inuktut.

These interviews can be read as stand-alone pieces and in any order, which I imagine readers familiar with Inuit cinema will be inclined to do. For readers unfamiliar with Inuit cinema, however, I strongly recommend you begin with Arnait Video Productions, which is presented first. As noted earlier, it is the only interview in this book presented in an Inuit language.

The idea that connects the interviews in this book is: Inuit should occupy a central role in discussions about their cinema. Each of the contributors takes up this idea in different ways. Arnait Video Productions have been involved in this discussion for many years. Established in 1991 in Igloolik, Nunavut, the company champions the voices of Inuit women. Their extensive work in television, documentary feature film, and narrative feature film is rooted in the oral traditions of Igloolik. In their discussion with Blandina Makkik, founding Arnait members Madeline Ivalu and Marie-Hélène Cousineau and member Lucy Tulugarjuk speak with equanimity about the challenges of making the films they envision. Theirs is a fully developed language for the process of local filmmaking for a global audience.

Stephen Agluvak Puskas speaks from a different place. Having worked variously for organizations such as the Canadian Broadcasting Corporation, the National Film Board of Canada, and now for the Makkivik Corporation in Montreal, he speaks with precision and force about the imbalance in power between institutions in southern Canada that control the means of film production and distribution and Inuit communities in both the North and south, communities that serve as the raw content for those institutions. For him, this imbalance is historically rooted and extends far beyond the making and circulation of films. Stephen has further developed this idea in his "Checklist for Making Films In and With Inuit Communities," which serves as a companion piece to his interview.

In conversation with her father, Jobie Weetaluktuk, asinnajaq speaks broadly about her training, her practice as a visual and textile artist and curator, and her work as a filmmaker. At the time of her interview, asinnajaq was completing production on her film *Three Thousand*, which was released by the National Film Board of Canada in 2017. Combining new animation by asinnajaq and archival film from the National Film Board collection, her work on the project provides her with a unique position from which to consider archives of Inuit film and how those might be better curated today.

Originally from Qaqortoq, Kalaallit Nunaat, and now based in Nuuk, Inuk Silis Høegh approaches the issue of representation from a different position. Having first established himself as a visual artist and then as a filmmaker, his work and his words focus on the issue of representation and self-determination more broadly. Inuk speaks to the connection between the current political moment in Kalaallit Nunaat and the ways we experience time-based art. He reminds us about the importance of simply being present and of the agency we all possess through our presence.

The final interviews in this book focus on the OKâlaKatiget Society. Established in 1982 in Nain, Nunatsiavut, the OK Society (as it is affectionately known) is Nunatsiavut's only radio broadcaster and television producer. Prior to 2004, OK also published the only Nunatsiavummiutut (in Inuttitut/Inuttut) newspaper, *kinatuinamot illengajuk*.[3] In the interview, former Executive Director Fran Williams and current Senior Television Producer Sarah Abel provide historical and contemporary context for the OK's audio-visual work. While funding agencies and government policies create practical differences between Inuit-made television and film, in this book both are part of Inuit cinema.

Inuit/Cinema

It is clear that there is no universally accepted understanding of what the words "Inuit" and "cinema" mean, but here is how I understand them and how they work together in this book.

In many Inuit languages, the word "Inuit" translates as the word "people." *Inuk* is one person, *Inuuk* is two people, and *Inuit* means more than two people. As a definition of a cultural group, Inuit refers to the related Indigenous Peoples from Kalaallit Nunaat, Inuit Nunangat (Inuvialuit Settlement Region, Nunavut, Nunavik, Nunatsiavut), and northern Alaska. Inuit lived in these regions long before Russia (which claimed Alaska until 1867), the United States, Newfoundland (which, as its own country, claimed Labrador until 1949), Canada, or Denmark ever existed or attempted to assert sovereignty. Historically, the range of Inuit occupancy and use extended beyond these regions to encompass southern regions such as NunatuKavut in southern Labrador. It is common to refer to Inuit as traditionally inhabiting the Arctic or Arctic regions of the countries listed above.[4]

The Inuit Circumpolar Council (ICC), an international, non-governmental Inuit advocacy organization, suggests another, more expansive idea. The ICC was established by Inuit representatives from Kalaallit Nunaat, Canada, and Alaska in 1977. In 2002, the ICC travelled to Chukotka (Russia), where it developed a regional office representing the Yupik and Chukchi Peoples. In a 2009 publication, "A Circumpolar Inuit Declaration on Sovereignty in the Arctic," the ICC adopted

....

3. Either "to whom it may concern" or "something for everyone."

4. "Basic Information About the Arctic" and "ITK Releases Inuit Nunangat Chapter of Arctic and Northern Policy Framework."

the following declaration, which positions the word "Inuit" as the demonym for all the Peoples it represents. The declaration includes the following assertion:

> **1.3 Inuit are a people.** Though Inuit live across a far-reaching circumpolar region, we are united as a single people. Our sense of unity is fostered and celebrated by the Inuit Circumpolar Council (ICC), which represents the Inuit of Denmark/Greenland, Canada, USA, and Russia.

It is beneficial to keep both senses of the word "Inuit" in mind when reading this book.

In the same declaration, the ICC also refers to a related term that is useful to remember: "Inuit Nunaat," which translates from Kalaallisut as "Inuit lands." The concept is defined as follows:

> **1.2 Inuit have been living in the Arctic from time immemorial.** From time immemorial, Inuit have been living in the Arctic. Our home in the circumpolar world, Inuit Nunaat, stretches from Greenland to Canada, Alaska, and the coastal regions of Chukotka, Russia. Our use and occupation of Arctic lands and waters pre-dates recorded history. Our unique knowledge, experience of the Arctic, and language are the foundation of our way of life and culture.

The term is not without its problems. As Inuit Tapiriit Kanatami (ITK) has pointed out, Inuit Nunaat does not encompass ice, an essential feature of Inuit life. For that reason, ITK adopted the term "Inuit Nunangat" to refer to the four Inuit regions in Canada.[5] Acknowledging what it does not include, Inuit Nunaat is still a useful phrase to use when thinking about a larger, circumpolar Inuit homeland distinct from "the Arctic," which is home to numerous Indigenous Peoples. I use the term "Inuit Nunaat" in this book on occasion and acknowledge its limitations in referring to the complete range of geographical features that are central to Inuit life.

....
5. "Maps of Inuit Nunangat (Inuit Regions of Canada)."

Today, many Inuit live outside of Inuit Nunaat and large expatriate populations exist in European cities such as Copenhagen, as well as in St. John's, Ottawa, Montreal, and Winnipeg in Canada. Many of these Inuit, including contributors Stephen Agluvak Puskas and asinnajaq, are deeply involved in Inuit cinema.

The word "cinema" also requires some attention. It has been well-theorized by many writers, and readers interested in theoretical considerations in circumpolar Arctic or small nation contexts would do well to refer to sources such as Lilya Kaganovsky and Scott MacKenzie, as well as Anna Westerståhl Stenport's *Arctic Cinemas and the Documentary Ethos* and MacKenzie and Stenport's earlier publication *Films on Ice: Cinemas of the Arctic*. Mette Hjort and Duncan J. Petrie's *The Cinema of Small Nations* also makes for good reading. None of these sources addresses the subject of Inuit cinema head on, but they provide useful academic context about how comparatively small circumpolar cinemas operate.

For me, the most pragmatic and generative definition of the word was given by Jerry White in his 2009 book *The Radio Eye: Cinema in the North Atlantic, 1958–1988*. "Although the term has colloquially become synonymous with the more intellectually ambitious forms of filmmaking," he concedes, "I think that cinema is reasonably understood as any form of moving-image arts."[6] Such a broad definition was important given the aim of his book, which was to tie together and advocate for moving-image making and watching in Quebec, Newfoundland, Iceland, Ireland, and the Faroe Islands and to advocate for these smaller, linguistically diverse communities. For White, there is little practical distinction between the various forms the media take: film, television program, or community-produced video. These forms were all unified in their expression of cultural-linguistic sovereignty. As I see it, there is something similar at work in Inuit approaches to making and watching moving imagery.

My understanding of the word "cinema" differs from White's in one regard, however. For me, it is best understood as any form of the moving-image arts *as well as* the discussions and expressions that follow from those arts. When discussing Inuit cinema, the inclusion of discussions and expressions that follow is crucial. Until 1950 or so, Inuit tended to find themselves in front of cameras being operated

6. White, *The Radio Eye*, 6.

by non-Inuit. There were few opportunities for Inuit to screen their performances, let alone work behind the camera. Now there are more opportunities to access and respond to this colonial archive of moving imagery. For artists such as asinnajaq, that archive has become source material for new work. For others, including vocalist Tanya Tagaq (Nunavut), that archive—specifically Robert Flaherty's (USA) 1922 film *Nanook of the North*—has become something to respond to through performance. It is a strange thing for a People to have had such restricted access to so much content that concerns them over such a long period. That condition, and Inuit responses to it, are a part of Inuit cinema, of *Inuit TakugatsaliuKatiget*: people, together, making something to be seen.

2. Interviews

Arnait Ikajuqtigiit

Taana katisimajuq apiqqsurutaulauqtut pingasuulingagaluaqtillugit, 2017-ngutillugu Laatina Makkik Tulaatumiutaq apiqsuqtiulluni. Uvanili, Makkik uqallaqatiqaqpuk Arnaikkunnit pigiaqsijinik Madeline Ivalu, Marie-Hélène Cousineau, ilagijausimalirmijuq Lucy Tulugarjuk. Makkiup Cousineau, apiqsulauqpaa qallunaatitut. Ivalulu, Tulugarjuk apiqsutaulauqput Inuktitut, Makkiullu qallunaatuliqtillunigit. Taissumani apiqsuqtautillugit, Arnaitkut parnalauqput ajjiliurinialisaaqlutik taijaujumik *Tia amma Pijuq*.

LAATINA MAKKIK (LM): Qanurli unikkaarajaqpiuk Arnait Ikajuqtigiit pigiarningat?

MADELINE IVALU (MI): Pigialauqsimavugut Marie-Hélène makkullaaluktillugu, suli qiturnngaqalaurani. Igulingmit nunaqaliqtillugu. Tusagakksaqalauqsimangmat naalautikkut arnaigguuq katimaniarmata. Uqallavikkut tusarnalauqsimangmat arnanik katimatittiniarnirajumik. Upalauqsimajunga, ununngittukuluulauqsimajugut. Tusaajiqaqluni uqallalauqsimajuq. Uqaqluni arnaigguuq tarrijausiurunnattiarmingmata angutitut. 1990nginnit pigialisaaqtillugit. Taissumani pigialauqsimavugut. Inuktigut [taissumanituqarnirmit] unikkaattinnik titiraqpaluaqsimannginnatta, taimanali papappalaunginnata unikkaatinnik. Pigialauqsimavugt ajjiliurivakluta inungnit unikkaaqtunik. Takutittinasukklutalu inuusittinnik.

MARI-ELENA KUUSINUU (M-EK): Iglulingmut nuulauqsimajunga 1990mit. Tarriujausiuqattaanilauqpunga Montrealmit, ilaak tarrijausiurasuqqattalauqpunga

Arnait Video Productions

Presented as a single transcript, this discussion amalgamates three separate interviews conducted in 2017 by Toronto-based Arnait member Blandina Makkik. Blandina spoke with founding Arnait members Madeline Ivalu and Marie-Hélène Cousineau, as well as Lucy Tulugarjuk. Blandina conducted the interview with Marie-Hélène in English. The interviews with Madeline and Lucy were conducted in Inuktut, which Blandina then translated. At the time of these interviews, Arnait was in pre-production for a film called *Tia and Piujuq*.

BLANDINA MAKKIK (BM): How would you tell the story of Arnait Video Productions?

MADELINE IVALU (MI): We began back when Marie-Hélène was very young, before she had children. When she started living in Igloolik. She made a public announcement that there was going to be a meeting for women. She was announcing this over the local radio station. I went to the meeting, there weren't very many of us. She was talking to us with an interpreter. She was saying that women were just as capable as men in creating videos. That women can learn also. So we became members, those of us who wanted to participate. This was in the early '90s. That's when we started. We Inuit [traditionally] did not write our stories down, that was not how we kept our stories. We started by filming people telling stories on camera. We were also trying to show how we live.

unikkaallattaaqsimajunit, sanaqatiqaqlunga Montrealmit katujjiqatigiinik ikajurasuktunit tarrijausiutiit atuinnaujjumiqullugit, unikkavulli atavut tamakkununga taisumani 1990nginnit qaritaujaqalauqsimanngimmat, uqaalutiralaaqaranilu, tarrijausiurnirlu akitullaalukluni.

Tarrijausiurnirli atuinnaulaunngimmat, timiujuinnarnut atuqtauluaqluni, tarrijauqsiuqtiit surlu NFB, uvvaluunnit talaviisalirijiittuat ajjiliurutinik atuinnaqalaurmata. 1985 pigiaqtillugu, mikinniqsait tarrijautiit saqilauqsimanngmata, nutaangummariqlutik arraaguujunik tallimanik nangminiq ajjiliurutitaarunnaqsilauratta akiqaqtunik $2,000, taisumani akitujummarialuulauqtuq. Nangmininnik niuvilauqsimagama tarrijautimik. Iglulingmut nuunnama tarrijautiqalauqsimavunga. Taassumingatuattiaq piqalausimavunga. Nakatirijjutinik piqarnanga, ajjiliurutituakuluga tagva. Nipiksamik illirijariaqaqtumik. Iglulinngmuaqlunga arraaguqalauqsimavunga 30nik, ammalu piqannaqtaarumallunga. Ujjirillugit Nuaman [Kaan] ammalu Saqqaliasi [Kunuk] ajjiliurivaktuuk. IBCkulli pimmariulauqsimangmata.

Angutiinnapaluit iqqanaijalauqsimanngmata [IBCkunnit]. Juuli Ivalutuaq arnaulluni, iqqanaijalauqpuq, tukimuaqtiulluni. IBCkutuattiaq tarrijausiuqpalaurmata, asiqaratik. Nagminiq ajjiliurutimnik atuqlutik, tarrijausiuqpaklutik, taimainninganut qinililauqpunga tarrijausiuqatikksannik. Ujirusulirama Arnait katippangmata aviksimallutik angutinik.

Isumaliqlunga arnanit ilauqattarumallunga. Upakpaklugit miqsuqatigiiktillugit. Kinauninnik qaujikkaivigiallalauqlugit upaqattalilauqsimavakka. Miqsuqpaklutik, uvangaluktauq miqsurnirmit qaujimallunga, alianaigillugulu, nangminiq annuraaliurunnalaurama. Ilippalialauqpunga asinginnik miqsuqtauvaktunik. Apirililauqpakka ajjiliurunnariaqsannik, ajjiliurijumamut, katimajut ajiliuqattalilauqpakka. Ilinniarvik mikittuugaluarmit nakatirivviqarmata taikunga apirilauqpunga nakatirijunnariaqsaq.

Isumalilauqpunga taakuaqai aturunnarasugillugit. Attauttikkullu Saqqaliasilu, Nuamanlu pigiarumaliqlutik tarrijausiurvingmit surlu ijjuaqsilutik Montreal pigiaqtaunikumit, Kuapakkutitut aulataujumik. Saqqaliasi Montrealmualauqsimangmat Nuamannmik piqatiqaluni ilaqaqlutik Raaput Muraimit, tarrijausiuqti iqqanaijaqtuq Kuapakkunginnit Montrealmit. Pikkugijaqalauqput nangminiq tarrijautinik piqarnirmit, tarrijausiurnirmiglu

MARIE-HÉLÈNE COUSINEAU (M-HC): I moved to Igloolik in 1990. I was already making films in Montreal, documentary and experimental videos and films. I was working with a co-op group in Montreal that was making the film-making technology accessible for artists. I think the history of Arnait is really linked to the history of the video technology because in 1990 there was no internet, no iPhone. Filming was something kind of expensive.

In these years, filmmaking was done in institutions like the NFB or through television broadcasters that had access to recording devices. There was the start, in 1985, of lighter technology, like VHS camcorders. In 1990, it was new that you could record, and you could even buy a camera yourself for $2,000, which was a lot of money. I had bought myself a camera. When I moved to Igloolik I had my own private camera. That's all I had. I had no editing system, just my little camera. One that you could put a cassette in. When I arrived in Igloolik I was 30 years old. I realized that there was Norman [Cohn] and Zak [Kunuk] making independent films. IBC[1] was sort of an institution.

It was mostly men working at IBC. The only woman was Julie Ivalu, who was working, producing television programs there. I tried to find people to make films with. I also realized that women were meeting together, doing activities together, and it was kind of separate in gender in the community.

I felt that I should hang out with the women. I went to where the women were and that was the sewing circle. I introduced myself and started hanging out with them. They were sewing and it was something I knew already, it was something I enjoyed, having made my own clothes before. I was learning to work with particular types of materials. I asked them if I could film—and I wanted to make films—I started filming the meetings. The elementary school had a small editing suite and I asked to edit there.

At this same time, Zak and Norman wanted to start a video access centre like there were in Montreal, like a co-op. Zak had visited Montreal with Norman and had been hanging out with Robert Morin, a filmmaker who was working at the video co-op in Montreal. They liked the idea of getting equipment and producing their own videos.

....
1. Inuit Broadcasting Corporation.

Asuilaak Takuminaqtulirijirjuakkunnut kiinaujanik tuksiralilauqpunga, niuvirumamut pijunnautinik ukiuqtaqtumit pitaqangittunik, Nunatsiamik, tarrijausiurvingmit, asittinnigli Kanatami pitaqauqtuinnaulaurmata asingit nunaliit. Taimaagli pigialauqsimavugut. Kinaujamik tuksirarvigijakka tujuqsilauqput $5,000nik. Katiqatiqqaqlungalu Piujurmit, Angutauqturmillu, tamarmiglu tarrijausiurnirmit qaujigiarumammagilutik, ilaalarik.

Ilaqalaurivugut Matiulla Hannilliaqmit, Maata Maktaarmiklu. Uqaqlunga, "Tarrijausiurnirmit ilinniarumavisi?" Kiullutik, "Iittiaq, ilittumavugut." Isumaliqlungalu kinaujanik tuksirakkanirumaliqlunga Arnait tarriujausirninganut Iglulingmit pigiaqtittijumallunga. Asulaak apiqsuliqpugut arnanik 15nik ilinniarumajarriaqsanginnit. Silina Utugik apiqsuqtiulauqpuq. Tamarmit pikkugusulauqput.

Taimannali pigialilauqsimavugut. Taanna ajiliuqtavut uktuutigillugu, Takuminaqtulirijirjuakkut tuksirarvigikkanirattigut tujuqtaulauqpugut $5000nik. Asuilaak pinasuarusiup iluani marruiqluta katimavalilauqpugut. Innait ilinniarvvinganik ajjiliurivalauqpugut, nakatirivaklutalu iliinniarvingmit, suqaimma asianik iniksaqanngittiaratta. Ingminik suurlu ingirratialauqtuq, qaijumajutuinnait qaivaklutik!

Uvannik apiriluaqpalausimanngilanga kina qainiarmanngaat, uvvaluunnit kisumik pijjutiqarninginik. Inuktitut uqarunnannginnama. Ammalu isumaalugijaujut qaujimanngittiaqlugit. Qaivaktullu suuq qaivangmangaangit qaujimanagit. Nunagijaujurlu qaujimanagu. Kikkullu nunalingmit aulattijiungmangaata qaujimanagit. Qaujimannangalu Anguttauqtuq aupaluktunuurninganut, Piujurlu sanningajuliurninganik, ammalu sunauvva ajjiunginniqarninginnik!. Ilagiiktullu qaujimanagit. Pinasuaqtavut quviagituinnaqlugu. Aksururinngiujaqluguluunnit. Imannattiaq Isumaalugijaqangittiaqlunga.

Asinnik ijjuaqsijumalaunngilanga ilisaivaktunik. Sillattuqsarvingmit ilinniaqsimalaurama, uqarunnarajalauqpunga "Atii tarrijausiurnirmit ilisailauqta!" Ammalu aturtaugajuktut ilisaijunik tarrijausiurnirmit maligunnarajalauqpakka pijumanniruma, taimannali pijumalaunnginnama. Isumaqarlaurama, unali uqausirinngimmajju. Utaqqituinnarluta, kisu saqqinniarunaqtuq. Iliinianikugali takuminarnirmit pijjutiqarniqsaulaurmat, tusarutilirinirmit suurlu, ammalu

I applied for some Canada Council grants and lobbied them to be able to purchase equipment so we could have in the Arctic—the NWT, at the time—a video access centre as they had everywhere else in Canada. That's how it began. I made a grant application, and we received a grant for $5,000. I then met with both Madeline and Susan [Avingaq]—they were both very curious at the start about making video, they were.

There was Matilda Hanniliaq, Martha Maktaak. I said, "Do you want to learn how to make films?" They said, "Okay sure, we want to learn." So then I thought it would be a good idea to apply for a grant to have a women's video workshop in Igloolik. We went around to ask about 15 women, to see if they thought it was a good idea to learn how to make videos. Celina Utugik was the interviewer. Everyone said yes, that it was a good idea.

That was the beginning. With this video we asked Canada Council for a grant to start activities. We received an Exploration grant of $5,000. I was able to organize meetings twice a week. We met and filmed in the Adult Education building and edited at the local school, as we did not have any other space. It was very organic. People who wanted to come, came!

I did not ask myself a lot of questions in terms of who's coming, what it represents. I did not speak Inuktitut. I did not understand local issues. I didn't know who was coming for what. I did not know the town, my first year there. I did not know the politics of the town. I did not know that Susan Avingaq was Anglican and that Madeline Ivalu was Catholic and that it meant something! I did not know the families. I was just having fun doing that. It was not very complicated.

I did not want to teach in a conventional way. I had gone to university taking film classes and I could have said, "Let's teach them how people make film!" I could have used the typical techniques: how to frame shots, etc. I did not want to do that. I thought, "This is not their language. Let's wait and see what will come." My background was more art than communication or broadcasting per se, and there was an element of empowerment I wanted to teach. I was a feminist and still am. They were saying things like, "We want to have these meetings only with women because sometimes when men are there, we cannot say what we want. We cannot really push our issues or questions. We trust this process with women."

ajunnginiqarnalaummarikpuq. Arnait quvvariaqtittumallugit isumaqalaurami, suli ullumi taimaipuq. Uqaujauqattalilaurama imanna, "Arnanik kisiani katimaqatiqarumavugut, ilaanikkut angutitaqaraangat, nilliqpannginnatta uqausiksaqaraluaqluta. Ajauqtualuujunnanginnatta isumagijattinnik, apiqqutigilugilluuniit. Arnauqatittinnik aulattijunnarniqsaugatta."

Taimaak tusarama, nalunalaunngilaq Angutauqtuq saqqittuniirmat, qainngiinaliqttuq, uingata qaiqurnngimmagu. Uqaujjuqluniuk angirraqsimaqulluniuk qiturngaliringaaqulluniuk, numaanalaukalauqpuq. Kisiani utilauqsimangmat, uqaqlunilu, "Qanutuinnaq"! Piujurlu kiulluni "Nutaqqait talaviisamik takunnatuinnalirmata, taimaittunik sanalauqta tusaatinniarattigut. Tarrijausiurunnaqtugut, uvatinnik takunnarniarmata." Piuttialauqpuq. Sivulliqpaatiamik Iglulingmit tarrijaqtittigatta, surlu pijuunautimik saqqituqalauqpuq, surlu "Uakallanga! Nunattinik ikajurunnaqtugut"! Pigiaqtittijunnaqtugut.

Nangminirli apurutiqalaunnginnama tusagaliuqtitut. Takuminaqtuliriningaamigli tunngaviqalaurama, Suurlu takujagaqarniup takuminaqtunik piniqsaullunga. Tusagaksalirijiniglu qassisuarjuklunga sanalaukaklunga iluarijaqalaunngilanga Montrealmit, taimaak sanavannginninnut. Ukpirilaunnginnakku taimak sananiq, quviaginngillugulu. Isumaksaqsiuvigijumanagulu. IBCmit takunnaliraangama, sanaujausimaninga isumagillugu ijjuarumanagu, IBC surluu CBCkunnit ajjiliusiquujilaurmat, tauutua gavamait timingitut aaqiksimajaaqluni.

LM: Uqaqsimagavit, "Arnait tarrijausiangit unikkaaqsimavut qaujisarnikkut atuqtauvaktutuqanit unikkausirnnit, nutauniqsaniglu unikkausinik." Qanurli taakkuninga saqitittiqattarumallusi pigiarniqpisi?

M-EK: Tukisiajumammarilausimagama. Inuktitut tukisiananga, kisiani isumaksaqsiurivalauqpara. Maana suli isumagiinnaqpakpara, qanuq uqausiq isumamut ataninganit. Unikkaaqpaktullu qanuq pivangninginnik, naalaktaujaraangamik. Suurlu, inarniq unikkaqtunik nalagunnapalaurama, inujunniqsimaliqtunik. Nua Pigattuq. Iqallijuq Ukumaaluk. Naalakkuviuk Iqallijuq unikkaaqtillugu, "Ataguttaaluup kaanirilauqtanganik", aksualuk

I liked that. Susan did not come for a while because her husband did not want her to come. He was telling her she should stay at home with the kids. That was pretty sad because she loved meeting with us. But then finally she came back. She said, "You know, whatever!" And Madeline said, "The kids are only watching television now, so let's make television so we can talk to them. We can make films, so they'll watch us." That was good. The first time we showed a film in Igloolik, there was a sense of empowerment, a sense of "Whoa! We can do something in the community. We can be active."

I did not have the boundaries of the traditional broadcast universe. I came from an art and cinema scene, more like experimental video art. For the few times I had worked in the industry in Montreal, I had felt very uncomfortable, not coming from that background. I did not believe in that style, did not find it interesting. That was not my intellectual preference. Also, when I was looking at IBC, I thought, "I'll not teach like that." IBC was more like CBC,[2] it was a governmental institution.

BM: You have suggested that "Arnait's productions are the expression of re-search into traditional and contemporary Inuit styles of narration." How did you come to decide upon this as an area of focus?

M-HC: I was intellectually curious. I could not understand Inuktitut, but I was curious about it. I'm still curious about it, how language influences your way of thinking. I was interested at looking how people tell their stories in films, if you're listening and not imposing a style. For example, I had a chance to listen to old storytellers that are passed away now. Noah Piugattuq. Rose Okkumaluk. If you listen to her tell a story, as in "Ataguttaaluk's Starvation," there is a respect when you're listening to this, and you have the feeling, "Oh, this is very, very rare what I'm listening to."

The way the woman is telling the story, the words she's using, how people are listening. This is not something you want to put into a little box. What do we do? We start the camera, she tells the story. When she finishes,

....

2. Canadian Broadcasting Corporation.

pimmariuninganik nalunnangimmat ikpingnarniqaqlunilu, "Uakallanga, una tusaajara pituinnaungittiaqtuq."

Arnaup unikkausinga, uqausiit atuqtangit, qanuq naalaktauninganit. Pimmariutittariaqarattigut, puukulungmuatuinnangillugu. Qanurli piniaqpita? Ajjiliurut ikillugu, unikkaaliqlunilu. Pianingmat, tarrijautit nuqaqlugu. Nalulilauqsimavunga qanuiliuriaqsaq, suuqaimma asianik pijakksaqarnangimmat. Unikkaaqtuq ulavisarumanagulu, suurlu, "Uattiaruai, una ajjiliurut maunngaalaglagu. Uqasaaqtait uqakkannirunnaqpiuk. Pigiakkanirniaratta." Tamakkua qallunaanit atuqtauvaktut iliqusittinnik.

Tukisiangilluni uqausirijaujunik [uqausirmik] kisiani ujjirusukluni pivalliajumit, qaujisattiarasuklunilu, Tukisiangilluni uqausirijaujunik [uqausirmik] kisiani ujjirusukluni pivalliajumit, qaujisattiarasuklunilu, ilinnattiarmat. Taimaak unikkaarniq uvannut aallaulauqpuq, inuusinnilli taimaak unikkaaqpalaunngimmata. Montrealmingaaqlunga, aullaruluujarnikuullungalu, tarrijarsimallungalu, kisiani iksivaatuinnarluni unikkaaqtuqaqtillugu, nalaktauttiaqlunilu, sivulliqpaamik aturiulauqpara. Naalattiavigjuaqtut, unikkaap tukingit, nutaanguttialauqpuq uvannut. Ajjigijaunginninga qaujilauqpara, ammalu nauttiqsuttiarasuliqlunga taimaininganik, nanilimaat pitaqanngimmat.

Nanilimaat asinngnik taimaak unikkaaqtuqarngimmat. Akkaugaluaqai asinginnik Inuit nunaliginnik, kisiani taissumani naalaktillunga, ammalu qallunaatuliqtitaungmata, tukisiliqlugit, uangilaak unikkat tusarniqtuqmarialuit. Asinngit taimaittunik unikkaaqtuqarngittiarmat. Ilavalliallutit, ammailaak apiqsuqattalirillutat irnisuksiijinik, ilangit apiqqut qaritaujarmuulauqtavut. Taikkuali apiqsuqattalauqtavut inuujunniittuinattiat. Upinnarani ningiungulaurmata taissumani apiqsuqattaqtillutigut. Taissumani singailauqsimagama, naalavigjuaqattalauqtunga. Ammailaak qallunaatungalirmata, tukisigakkit, uakkalaluaraalunga! Unikkaangit, qaujimajurjuamarialuulauqtut. Taikkua Arnait, ingminiinaq ikajuqattautillutik, irnivalaurniqput nunainnarmit, taimaak, iliqqusituqaalugigamiuk taimmannganik, arraagunik amisuuniqpaanik.

Nunarjuarlimaamit kikkut taimailiurivat? Unungittummarialuit! Qaujimalauqtut unungittukulungnit iqqaumajaujunit. Tamannalu qaujimaniq aksummarialuk annirnaqluni, qallunaanit piijaqtaummarilirmat, inuusirminut we stop the camera. I did not know what else to do, in some way because there is nothing else to do. You do not want to interrupt the person, like, or say, "Wait, I'll position the camera there. Repeat what you just said. Oh, we'll start again, we'll ask you a question." All those things that people do in our White culture.

When you're not understanding [language] the words but you're understanding the process of what's going on, and if you're attentive to that process—you can learn from it. This was a process I was not familiar with, I had nobody else in my life telling stories like that. I was coming from Montreal, had travelled places, had watched movies and all that, but I had never been in a situation where you actually sit down and let a person tell a story and everybody is reacting to it. The respect that is there, the meaning of the story—this was all new to me. I knew this was unique and that I had to pay attention because you can't see this anywhere else.

I really had that feeling of awe when I was listening and, when it was translated—oh my gosh—those stories were amazing! Nobody else is telling those stories. We did a series of interviews with midwives; some of those interviews are on the internet, we were able to digitize them. Those women are all passed away now. They were already old when we interviewed them in 1991. As I was pregnant at the time, I was really paying attention. When we translated this then, it was, "OMG." The stories they told, the knowledge they had! These women were, by themselves, helping each other giving birth on the tundra and this had continued for thousands of years.

This knowledge was very precious, because somehow civilization was erasing it with colonization, erasing it with science, with language. Those women were not on regular television saying, "Hey! This is how to do it! This is how we're doing it." Our work, although very discreet, was revolutionary. It is revolutionary. To listen to those women and say, "Talk, talk your talk, say it. We're going to share this because, it's unique, and when it's gone, that's it, on the face of the earth."

BM: How would you describe traditional Inuit storytelling?

kipullugu, qaujisarnirminut, uqausirminullu. Taikkua Arnait qautamaaqsiutikku talaviisamiilaunngimmata, ima uqarnatik "Ihi! Imanna pijariaqaqtusi!" Taimana atuqtavut. Takuqutilaungittut. Ajiulaungilaq, maana suli ajjiqarngilaq. Naalaklugit taikkua Arnait, "Uqautillugillu, uqarissi, uqausisi aturlugu, uqaruk." Tamana unikkaq takuksautiniaqtavut, ajiungimmat, ammalu pitaqarunniqpaat, taimalu! Asiuvuq, nunarjuarmillu pitaqarunniqluni.

LM: Qanurli uqausirinajaqpiuk Inuit unikaaqtuarninga?

LUCY TULUGARJUK (LT): Nutarautillunga angajuqqakka unikkaaqtuaqtiulaurmatik. Surlu, uqausiqalirnirutik qanuittuqarniqpat ajjiungittumik, uvaluunnit nunaminngaaqtumik sunatuinnamik, inungnilluunit qanuittuqarnirpat quvianaqpalluunnit, quaqsarnaqpalluuniit, taimaittunik pijjutiqaqlutik unikausiqarajaqtut. Ullumi iqqaumagaluaqpunga ataatatut unikkaaqtuqaraangat, sulijunit uqausiqaqtunik, kisiani taimaittunik tusagajunngiliqtugut. Ullumilaak, puiguttiammariliqtunga, unikkausituqarmit tusarniruma iqqarajaraluaqlugu, puigujatuliraluqalunga. Maanali ilinniaqtitausimamut qallunaatitut, inuusiriliqtattinnik, asijjiqtuq.

Uktuutiqarluni, unikkausiujarangatta ulumiujumut tunngaviqatuinnariaqaqput, kisiani, ilasimalutik atuqsimajattinnik, uvvaluunnit nutaraulluta isumgijavinittinnik, paurngaqtarniq, pisujunngniq, ningiuq unikkaaqtuaqtuq, tamarmik taakua katillugit, saqqitittummallugit, uvangaliasiit, takukksaukkaniqullugit, unikkaat puiguliqtavut-surluuniit piruqsiat tailugit nunaminngaaqtut-niviaqsaakulungmit ilisaqtiqarluni. Pinnguarniugaluaqpat, pillattaanguarluni, takuksauniaqpat tarrijautikkut talaviisakkullunniit. Unikkaarusivut asijjirmat.

Taissumani, unnukkut unikkaaqtuaqtumik naalakluni, aksualuk iqqumanasunngnalaurmat! Unikkaaqtaujuq tamarmik tusaajumaluarnikumut. Ujjirinngillutaqai ilisaqtaulauqtugut inngiusini, suurlu, taassuma unikkaap ilagilluniuk. Ullumi, kamammarikpakpunga sivullitta iqqaumajunnarninginnik, kisiani isumanik atuqlunigit, suuqaimma titiraqsimavalaungimmata, ullumititut, iqqaumajumaguma kisutuinnarmit kisiani titirarlugu. Taissumani naalattiariaqavigjualauqsimavugut, tusaattiarasugvigjuaqluta.

LUCY TULUGARJUK (LT): As a child, my parents were my storytellers. For example, if they were relaying an event that was out of the ordinary or unusual, coming from the land, or something happened to the Inuit, whether it was joyous or threatening, this is the type of event that would lead to the story being told. Today, although I recall my father's way of storytelling, speaking of factual events, now it is rare that we hear of stories. Today I'm even forgetting many of them, although if I were to hear an old story, I could recall it, although I'm prone to be unable to recall. Today, as we are now taught in the Qallunaat way, in this modernized world, it is changed.

For example, when we create fictional stories it may be based on contemporary events, however with elements that we may have experienced or thought as children, like young girls berry-picking, hiking, a grandmother telling a story— gathering all these together and wanting to show, at least in my case, wanting to have them shown again, as the stories that we are forgetting, even naming the plants that come from the land, usually the young girl as a teacher. Even if it is a fictional event, to make it seem real, if it is going to be presented in film or video. The way of telling stories is now changed from what it was.

Back then, hearing stories in the evening, we would try so hard to stay awake! Not to miss any part of what was being said. Without realizing it we were probably being taught songs, for example, which were part of the story learning. Today, I am awed by the mental ability of those before us, the reliance on memory of things that were not written down—as today, if I want to remember anything, I must write it down. We had to try and listen very carefully, paying great attention.

MI: In the evening, when all chores were completed, when people were all inside, perhaps getting ready to sleep, when everyone was settled in, that is when the stories would be told. We listened attentively, never interrupting, unless the storyteller paused, to ask a pertinent question relating to the story being told.

Because if an Inuk is telling a story, and is being bombarded with questions, that person would cease telling the story. Because they were relying on their memory and had to focus on that memory. Inuit were and are capable of

MI: Unnukkut pilirijaujariaqaqtut pianiktaujaraangata, isiqsimaliraangamik, imaqqa sinnaksarnialiraangamik, taimali unikkaqpalauqput. Naalattiavigjuaqpalauqpugut, nillirparngilluta kisiani unikkaaqtuq nipangilakakpat, apirilitainnaqluta unikaaqtaujuup misaanut.

Inuk unikaaqtuaqtuq apiqsuqtauninnaruni, unikkaarunniirajarmat. Suuqaimma iqqaumajaminik unikkaaramik ammalu iqqaqsariaqaqlutk iqqaumajaminik. Inuit taissumani manalu imannamaraluk iqqaumajunnarmata. Isumavunga qallunaaqalisaaqtllugu, taiikkua inungnit tukiqargninnasuginnnaaluaqtut. Inungnit, suurlu qimmitut, Inukuluk qungajaanginnaujaqtuq. Immaqaa qallunaat uvattinnik isumaqattianginnasugilaurmata, qungajaangnnaujaratta. Aakkaugaluaq, taikkua Inuit aksualuk isumaqquqtulauqtut.

LM: Ullumili Inuit unikkaarusiangit?

LT: Tussangujaqlunga iksivaaqlunga, Akunialuk taimaak pijunniiqtunga. Kisiani tarrijausikkut uvvaluunniit titiraujaqsimajunik tarrijausinik surli *Qaggiavik*, takunnaqluni Inuit Takunnagakksalirijikkunginik unikkaaqpaktunik, maanaujuq taimaittunik unikkaaqtunik naalakpagunniqtunga.

MI: Suli manna unikkaaqpaktunga qiturngannut, unnukkutuinnaungittuq. Suli ilaannikkut unikkaaqpaktunga. Ilaak, ippasasaaq qiturngakka ullurummitariaqturtillugit. Unikkaatuatuqarmit unikkaarasulauqtunga. Ullumi, igluqaratta iglurusiqauqtunik, unikkaaqtuaqtiarnangimmat, taissumanitut. Ajurnanginnisaujuq aullaqsimaliraangatta. Taimali aullaqsimaliraangatta paniga, naalagummaaluungmat, unikkaaqujiinnaujaqtut.

LM: Ajjigiingippat Inuit uikkaaqtuarningit taissumani maannaujurluu?

M-EK: Iinguqquuqtuq. Kiunaqpara immanna. Nanisilaurama apiqsuqtautillugu Gabrielle Rua, naalautikkut Sipisiikut apiqsuqtautillugu 1961-ngutillugu, arraagut 55 qarngiqsimaliqput. Apiqsuqtaulluni alianaigilaunngimmagu, tannali apiqsuqtanituaripaluktanga.

holding on to incredible volumes of memory. I think that with Western contact, those people thought that we were no smarter than dogs, the image of the happy smiling Inuk. Perhaps the Qallunaat thought we were simple-minded, since we were always smiling! But no, those Inuit were very intelligent.

BM: And Inuit storytelling today?

LT: Listening while sitting down. I have not experienced that in a very long time. Only by films or animation such as *Qaggiavik*, viewing IBC programs of storytellers, but personally I am not listening to that personal style of storytelling anymore.

MI: I still tell stories to my children, not necessarily in the evening. I still occasionally will tell stories. Why just yesterday my children came over for lunch. I was attempting to tell a legend. Today, when we live in homes that have separate bedrooms, it is not conducive to tell stories as in the past. It is easier when we are away on the land. That is when my daughter, who loves to hear stories, will always request a story.

BM: Are there differences between traditional and contemporary Inuit styles of narration?

M-HC: I suspect there is. I'll answer it by talking about something else. I found an interview from 1961 with the French Canadian writer Gabrielle Roy. She did not like being interviewed, so this was one of the rare interviews she gave.

To see Gabrielle Roy, whom I had never seen talking, was very moving for me. It really felt that she was coming from another time. She was speaking French very differently than the way people are speaking right now.

The words are the same but the way the sentences are put together, the rhythm, the choice of words is different. Her thinking, it was just beautiful—very eloquent, very elegant. Nobody speaks like that anymore.

This is one kind of storytelling that does not exist anymore. To answer the question, I am certain that the storytelling I was exposed to, and that

Tainna Gabrielle Rua, takulauqsimanngittiaqtara uqallaktu uangilaak ikpingnaqtummarialuulauqtuq, uvannut. Imanna taissumaningaalarilqtuq. Uiviitut uqallakktanga manna uqallakktauvaktumit ajjigijaugnittialiqtut. Kisiani uqausilimaaq tukisilauqtara.

Uqausiit ajjagiikktuugaluat, kisiani aulaninga, ammalu qanuq uqaqtauninginnik ajjigilaungimmagu. Isumajanga, uangilaak tusarnilaurmat, uqattiaqsimalaurmat, pikkunattialaurmallu. Maannaujuq taimmaak uqallaktuqaqpagunniittiarmat.

Taimanna unikkaarniq pitaqarunniirmat. Apirijait kiulugu, qaujimattiaqpunga, unikkaaqtaujut tusaavalauqtakka ammalu Inuit tusaavalauqtangit arraagunit 25nik qaanigsimajunik, maana unikkaaqtauvaliqtunik ajjigijaunngittiaqtuksauliqtut

Taimannauluni kisianiungmat. Arragut 25ngulirmata qaangiqsimajut, apiqsuqattalaurnivut innatuqarnit. Maanna tuqungaliqtut ilangit. Suurlu Piujuq, unikkaakkammarialuujuq. Pisimavuq- Angutauqturlu-70-ungataanik ukiuqaliqtuuk, kisiani pisimainnaqput unikkausinik. Kisianittauq ajjigijanngittuksaugivuq anaanangitta anaanattiangittalu pigilauqtanginnik. Uqausingat asijjiqtuksauvuq, inuit uqallanningit. Ammalu taimainnik unikkausinik iqaumavat suli?

Iqqaumajut amisummarialungnit. Piujuullu Angutautuullu nalimungillu qaujimajuvigjuaraaluit, ilakuugillutiglu. Asigituinnariaqaqpa asinginnik nunalingnit, nunaliralaangunnirutigluunniit, ilinniariannirpataluunniit, qallunaujarunnarutik. Kisutuinnat tamatuminga unikkaqarnirmit aktuutiqarmat.

LM: Nipiliuqsimajut ajjiliuqsimajullu ikajuqpat uvvaluunnit ikajunngilak unikkaarniup asijjirninganuut?

M-EK: Ilauqataujariaqaravit nunarjuarmit, ammalu tusarutilirijinik ajiiqatiqariaqarniaravit, taimali qanuiliurnialiqpit? Pilirijariaqaarniaravit-taimanna uqausiqalauqsimagatta-taissumani tarrijausiulisaaqluta Iglulingmit Arnaittigut, sanalauqsimagattigut Iglulingmiut tarrijarunaqullugit. Taanna tarijausiuqtavut takuksautinniarlugu pinnguarvingmit. Taimali nunaliup Igluliup silataanuaruttigut-sivulliqpaamik tarrijausiavut

Suurlu sivullirmit, Canada Councilkut kiinaujannginnik kisiani atuqluta tarrijausiuqpalauratta, qanutuinnattiaq tarrijausiurumajattinnik isumaqsuttialauqsimajugut. Aulataunnittiaqluta kiinaujanik tujuqsijunik.

Inuit were exposed to, 25 years ago is very different than what they are exposed to right now.

How can it be otherwise? We did interviews with Elders 25 years ago. Most of them have passed away now. Madeline and Susan Avingaq—they're both 70-plus—they kept that storytelling skill. But it must be different than what their mothers had or what their grandparents had. The language must be different, the way people were talking. And do they remember all the stories?

They remember a lot of stories. Madeline's and Susan's generation have knowledge, but not all of them. It might be different in different towns and regions, if they lived on the land, if they went to school, if they speak English. It depends on a lot of things.

BM: Do you think audio-visual media contribute to or diminish these differences in narration?

M-HC: You're going to participate in the world and you're going to have to participate with the media, so what are you going to do? At first when we made films or videos in Igloolik with Arnait, the audience was the audience of Igloolik. We are making this and we'll show it at the community hall or church basement or in our house. People are watching it. It is made for the community. Then, as soon as you take it outside Igloolik—it will come with conditions.

For example, at first, we only made films with Canada Council money, some grants, so we could do whatever we wanted within the project guidelines. You could do pretty much what you wanted, there is no aesthetic conditions. If you want to have more money, and we did get more money to make films, then it comes with a lot of conditions—enormously—constraints and expectations.

You can play with those. We tried to play with those as much as we could and to keep a style that is particular to our process. But, certainly, it is not just putting the camera there and letting someone talk. It is not. We're doing this, and Zacharias Kunuk is doing this, too, in Igloolik, and working with those questions, too. Films that are coming out of Igloolik probably have a style that is more original than, let's say, those coming out of Iqaluit. It is because of the process in which those films are made.

Unurniksanik kiinaujanik pijumaguvit-ammalu unurniqsanik kiinaujanik pilauqluta, tarrijausiurutiksanik-aulataunnaqtummarialuk imannarjuaq-piqujaujut pijariaqalugit, niriugijaujullu.

Taimaikkaluarluni aaqqiksuinasugunnarmijuq. Taikkua maligiaqaqtavut silataagut pinasukpalauqpugut, iliqqusivut tarrijausiurnivut pigiinnarasuklugit. Ilaak tarrijaummik aaqiksituinnarluni, uqallaktuqatuinnalirluni tarrijausiuqtaujumik, taimaingimmat. Taimmaingimariktuq. Sanagatta, Saqqaliasilu sanangmingmat Iglulinngmit, taikkualu isumaksaqsiurijariaqarillugit. Iglulingmingaaqtut tarrijaat sanasimaningit ajjigijaungimatta pillattaanguniqsaullutiglu suurlu Iqalungnik sanajaujunik. Apiqquti, aulajinirmut apiqquti.

LM: Unikkaat tarrijausiutautillugit, talaviisakkuuqtillugit ikajurniqaqpaa Inuit unikkaanginut?

LT: Sanajausimaninga maliklugu kisiani kiujunnaqtunga. Takunnaqsimavunga unikkaanik malittiarsimavigjuaqtunik ajjiliurinikkut. Kinamut sanajaungmangaalu ajjiliuqsimajuq maliklugu ajjigiinngittunarilluni, titiraqtigijaujurlluunni, ilaannit anngaaqatigillugit, uvaluuniit aaka. Ilangit unikkaaqtuamit malittiarmata aulajunik titiraujaqsimajunik, malittiaqtillugit unikkaaqtaujumik, taimaak takusimavunga.

Ukpirusunngmarikkpunga [ikajuqsimavuq] tarrijaqtillunga, naalaklungaluunnit puiguliqtaraluannik. Taimaittu takuksaugajugjuumikpata, unikkaatuqait, qiturngavut qaujimaniqsaunajaqput. Ilaannit iqqaraangama, unikkaarasukpakpunga anaanama unikkaaqpalauqtanginnik. Ajjittiamarikulugingikkaluaqpagit.

Tautuujaqlunga Mary Kunuup tarrijausiulauqsimajanganik ningiuq irngutaminik quinaksaaqliluarnikumut tinngmianguqluni. Marie-Hélène taana unikkaq uiviititut saqqqilaurmingmagu. Uiviititut tukisangikkaluaqlunga, tainna tarrijalirakku, iqqattialauqsimajara. "Uinna, inga unikkaaqtuaq"! Iqqarnaviggjuaqtuq.

MI: Ii, iqqaumajunnarnirmut ikajuqtut, unikkaaqtuaniglu iqarnarillutiik. Uangilaak puiguliqtavinittinik iqarnavignuaqtut.

BM: Does having stories on film and television help Inuit storytelling?

LT: It depends on the type and what show it is. I have seen stories that follow through, true to the original. Depends on who filmed the story or legend, whichever, depending on individual scriptwriters, I would agree or disagree. Some presenters follow the original story, say an animated version, when it is presented in the original story. I have seen this form of presentation.

I sincerely believe [it has helped] when I'm viewing or listening to things that I may be forgetting. If that type of story was aired more often, those stories that were told, our children should be exposed to. When I sometimes recall, I try to pass on stories my mother told me, to my children. Even though I may not completely accurately relate them exactly.

I was watching Mary Kunuk's animation story of an old lady who tickled her grandchild so much she turned into a bird. Marie-Hélène presented this story in French. Although I did not understand the French language, when I viewed this animated story, I totally recalled it. "Oh, here is that story!" It really jogs memory.

MI: Yes, they help to bring back memories and remember legends. It really helps to recall stories we may have started to forget.

BM: What roles did women play in traditional Inuit stories?

LT: Strong women. They were very capable, helping out other people, being good caregivers to their children, always sewing, always occupied and busy. They were incredibly competent. Then I have heard of giant women from/ of the land, when they would sight children on their own, they would snatch them. Then there are women who reside in the sea. *Qallupilluks*[3] who are female that kidnap children, put them in their pouch, and take them to the sea! How frightening!

....

3. *Qalluplluit* are sea-based creatures with scaly skin. They prey on unattended children near the sea edge.

LM: Arnaili qanuq iniqaqtitaulauqpat Inuit unikkaaqtuatuqanginnik?

LT: Sanngijuvinialuit, Arnait ajungitummarialuulauqttut, inuuqatimik ikajuqpaklutik, ilaminik kamattiarunnaqttuvinialuit,. Miqsuinnaujalauqtut annuraaksanginnik, piliriinnaujalauqtut nuqangaattuinnalausimanatik. Unikkaaqtuakkut tusaumangmijakka Inukpasugjuit, nunamingaaqtut. Nutaqqanik takunnirutik inutuujuni tigusinajaqtuguuq, nunamunngaujjaulunilu. Taimalu arnait tariurmiutat, Qallupilluit, nutaqqaniguuq amaqsijumavakttut imaanullu nasasikallagllugu. Kappiannamiiglikiaq!

MI: Tusaumavunga arnanik sangijummarialungnit, aggainnarminut iqalugunnaqtut, pinnguaqtinik unikkaaqtuanit. Isumanaqput arnait unikkaaqtuarniigajunngniqsaulauqtut. Isumavunga angutiit angunasuinnaujalaurninginnut. Angunasuinnaujariaqalaurmata, taissumani niuvirvingmit niqitaakpanngata. Isumvunga, taimmamaqai arnait unikkaaqtuarniiniqqsausuunguvut angirraqsimaniqsausuungulaurmata.

Taikkua unikkat inuusiqattiarnirmut turaangavalaurivut qiturngiurnimut. Suurlu, arnaq surainniruni, uqausirinnagulu. Uvvaluunniit ningaqtauvanngniruni uiminik ikajuriaqaqpaklugulu- aksuruluamut surainnirunni, uqalaurani, nunalilimaat aksururnaqtuqsiulirajakput. Nirjutiqarunniirluni, inuit kaalirlutiklu.

LM: Ullumili arnait qanuq unikkausinik iniqaliqpat?

LT: Ullumiujuq arnait tarrisauninik takuksaujariaqammariktut, amisummarialuit saqqitaujariaqarmata, suli amisummariungmata qaujimajaujarialiit takukksautitaujariaqarmata suurlu amausiurniq, qisiliriniq, pigiarninganik isuanut, amiliriniq, qulliiup miksaannut, missuqtiarniq. Taakkualimaat arnanit pilirijauvaktut, uqiuqtaqtumi nunaqarniarluni, tamakkua qaujimajariaqarattigut. Puigugiaqanginnattigut. Arnait pilirivaktalimaangit nipiliuqtaujariaqaqtut, asinninnit arnanik takujaujunnaqullugit, sivuniksattinnut, qaujimajauniarmata.

LM: Ullumili unikkaarnik qanuq aturniqaqpa?

MI: I have heard of very strong women, women picking fish with their hands, women in sporting events, in legends. It seemed that women characters were more common in legends. I think it is because the men were always hunting for food. They always had to be looking for food, before we had any food we could purchase from a store. I think, perhaps, that is the reason women figured more prominently in stories, as they were the ones staying home.

Often moralistic stories involving women had to do with bearing children. For example, if a woman miscarried and she did not inform anyone. Or if she had an abusive husband whom she had to physically assist—if due to this exertion she miscarried and did not tell anyone, then the whole camp would undergo hardships. There might not be any game, to the point where the people would be facing starvation.

BM: What role do women play in stories today?

LT: It is important to portray women today. There are many, many things that need to be shown. There are still many skills to be shown and passed on, for example steps for making *amautis*,[4] preparing skins, showing the steps in preparation and way of treating skins, from beginning to end, preparing hides, *qulliq*[5] maintenance, good sewing techniques. All these responsibilities that are in the woman's domain, in order to live in the Arctic we have to know these skills. We cannot forget them. All these women's responsibilities have to be recorded, to share with other women, for the future, so as to pass on the knowledge.

BM: What is the purpose of storytelling today?

LT: I think the purpose is still the same: to pass on messages that are important to us. The style may have changed, since we use recordings now, we can use computers, some may edit the recordings, upload it to the internet for people to view. Back in the day you had to be present with the person to hear their story. I think their story also changes [to something] more to modern.

....

4. A traditional female parka.
5. An oil lamp.

LT: Aturninga asijjingittiaqttuq: tusaumatittinirmit tamakkununga uvattinnut aturniqallariktunut. Nutaanik atuliqtilluta, nipiliurijunnaqsigatta, ilangit nakatiqtaullutik, qarisaujanik aturatta, ikiaqqivikkullu nuitippaklugit takujauniarmata. Taisumanili kisiani upaksisimaqattautiliraangamik unikkaarpalaurma.

Arnaikkunit ilaumariliqtillunga 2017mi, sanalauqtavut taijaujuq *Tia amma Piujuq*, pingasunik unikkaaqtuarninngaaqttunik ilaqalauqttuq, Inungnut tusaumajaujutuqaulluti tamakkua nunaminngaaqtut. Unikaartuatta ilangit tarrijarunnautirjuakut tarrijaqtaujunnaqsinniqpata pikkunarlikiaq.

Tusaqtitaulauqsimajunga innarmmin Tarriaksuit kappiananngittuguuq. Takulauqsimajaminik iqqaumattiaqluni. Tusaajaujunaraluaqlutik, takujaksaunngitut. Qiksimigillugit takunnattuugaluat, qiviaqlugit pitaqaqpanngitut. Niviaqsaangutillunga; aullaanginnaujapalauqsimagatta aujalimaaq, iqqaumangmijungattauq anaanaga uqautijara "Anaanaak, silamiittuqaqttuq, ikiraqpalattijuq", tupitta qanigijaaguqpalattijuq, takunasukkaluarakku angmajukulukkut takujunnangillugu.

Anaanaga miqsuqtillugu sailillunuk tupittinni, qimmivulli muggulaaqtummarialuuliqluni. Qiraaqpalattiju ungasikpalattilauqlluni, tusaalirillutiguk tupittinnut qanippalattijuq. Anaanaga nilinngisuujalauqluni, uqaliqluni avunngaungmaguuq. Anijumagaluarama takugiarumallunga aniqujaunnginnama, Anaanama ittuaqtturvikuluagut angmmajukulukkut takunasukkaluarama, inuktaqanngittiaqtuq. Anaanannut uqaqlunga, " Ingna qimmiq kisuungittiaqtumik kappiasusaaqtuq." Isumavungali qaglisuunguqquurmata aullaarsimavvittinik, iinguqquuqtuq, ukpirijara.

LM: Unikkaaliurusiriqattaqtait asijjiqpaa?

MI: Aakaunasugijarali. Arnait sanaqatigiikangamik, angiqatigiisuungungmata ikajuqatigiiklutik. Katujjiqatigiiliraangatta, angiqatigiisunggatta.

M-EK: Unnikkarumaujuinnaugatta, iliqusigigattigut unikkaaqtigut. Immaqaa Inuit ilangit naalakkauniqsaunngamata, amiqqaarunnarniqsaullutiglu. Uvagulli Arnaitmiittugut, unikkaaqtiugatta ammalu alianaigillutigut unikkaarniq,

I first became involved with Arnait in 2017. The fiction I was involved in, called *Tia and Piujuq*, we included three supernatural characters that are known to Inuit legends and myths for millennia, from traditional oral storytelling to modern technology on [the] big screen. I am looking forward to the release of this film.

I heard an Elder tell a story of *Tarriaksuit*,[6] which are not to be feared. She vividly recalls seeing them. You may hear their presence, although you may not see them. A Tarriagsuk can be seen from your periphery—when you look directly it's not there. I do also recall: as a child we were always travelling to the land. Every summer we were travelling, I told my mother, "Mother, there is someone outside, I can hear someone walking." I could not see it through a peek hole, but I was able to hear the footsteps near our tent ring.

We were sitting and relaxing, she was sewing, she was not alarmed. Our dog started really howling. We can hear the sound of the footsteps from the distance, then we heard footsteps closer to our tent. My mother did not say anything for a while, then told me they went away. I wanted to check what was out there, but I was told not to go outside. I peeked through a peek hole on the side of my mother's tent. There was no person there. I said to my mother, "Mother, the dog was scared of nothing." I think there was a Tarriagsuk close by our tent that summer. I think so, I believe it.

BM: Have your reasons for telling stories changed?

MI: In my opinion, I do not think so. When women work together, coming to a decision by helping each other. When we're in a situation, we achieve consent amongst ourselves.

M-HC: The reason to tell stories is a compulsion—a human compulsion for us storytellers. Maybe some people are more likely to listen to stories, to share. At Arnait, we are storytellers, and we like to tell them whether it is

....
6. Shadow people who are only visible in this world by the shadows they cast or once they are killed. The singular form is *Tarriagsuk*.

tarrijausiakkut uvvaluunniit uqausikkut. Alianaigillariktavut naalaklugit. Nangminirli isumavunga, inuktigut ajjiungiujaqtugut ilaak qanurli asianik piniaratta unikkaarniup asiagut?

Asianit qanuq piniaravit? Avaluttinnik tukisiumanasukkatta, ullaatamaat tupakpugut isumalluta " Ua, ullu nutaaq"! Iqqummaqpunga. Qaujimanngilanga. Tukisianngilanga nunarjuarmit qaniuliuqtunik. Qaujisausiriniq tukisianngilara. Avatirjuaq tukisianngilara. Nangminirluunniit tukiusiumannginnama. Suurlu qanuqlaalunguna? Tukisianngilanga naisausirirjuarniit. Ullurijjaaluit tukisiangilakka. Ammai, qanuimmakkiaq. Suurluliqi tukiqaqtittinasuktugut inuusikuluktinnik, tukisinasuaratta takujattinnik, ikpigijattinnik. Qanuimmat ullumi quviasukkpunga? Ippaksaq quviasulaurnanga? Kisu asijjirmat? Una kina inuk? Qanuimmat aivavat? Kisuungmat kinguniqput? Qanuq iqqaumavavut? Ikaaqsimajut unikkaaqtavut sulijumit unikkaaqpavut? Aakkallammarialuk!

LM: Tarrijausiasi asijjiqsimalirmata, unikkaalattaangujuniirlutik, pinnguanguniqsauliqlutik, qanuimmat taimaipa?

LT: Tarrijausiuqtiulluni nutaanik saqqitittinasungnarmat, qanuqtuurnarmat, alianaigijaunajaqtumit unikkausiliurumannarmat. Titiraliqtilluta *Tia amma Piujuqmit*, nutaangulaanik nipiliurutinik, nakatirijutinilu aturumalauratta, takujuminaqsitilugu. Tisamanik uqausirnnik pinnguaqtinnik uqallaqatalaaqttut, nakinngaaningillu ajigiinngimarialuklutit.

MI: Isumajunga unikkaaliurniq ajigijanga suli. Sulijumit sanagutta, iqqaumanittinnik tunngaviqaratta, tamakkua titiraqsimalaunngimmata. Isumavut atuttiaqlugit, iqaumalluni qanuuvalaurninginnik, iqqaqpasaaqattaqtugut uqausirnik atuqtauvagunniiqtunik. Angutauqturluluaq uvaguk taimaak aaqqiksuisuunguvuguk. Isumaksaksiuvigjualunuk, aaqiksuillunuk qanuk pijauvalauqtunik. Angutauqturlu iqqaumajattinnik atusuunguvuguk sanaqatigiilirangannuk.

M-EK: Ajjiginngittunik aaqiksimasuungujut. Ijurnasuunguvuq tarrijausiavut pinnguangugaluaqtillugit, pillattaangunasugijausuungunngmata. Munturiamit tarriujaqtautillugu *Uvanga*, apiqsuqtaunginnattialaurpunga pinnguaqtit with film or words. We love to listen to that. Personally, I think that the human condition is so weird because what else is there but to tell stories?

What else are you going to do? We're trying to make sense of the world around us, it's every day we wake up thinking, "Whoa, another day!" I wake up. I don't know. I don't understand what is going on in the world. I don't understand time. I don't understand space. I don't understand myself. It's like, "What the fuck is this?" I don't understand physics. I don't understand the universe. I don't know why. It's like we're trying to make order in our little thing, trying to give meaning to what we see, how we feel. Why am I in a good mood today? Not yesterday? What is the difference? Who is this person? Why are they arguing? What is history? How do we remember it? The history that we tell, is that really what happened? Obviously not!

BM: There has been a shift in the style of your productions, moving from something that *looks* less like documentary and more like narrative. Why?

LT*:* When you work in film there is a constant change—looking for ideas, looking for interesting subject matter. At the beginning of writing the script *Tia and Piujuq,* we planned to use the most updated technology available and use special effects. There are four different languages spoken by actors, coming from different backgrounds.

MI: I think that we still use the same techniques for telling our stories. If we are making a docudrama, we are still relying on memory, as these stories were not written down. Exercising our memories, remembering how things were, we even start to recall language that is no longer in use. That is particularly how Susan and I develop our videos. We think a lot, recreating how things were done. Susan and I still use the memory process when we are working together.

M-HC*:* There is a mix of styles. What is funny is that people think our films are documentaries even though they are fiction. When I was showing *Uvanga* in Montreal, people kept asking questions about the actors—that they are so good, they think it is a real story. It is not a real story and I find it interesting that

misaannut-ajunngiluarninginnut, unikkaaq sulinasugijausuungujuq.
Pillaataangungimmat, kamagiujaqparalu taimaak apiqsuqtuqaraangat.
Maananisautiungmat, ulumimullut aaqiksimalluni. Makkuali tarijaqtut
takunnaraangamit Munturiamiinnguaqtumit, tarrisausiugaluaqpat,
talaviisakkuugaluaqpat, taimaagli isumagijausuungungimmata! Qanuimat
pillattaangunasugijaunginnaujaqpat snavut tarrijaqtaugaangamik?
Qanuimmakkia naluvinga. Inungnit takulluni pinnguangujariaqanngimmaat?
Uvalukiaq pinguaqtiit pisitiuninginnik pillattaarasugijausuunguvat? Ammalu
ajjigiingittunik sananasukpangmigatta. Pillataanik, pinnguatunik. Sanavaktavut
takuninga atuqsimajuinnaungmata: unikkaaqtuarniq, pillattaanik ilasimallutik
pinnguaqtunik isumasaksiurnartunik.

Immaqaa tarrijausiurniarluni atugauniartut pijjutigillugit. Qanuq kiinaujanik
tuksirarnarpa pillataamik sananiarluni? Qanuq kiinaujanik tuksirarnarpa
pinnguartunik sananiarluni? Ajurnanginiqsauvuq pinnguartunik sananiarlunik
kiinaujanik tujuqtauniq, kisiani akuniuninga ajjittiarivauk pillattaarmit sanalluni.
Qanuimat sanatuinnarluni pilataanguaqtunik, arraaguunnit marruunit sanalugu-
pilattaatuinnamik pinngingaarluni- asianigluunniit

LM: Arnait tarrijausiangit suukkainniqsauqquujisuungungmata. Ilaanikkut,
qaangiqpalliajut akuniuniqsauqquujisuungungmata attuqtaujut tautuklugu. Tamanali
qanuq uqausirinajaqpiuk?

LT: Inuit inuusingat sukkainniqsaungmat, tuaviinnaujaalungilluni,
sailiniqsaulluni unikkaangujarjungniq, pilirijarialiilu tuavingiujarlugi.
Qallunaanigli, sunalimaat tuaviqtummarialuungmata, pijaksaqauvijjuattut.
Ingirranirluunniit, ikunngagariaqaqpuq, upaluqtualuulutit, nuqalaukakparnirlu
upagasuktani tikiniasaarlugu. Inuilli nunangani nunaliit mikimmata,
qaujimaqattautijuinnauttiarlutiglu. Taimainninganuunasugijara, isumakkullii.

M-EK: Pituinnakuluungittuq, naluvunga qanuq apirijaujuq kiujariaqsaq.
Ukiuqtaqturmiinnatta uvvaluuvva uqiurmiut unikkausingit, Inuit, qaujisaulluu
ikaarninga ajiginngimmagu. Takpaungaraangama sanaqatikka Inuulutik,
qaujisaup qaangirninga ajjiginngitanga uvaanut. Upaksimajavuqqai pijjutigillugu?

people ask that question. It is modern, within a modern setting. When people see a film set in Montreal, whether it is a film or a soap opera, people don't think it is a documentary! Why do they think it is a documentary, when they see our films? I am not sure why. Is it that you see Indigenous people, you think "documentary"? Is it because the actors are so good that people think it is real? We're playing with the style also. We're doing documentaries, we're doing fiction. Our style is a mix coming from those two traditions: storytelling tradition and documentary tradition mixed with drama.

Maybe it is a question of production. How do you raise money to make a documentary? How do you raise money to make fiction? It is easier to raise money for fiction, but it takes the same amount of time to make a documentary. So why not make a fiction film, take two years to make it—as opposed to having less money to make a documentary—then another?

BM: Time works differently in Arnait films. Often, moments *feel* longer than the actions contained within them. How would you describe your approach to time?

LT: Inuit have a slower paced lifestyle, not always in a hurry, a more relaxed way of telling a story, taking time with chores. In a southern environment, everything is more rushed, so much to do. Even getting places, one has to go here, then there, making hurried stops before reaching a destination. In the North, communities are small, everyone knows everybody else. I think this has to do with the pace of life, in my opinion.

M-HC: It is complicated, I do not know how to answer this question. We are working in the North or with the northern kind of storytelling—Inuit—and time is different. When I go north and work with my Inuit colleagues, I find time passes differently. Is it because of the place where we are? Is it because of the way people are? Or is it because of the use of the language? Is it because I don't understand? Because it is cold? When we're filming, it's different. Also, even the space looks different.

It is physical. For example, if you have to walk from left to right in a shot, it takes a long time to walk from there to there and you see it on the screen.

Uvaluunniit Inuit iliqqusingit. Uvvalukiaq uqausiup atuqtauninganit?
Tukisianngiluaramaqai? Niglasunngninganiik, uumunga iksumungaluunniit.
Ajjiliuriliraangatta asigijanga. Suqqaimmaluunniit avatigijavut ajjiginngimmagu.
Qaulauqtinnagumit, napajunit takujaksaqtaqanngimmat, avati qaujisaullu
ikaarninga.

Ilaannit timmi pijjutigillugu, pisugiaqaruvit saumingmit taliqpingmut,
akunialuk pisugiaqarnarmat, ikangnat ikunga, tautuklugulu. Napaaqtuqtaqaranit,
napajuqtaqarani, nunasiutitaqarani. Taimaitillugu, asijjirnarmat. Akuniunarmat
uvangat ikunga. Sunataqanngippat, suurlu maanippat, avatigijaq asiagut
aaqiksimakpat, ikaarniq ajjigijjaangimmagu. Aulaniq asigivauk. Taimmaak
isumaliqpunga takunnaqlugu *Maliglutit*, igluvigarmit iksivaaqtillugit, nipiqaratik.
Imannali uqaluutiralaaliringitut, imaagluniit qanuruluujaq. Taikautuinnaqpuq,
nuisavuq, ammalu akuniuniqsauvuq ajigingitangannik aturavit.

MI: Isumavungali sanajavut aaqittiaqsimagattigut, sulijumit takuksautittijumamut
piqqusiulauqtunik.

LM: Qanurli nakatirinialiraangassi parnasuunguvisi?

M-EK: Nakatirilluni, ujjiqsutiariaqarnaqtuq avatiujunik inigijaujuniglu.
Nakatirijittiavak qaujimajariaqaqput ikpigijariaqarnirminit. Ilurilugu.
Nakatiqnasaaliqtungali.

LT: Uvangali nakatirivanngittunga. Apirijaujaraangama, ujjiqsugasukpaktunga
unikkarmit tauttunginiglu. Ujjirusuttiarnit avatimut, silami ajjiliuqtaukpat.
Ujjirusuttiarniq upaksimajamit avatimit: sukkasarninga, sunalimaangit, tupiqaqpat
suurlu. Ujjirusuttiarnirmit qangauninganit, malittiarluni ingirrattiaqumut.

LM: Qanurli parnasuunguvit tukimuaqtinialiraangavit?

MI: Innarmigli uqaqatiqaqaanginnaujaqpunga, tarrijausiuqtamit
nalunngittulirijaujumit. Immagluunnit katimasijuqasikkaallapagluni
sivumuaqpallialluni, uqausiuniaqtut pilluanguaqlugit.

There are no trees or poles, cars that enter the scene. That changes your perception of time. It takes time to go from this area to this one. If there is nothing, just like a flatness, if a space is organized differently, then time is going to feel different. The actions are different. I was thinking that when I was watching *Maliglutit*,[7] when the characters are sitting in the igloo and they are not saying anything. People are not playing with their iPhones doing this and that. It's just like they are there, they exist, and the time is long because you're doing something different with it.

MI: I think it is because we want everything to be well created, really to have a true portrayal as to how it was.

BM: How do you approach editing your films?

M-HC: Editing style is respecting the approach to time and space. A good editor would see that, they would have to feel it. Respect it. I myself have not edited lately.

LT: I am not physically involved in editing. Although when consulted, I pay attention to the storyline and the visuals. Pay attention also to the environment, if it is being shot outdoors. Pay attention to that particular environment: timing, details, if there is a tent, etc. Paying attention to seasons, to make continuity flow.

BM: How do you approach the task of directing?

MI: I will always consult first with an Elder, one who is on the set as a consultant. Even to have quick meetings, as to provide direction as to how to proceed, especially regarding dialogue.

M-HC: Every project is different, so the style of directing will change depending

....
7. *Searchers.*

M-EK: Sananiaqtup ikpingnia. Ajjigiingittuinnaumata, tukimuarniglu asijjirniaqpuq ataluni kisu pilirijauninganut. Suurlu *Qaulauqtinnagumit*, Madeline aksualuk pinnguaqtimmariutillugu, tarrijausialirmattiarmut tunngaviulaurmat. Irnngutanilu tarijausiuqtauqatigilluniuk sanaqatigilliniuk. Ullaatamaat ajjiliuqtaulaurattik, ulluulauqtumigluunniit, katimaqatigiikpallauqpugut aturnniaqtattinnik.

Madelinelu parnaqatiqaliqpakluni Atuarmillu [Akittiq] Marymiglu [Qulittalik]. Qallunaatitut titiraqsimajuq aaqigiaqlugit titiraqlugillu Inuktitut. Uqausiit uqakataklugit nipiqaqluni. Uvangali ajjiliuqtauniaqtuq uqausirillugu, ajjiliuqtiit iqqanaijaqtiillu qallunaujatuinnarmata. Ajjiliuqtauniaqtuq uqarukku Madeline pigiaqpakluni, pijariirluniuk, ajjiliuqtausaaqturllu takkunnaliqlutigut. Imanallarik unikkaarunnanginnakku. Ilagagut pillattaatitut aulattialauqtuq. Madelinetauq ilitarijausimattialauqtuq Puvirnirtuurmit innarijaullunilu. Ilitarijauvaklunilu *Atanarjuat*-milaurninganit. Qaujimajauvigjualauqtuq. Nunalingmiunit kamavakluni, uvangali sanajivut qallunauqjaqtut, uiviitituuqtullu kamagivaklugit, aulattijiuqataujurrlu uiviingujuq. Taimaak tavva tukimuaqtilauqtavut *Qaulauqtinnagu*.

Sol-milli sanalluta, aulatuaninga ajjigilaunngittiaqtanga. Susan tarrijausiurumalilaurngmagu tillinanngittumik. Paninganik uqaluutirallakkut titiqqartaarama. Uqaqluni Susanguuq isumaaluutiqavigjuarninganik taissuma Suulumuuniup ilangit kamagijauninginnit. Ingminirasuginngilluniuk Suulumuuni. Asiangunasugilluniuk. Unangilaak isumaalugviguatuq. Isumallunga, "Qanuimmat tusaqtitauvunga paniagut Ruthiekut? Innaqai Susan uvannik tiliuqsinasuktuugaluaq?" Ruthie uqaqatigikkanilauqlugu, Susanlu titiraqlunuk naittumik unikkausimik, takuksautittijunnalaaqtumit [talaviisakkut] nanisillunga, qilamialuglu aqqiksuiliqluta. Tainna ajurnanngitualuulauqtuq kinaujamik pinasunngnikkut. Qilamialuk aaqilauqtuq.

Susan unagilaak pivikksaqarniqpaangulauqtu qaujisaliqtilluta tarrijausiattinnik. Tainnaulaunngippat, uvannut uqallaktuqarajalaungilaq. Inungit upagialinngnit qaujimalaurmat. Suulumuuniullu ilanginnik uqaqatiqarunnalauqluni, piqannarijanginiglu, makkuktunnut innauniqsaniglu. Apiqsurnilimaattiat upaksimaqattalauqtangit. Apiqsuqpaklunilu. Kisiani apiqsuqtituinnaulaungilaq. Ilurirrajulauqtuq. Imanna uqausirijaunnajalaunngittiaqtuq tainnaulaunngippat. Aksualu innauninga ikpigijaulauqtuq.

on what is going on. For example, in *Before Tomorrow*, where Madeline was really involved in acting, she carried the whole film on her shoulders. She was working with her grandson as her main actor and partner. The process was that every morning before shooting, or the day before, there was discussion on what we were going to be doing.

Then Madeline would prepare with Atuat [Akittiq] and Mary [Qulittalik]. She would redo her dialogue in Inuktitut from the English script. Checking the words, saying them out loud. Then I would call the shots for the camera and sound crews. They spoke English only. I would call the shots, then Madeline would start, complete the scene, we would review it. I am not quite sure how to describe it. It was organic in some way. Madeline also had a role in the community of Puvirnituq [where the film was shot] as well as being the Elder on the set. She was also recognized from her role in *Atanarjuat*. She had some fame. She dealt with the community and I dealt with the English- and French-speaking crews. This is how we directed *Before Tomorrow*.

On *Sol*, working with Susan, the approach was very different. Susan came up with the idea of making *Sol*. I got a message from her daughter on Facebook. She told me that Susan was very troubled with what was happening and how the family [Sol's family] was being treated. She did not believe it was suicide. Maybe it was something else. She was really troubled. I was thinking, "Why is this message coming to me through her daughter Ruthie? Maybe Susan is trying to ask me to do something?" I spoke with Ruthie, then Susan and I came up with a one-pager, found a broadcaster, and started to work on the film very quickly. That film was very easy to finance. It came together really fast.

Susan was so very important in the investigation of the film we were making. Without her, I doubt anybody would have talked to me. She had access to people. She had access to Solomon's family, access to his friends, both young and old people. She attended every interview. She did the interviews. Her role was more than just being an interviewer. She was the catalyst. Otherwise, nobody would have talked about that subject. She also commanded respect as an Elder.

For people, having an Elder wanting to discuss the subject matter of suicide was incredibly important. It was difficult for both of us to make this

Inungnu Inungnut inarmit uqallagunnaqtumit pitaqatillugu pimmariulautuq. Tamattinnuk aksurungnalauqtuq taana sananasuklugu. Ajurajalauqtara tainnaulaungippat. Aksururnalualaurninganut. Ajjiulaungittuq. Ilaak kamanaqtuq, uqausiqatiginnginnannuk. Kisiani tarrijausiurnikkut tukisiumaqattautittiarannuk, turaagavullu ajjigingmat. Ammalu manna arraagunit 20 ungataanit sanaqatigiilirannuk.

Niriuktunga Lucymit sanaqatiqariaksaq, ajjigijjaangikkivauk aullattijiuniarama tukimuaqtijiutillugu. Qanuinniaraluaqpakiaq. Apiriniaqtara qanuiliuquniarmangaarmma tarrijausiulirutta. Najurniaraluaqtara, kisiani unuqtunik Iglulingmit tarrijausiuqatausimalirmat, katujjiqatiqalimallunilu. Kinaujanik tuksirarrasugluni tarrijausiurniarluni, sanaluni uangilaak taiggusiit aviktuqsimajariaqarngmata qallunaatitut; kamaji, tukimuaqti, ikajuqtii, sialaaq makualimaat. Taimaak titiqauniaqtut tarrijausiurluni taimaak taijjusikkut kisiani saqqijaariaqasuungungmata. Imannatuinna uqarunnanginnatta, "Una tarrijaksaq tamatta sanjavut"! Kisiani iluunnata taigusiqsuriaqaratta, piqqusiit maliglugit, ilisarijaujjutiit. Qanurli pijariaqaqpita? Nangminiq pilirijaksattinnik pilirijariaqaratta tarrijausiuliraangatta. Lucyli pinnguqtinik tukimuaqsiniaqtillugu, akauksaqujara unikkaani saqitiliruniuk. Kisiani aksururnarniaqtuq nutaqqanik ajjiliuriluni.

LT: Uvangali ujiqsurniaqtunga niviaqsaakuluuk [pijjutilik *Tia ammalu Piujuq*] sailittiaqullugit, akauksaqullugillu. Ajjiliuqtaulauqtinnagillu uqalimaattiaqsimatinniaqtakka uqausiriqattaqniaqtanginnik. Uqalimaaqsimavagirlutik, parnaksimalutik, ajjiliurimmariliruttalu sulijunik uqaqatiqaqpagluta pijariaqaqtattinnik, takujumajattinniglu. Taimaak aulanasungnniaqpugut tassuminga sananiaqtattinnik tarijaksamit.

Taimali iliqsituqarnit aturiaqaraangatta, Piujurmut apiriinaqpalauqpunga, ungasigiikkaluaqtillunuk. Suurlu imanna uqarutta akauvaa? Immanna tauttua akauvaa? Apiqqsuinnaqpallauqpara tarrijausiurniaqtavut titirasungaqlugu kappiasaarijumangilunga uvvaluunniit ukpirijaujunik malikkaluarmangaarma, tukisigirvigivaklugu. Anaanagali uqausiqarummaulaunngimmat tarriagsuit misaanut, tuksiariagajuktugu. Piujurli apiqqutinnik kiujunnaqtillugu, aksualuk qujagilauqtara. Susan Avingaq, akunialuk Arniakkunit ilagijujuq, aksummarialuk ilaujumalaungittiaqtuq Tarriasungnit uqausiqarniatuaqpat.

film. I do not believe I could have made this film without her. It was too difficult. It was a different process. Obviously it is a strange thing, because we don't speak the same language. But we speak the language of the medium and have the same goal. Also, at this stage we have been working for over 20 years together.

It is going to be interesting to work with Lucy. It will be very different for me, as I will be the producer of her film. We'll see how it goes. I'll ask her what are her expectations for me on the set. I'll be on set, but she has worked on many films in Igloolik and is used to collaborative works. It's interesting because, to finance, you need specific roles: director, producer, coordinator, assistant. This is a requirement on the screen credits. What you cannot do is say, "Oh! This film is made by us!" We have to give each other titles like this, officially, for the credits. What do we do? It is up to us as to what we do individually on filmmaking. Lucy will be directing the actors and I want to help her to be comfortable telling her story. It is going to be difficult, as it is difficult working with children.

LT: In my case [referring to *Tia and Piujuq*], I will make sure the young girls are relaxed and comfortable. I will ensure that they have read the script ahead of time, prior to shooting. Script reading in advance and during the shoot, making sure there is honest communication about what is the expected outcome. That is how we will try and move things along with this film.

In terms of content dealing with traditional beliefs, I constantly deferred to and consulted with Madeline, even though we were in different places geographically. Things like: is this dialogue acceptable? Would it be all right to portray the scene this way? I was always consulting with her as I was writing the script to make sure it is non-threatening, or that it is respectful to beliefs, understanding from her. My mother, being a more churchgoing person, was hesitant to answer or discuss traditional beliefs with me, while Madeline could answer my queries. So I was very grateful to her. Susan Avingaq, a long-time member of Arnait Video, on the other hand was absolutely adamant not to be involved in a script involving Tarriaksuit.

She was not comfortable with the subject matter. As a young woman—or rather, as a woman in between youth and middle age—and because, I think, having seen Tarriaksuit in my childhood, having heard them while out on the

Uqausirijavut, illuarilaungitanga. Makkuktuullunga, uvaluqai, inarlauliraluaqlunga, ammalu Tarriaksunik tusaqsimagama nutaraullunga, aullaarsimalluta tusarnikugillugi, ukpirijakka. Kappianarasuginngillugillu. Angajuqqaakka uqaqpalaurmata kapianangimmataguuq, uvattitu inuusiqaramik. Tusaumalaurakkit ilaliutijumalauqtakka, kappiananngimata. Tanna pijjutigilugu, titiraqtannik ilaliutijumalualauqtakka.

Sivullirmit taakkuak niviaqsaak Montrealmiinnialauqtuugaluak. Titiralisaaqlunga-M-Elu Samlu titiraqatigilaurakkit-apirillugit "Nunavummuangaaruttali? Nunattinnut, pilluaqtumit aullaarvigivaktattinnut, nunalingni ajjigingitangit pivakktillugit. Tarriasunngnit apuqsinatuinnariaqaqtillugu." Nutaqqanut, quiliqtanarujugluni, aliasummarikkaluarlutik aliannainiqsaujunnarasugillugu. Taimaak pililauqpugut.

Aksualuk tarrijausiurluni alianaigigakku, sanajakka pianigumammariliraangakkit, uglaqtuqaqpat, uqautisuuka sanajariaqarninnit, tukisiumatillugi pijariaqaqtannik. Ukpiriniqarniungmat pilirijamit, aksuruutigillugulu.

LM: Qanurli parnasuunguvit pinnguarnmedialiraangavit ajjiliuqtauniarlutit?

MI: Pinguarniaqtara isumaksaqsiutigijariaqallarisuura. Inarnut apiriinnaujaqtunga sulijumit aturaluariaksannik. Piluaqtumit sulinnguaqtunik sanagutta, tukisiumattiariaqarnaqurmaringmat. Ikajuqqattautiqattarpugut, ikajuqatigiikpakluta, ammalu suqquisugasukkpakluta qanuq taissumani atuqtauvalauqtunit.

Parngnarniq ajjiliutauniarluni ajjigiikpuk pinnguarniaruniluunniit, sulijumilluunnit sananiaruni. Uqausiriniaqtat iqqaumanasuglugit ajjigiimmat. Qungattailijariaqarniruni naliatuinnarnit, attausirrmit aturnarmat pijjunnautimik.

LT: Tarrijausiuqtauniaqtuq uqalimaqaalauqlugi tukimuaqtiuju pijumajangit maliklugit. Pinnguarnirli ajurnarinnginnakku. Alianaigimut, pinnguarniq. Iqqaumavunga-niviaqsaangullunga, ukiuqarlunga 5-6, talaviisaup iluaniinnguaqsirtuqpalaurama taissumani Inuit talaviisakkut takuksauvaluanngitillugit. Iqqaumajunga unnullaalukkut, 12minngaaliqtillugu Iglulingmiunik ilaujuqaqluni, taissumani CBCkut saqqijaaqttitillugi *Inuksuk* land, I believe in them. I do not think they are to be feared. My parents used to say that that they were non-threatening, they live as we do. Because I had heard about them, I wanted to include them in my script, that they are not beings to fear. That is really why I decided to include them.

Initially, the girls were going to be based in Montreal. Early on in script development—I was developing this with M-H and Samuel Cohn-Cousineau—I asked them, "What if we move the location to Nunavut? To our land, and especially out on the land/tundra, where different things happen. Where they might be in contact with Tarriaksuit." For children, there is a bit of an eerie element that might make it more interesting, although non-frightening. That is how it developed.

I truly enjoy filmmaking. When I really want to accomplish something with my work, if someone visits, I have to say that I have to work, make them understand my priorities and commitment. It is commitment and passion.

BM: How do you approach acting?

MI: I really do concentrate a lot on the role that I'm playing. I will always ask Elders for an accurate portrayal. Especially if we are working on a docudrama, it is very important to consult properly. We help each other's memories and recollections of how things were done in the past.

I find preparing to act for a feature and being in a documentary is the same. Memorizing dialogue takes the same preparation. If we have to keep a straight face for either style, we use the same process to control our emotions.

LT: I read the script first, listen to what the director wants, and I take it from there. I find acting to be natural. It is my passion, to act. Since—I remember as a young girl, 5 or 6, I used to pretend to be inside the TV when there was hardly any Inuit on TV. I remember the launch of the first ever Inuit TV Live Stream, called *The Inuksuk Project,* on CBC. It was after midnight, 12:30. It included *Igloolingmiut,*[8] as we were living in Hall Beach. I begged my mother to wake me up so I would not miss it.

....
8. People from Igloolik.

*Project*mit, Sanirajangmiutautilluta. Anaannannut tupaaqtaujumalauqsimajunga, takkujumalluarnikumut.

Taimaatigi talaviisamit pikkugusulauqsimajunga. Taissumanilu isumavakkaluaqlunga qanualuk inukulungnit mikittullaaalungnit talaviisaup iluanuaqsivangninginnik, kisiani qaujimaniqsaulilauqtunga, Inuillu ilauniqsauliqtillugit. Ivvit ilaulauqsimajutit, ammalu Apak Angilirq. Pikkugivigjualauqsimajakka, quviagillugillu, suli nutaraugalluaqlunga. *Takuginai*millu saqqitittigavit, Apaullu sanajangit takunnaqlugit. Nangminirli, pinnguarnirmit quviagijaqqaanilaurama. Taimaaqai, pinnguarniq aksurunnarinngilara.

Uqalimaalisaaqlugu *Atanarjuat*, ilauniariaksannik nalulauqtunga, pikkunaqtualuulauqtuq, suurlu, "Naruluk, qiiminaqturuluk"! Ilangagullu sirnigillugu, nuliarijaulluni, manisaqluni, iniqtirumallugu. Inngnarlaaluk!, qanuittualunguna! Taimaak ikpigitigilauqtakka ilukkut Pujamik pinnguarasuktillunga. Ilaunialirama, isumalilauqtunga, "Ainna, taimaktauq arnaqatiga Sylvia, piruqsaqatigilauqtara." Ilirasurujulauqsimavunga pittiannginguariaqarninnit. Ilaanikkut ajjiliuqtautilluta, iluarnattiaqattalaungittuq qanuiliuriaqaraangakku, pittiannginnguariaqaraangakku, suuqaimma pinnguatuinaraluaqtilluta ajjiliuqtaugatta.

Illaanikkuttauq ajjiliuqtautilluta ijingit ujjirinajaqlugit nagligillugulu isumalungalu "Mamianaq, taimailiuriaqarniarakkit." Pinnguatuinnaralluaqlunga, pijumanngikkaluaqtillugu pillugu. Ikpinnaqattavijualauqtuq. Pinnguaqluni annuraaqsimaliqluni, piusaqtaulluni ikajuutiqarnammariktuq, aturniaqtara, isumakkut parnattiaqlunga, timikkut, taikunngarluni pinnguarlunilu.

Uvagulliqai ujjiqsurniqsauqquratta uvattinnik, inuuqatittinninni, silatittinnilu. Taimannganit mikinnittinnik piinguaqpalauratta, nutaraugatta, nutarautitaulluta. Inuganguaqpakluta ujaratuinnarnilluunii pinnguaqasikallakpakluta qarmannngualiurluta, ujaratuinnakulunngnut. Qiturnnngaujaqariaqanngilluta, isumavut atuqlugit, taimaitillugu, pinnguarnialluni ajurnnannginniqsauqquqttuq.

Iqqaumavunga nutaraullunga piqannarijaqalausimagama, qallunaakulungmik pairijariaqaqluni, ilisaijinik angajuqaaqaqluni. Uangilaak piqujaaqauqtummarialuulaurtuq, isumavaklunga, "Qaunuimmanuna nutaqqaujunnangilaq?" Maligaqavigjualaurmat: "Iglumit ullajanngillutit.

That is how enthralled I was with TV. I did used to wonder how they manage to fit really tiny people inside the television. But I [came] to realize later on, [especially] when Inuit were more involved. You were involved, as was Apak Angilirq. I was impressed with it and had passion for it even as a young child. And when you introduced *Takuginai* IBC, watching Apak's work. I was already delighted with the acting component. Perhaps that is why I consider acting to be a natural part of myself.

When I first read the script for *Atanarjuat – The Fast Runner*, I was not sure whether I would be cast, it was so interesting. Her character popped up a lot, like in, "Arrghh, she is so spiteful!" But then I would feel defensive for her, as someone's wife, admiring a man, thinking to caution her behaviour. Bitch! Or, How dare you! Those are emotions her character raised in me. When I was to be in the film, I suddenly realized, "Oh, there is also my cousin Sylvia, whom I have grown up with." I was in trepidation of having to act aggressively towards her. During filming, it was sometimes uncomfortable when I had to do something to her, being negative towards her, although it is in character and we are acting.

When in some scenes, I would notice her eyes and feel for her while thinking, "I'm sorry that I am going to do this to you." Although, again, it was totally the character and not me personally. It was quite emotional. Getting into character by putting on costumes and make-up is an immense help. I would take time, at least take five minutes to myself alone, find a private space, concentrate, get into the role and prepare myself, my body, go there, and perform.

I think we are more in tune with ourselves, the people, and the environment. Since we were little, we played—it was natural to pretend, kids were allowed to be kids. We played with *Inuganguaq*[9] or even with rocks, just simple rocks as human sticks, and make circular form of *qarmmaq*[10] on the ground. We did not need a Barbie to play, so we used our imagination. When you adopt this imagination to acting, it is easier that way.

I remember as a kid, there was this friend of mine who had to babysit a child of Qallunaaq teachers. He had so many rules to follow and I would wonder, "How come he can't be a kid?" So many rules: "Don't run around the

....
9. Hand-carved wooden dolls.
10. A type of dwelling used in spring and summer.

Qarliikkit maramittailikkit" Isumavungali, "Aww, nutarautituinnalauqsiuk"! Piruqsainiq ajjiginngimmata Inunngnit, Qallunaaniglu. Inuullutali, nutaqqanik nutarautittisuungugatta, anirajakktillugit. Taimainninganut pinnguattiluta iluriniqsausuunguvugut tarrijausiurnialiraangatta.

Pillattarmit tarrijausiuqluni, pinnguarniunngimmat, pillattangungmat. Inuusiungmat. Manna pivalliajunik, qanuimmat pivallianinganik, ammalu ikpigijait: pillatangujuq, pinnguanngittuq, sulijuq, qanuq sulijut pivallianingit, tusaumatittiniq, saqqititittiniq pillattaaqtunit.

LM: Arnailli sanajangit qanuq tautukpigit, ullumi Inuit tarrijausiurnirivakktangit isumagillugit?

MI: Uvannulli sanajavut ajjiungiginnginnakku asittinnik sanajauvaktunik.

M-EK: Apiqqutiksattiavak, kisiani asinnit kiujauluarquurmat. Taimmaak uvattinnik uqausirijariaksaq ajupalukkatta. Uqausirillugit qanuq aulanirivaktatinnik, qanuq uvagut pivanngnittinnik. Taimali uqausiuniarangatta, asinnginniktauk tarrijausiuqpakktunit, asittiniqai uqausiukpat akauniqsausuungujuq.

LT: Arnaikulli tarrijausiangit arnanut turaangasuungungmatta. Tamakkuninga arnanik pimmarigijaujunik, akturniqaqtuniglu. Inunngnit tarrijausiuqtauvaktunik, arnanut turaanganiqpaangujut: miqsurniq, tiguarniq, amiliriniq. Tamakkualimaanit unikausiqarniqsausuungujut.

Isumakkulli sanajangat, *Atanarjuat* angutisiutaulauqtuq, sivurliq takijuq tarrijausiangat, tuglingallu *Kunutiup Titiraqtaviningit*, pingajungallu Maliglutit. Ii, taikkuali tamainnik saqitittisuungujut angutisiutinik, uvagulli arnanut turaangaluaqtunik.

LM: Uqaqsimagavit sulijunit sanagaangassi, inulimaanit inungnit nipitaaqtittisuungujusi, qanuimmat tamaippa?

LT: Nangminirli isumagillunga, uqalauqtakka iqqaqlugit, sulijunik sanaluni utiqtitisuungunngmat puiguqtavininnit, suuqaimma pillattaanik house. Don't get mud on your pants." I'm thinking, "Aww, let him be a kid!" There is a difference in upbringing a child between an Inuk and a non-Inuk. I think, being Inuit, when we are raising kids, we allow them to be kids, play outside. I think that is why we're more natural when it comes to acting.

In a documentary, you are not acting. It is a fact of life. What's happening right now, why it's happening, and how you feel—it's real. It is for factual, not playing, really occurring, how real events are happening, relaying information, showing visuals of reality.

BM: How do you see Arnait's work within contemporary Inuit film tradition?

MI: I do not know in what aspect our works differ from others.

M-HC: It is an interesting question, but I think that somebody else should answer. It is hard for us to talk about ourselves like that. We can talk about our process, what we do in particular. When it is time to make such comparisons, I think it takes some kind of external eye.

LT: Arnait Video make the majority of their films for women and women's issues. Content on what is important to and what affects women. Compared to other Inuit films, they are all geared to women: sewing, adoption, preparing skins. All those things, they concentrate more on those topics.

With Isuma, *Atanarjuat* was masculine, their first feature film. The second feature, *The Journals of Knud Rasmussen*, and third feature, *Maliglutit* (*Searchers*), are all masculine, but Arnait's emphasis is on women's issues.

BM: You have spoken of the docudrama as permitting you to "take on [your] own themes by giving voice to several generations of Inuit." Why does the genre allow you to do this?

LT: I think, for myself, recalling what I said earlier, that the docudrama style relives, reconstructs events or practices that I may have forgotten, because the basis for the docudrama is factual events. It provides a vehicle to remind us of unikkausiqarmata. Aqqutauvuq iliqqusittinnik puigujjailluni, puiguliqtavut nuitillugit. Makkunngniqsanut, uvaluunniit inuusiulauqtumit atulanngittunik, irngiinnaq takuksautittisuungujuq, atuqtauvalauqtunit. Iqaqtitauvakpugut, qanuiliuqpalaurninginnik. Inuusiulauqtuq iqaqlugu, iili uvannuut, taimaak isumasuunguvunga. Pikkugijara, ammalu alianaigijara sulijunik saqqittuqaraangat.

M-EK: Uvattinnulli pimmariugijavut arnalimaanit sanaqatiqariaksaq, qanutuinnaq ukiulingnit. Pimmariullattaaqtuq. Makkungniqsaujunit ilauqujivigjualauqtugut, kisiani, uqallaktinnasuklugit ajurnapalulauqtuq. Kanngusunngmata, apirillaqtaaqlugillu, surlu "Qanuimmat immaippa?" uvaluunnit "Qanuimmat taimailiurajaqpit?" "Taana sungmat isumaksaqsiurutauva?" Kiujariaksaq qiksaakpalauput. Sulinnguaqtunik sanalluni-ilangagut pillataangunnngimmat-ajurnangigijauniqsausuuq nangminirijarmininngaangimmat tavvani nunagijaujunni.

Pinnguarniqsaumut, atannginniqsaujut pinnguartiujumut, uqallagunnarniqsaujut. Sulinnguaqtunik pinnguarniarluni suurlu inuk atausiq tikkuaqtaunniqpat, tainnaunguarumaluni, sulirlakkaluarluni pillattaangunnngimmat. Makkungniqsanut ajurnanginniqsaulirlunilu. Qaujimanngilanga arnait makkuktut uqallagunnarniqsaulirmangaata inugiaktunik nunalingnit. Asinngirniqai anginiqsanik nunalingnit taimaingikkaluarpuq. Nunaliit ajjiginnngimmata, nunalingnit anginiqsaniqqai uqalagjuariaksaq ajurnannginniqsauvuq.

MI: Nangminirli, alianaigijaqarniqsaujunga pillattaanguniqsaujunik, uluminisaunnginniqsanik, imaagli, isumalluni qanuq taissumani pivalaurninginnik, inuusirilauqtattinnik. Uvangali ujjirusukpunga tamakkuninga sanajumaniqsausuungujunga. Nuttaqqait sanasimajattinnik, ilaanikkut ijjuaqsisuungujut. Iqarnasuuq. Suli tarrijausiurluni alianaigijara, kisiani ningiungulirama, qaujimajunga suli alianaigigakku! Unikkaaqtuanit tarrijausiurumavigjuaraluaqtunga. Tautunnguasuunguvunga unikkaqtuanik tarrijarlugit alianaittualuunajaqtunik. Unikkaatuqait.

LM: Qanurli tautukpiuk piliriarivalauqtatit isumagilugit ikajurniqaqpat sivunirnit piliriarijumaniaqtarnik?

52 | Inuit TakugatsaliuKatiget / On Inuit Cinema

cultural values, providing a repository of traditions that we are losing. For the younger generation, or those who have not experienced these cultural practices, it brings life to past reality, as to what was done in earlier times. We are reminded of how past life was lived—at least in my case, that is how I react. It makes me proud and I'm grateful that this method is used.

M-HC: What is important to us is to work with women of different generations. That is important, for sure. At one point, we wanted to have much younger women joining, however it was difficult to get them to talk. They are shy. It was hard for them to state an opinion. When you use the docudrama—because it has some fictional element—it puts them more at ease, because it doesn't necessarily come from them personally as an individual in this community.

Because there is an element of dramatization, they are able to distance themselves and verbalize more. With docudrama, we are creating a composite character. And if I am in this character's role, it is a bit of truth, but not really. So for younger women, it becomes easier. I do not know if younger women are finding it easier to talk today publicly in the communities. It is probably different in the larger communities. Every community is different and perhaps it is easier in larger communities.

MI: Personally, I am more inclined to prefer the docudrama style, not contemporary; rather, reflecting on how things were done traditionally, the way lives were lived. I find that I am more drawn to these topics. When children watch our films, they sometimes re-enact scenes. This brings memories back. I still do enjoy filmmaking, however I am becoming an old lady. I know I will still enjoy this profession! I have a real desire to bring some legends to life. I imagine certain legends that would be riveting to watch on screen. Old myths.

BM: What role do you see your past work as playing in shaping your future work?

M-HC: Somehow it does. I'm not sure of the future at all. Technology is changing. Politics are changing. There are new people making things. Every

M-EK: Qanuugaluaqiaq ikajurniqaqtuq. Sivuniksara qaujimanngittiarakku. Sunakkutaat uajamuulingajut asijjiqpallianginnarmata. Innaruqpalliajuinnaugatta. Inuillu nutaat pilirijaqaulirmata. Tarrijausiuraangama, isumainnaqpaktunga, kiinaujanik tujuqtauniq pituinnaungittummariutillugu. Immaqai tarrijausiutara kingulliqpaangunialiqtuq, ilaak qaujimannangitiarmat. Suvuniksavut tautunnginnakku.

Alianaillaalunga aujaq Iglulingmiinniaratta ammlu titiraqluta *Tia amma Piujuq* tarrijausiuqtauniaqtumut. Ikajuqatigigluta, sivullipaattiamit Lucy tukimuaqtittijiuniaqtuq. Paningalu ilauniaqluni. Aulattijiuniarlunga. Ikpigusuttiartunga suli taimailiuratta, sanaqatigiigunnattiaratta. Taissumani araagut quliit qaangiqsimaliqtillugit, piliriniqput asijjiqsimalirmat. Maana 2017mit asianit tukiqarmat. Pimmariuvuq suli kajusiinnaratta. Amisuit nuqqasuungunmata!

Susan tauttuginiaqtanginnit, annuraanguanguniaqtunit tamakkuninga kamajumajuq, alianait! Pikkunavigjuaqtuq suli sanaqatigiigumagatta, Madeline anaanattiannguanguniaqtuq. Aksualuk quviasugutigijara ammalu pikkunaqquuqtugut.

LT: Piliriaginikukkali ilisimavakka Saqqaliasimik, Marie-Elenamit, Madelinemit, Susanmillu, ilisimavvigijakka. Ilisimajakka aturniqarniaqtut sanaliruma *Ababa*mit sanalaaqtakkalu sivunnittinnik, kingulliriniartannillu makkungniqsaujut ilisarijumajakka. Uqallaqatigiiktiarniq, tukimuaqtinik pinnguaqtinik, ajjiliurijinik, tammakkiit tukisiumattiaqullugit. Uangilaak qautamaattiak quvianaqtuq, ulaarnit pigiarluni, uqaujjuiluni—"Ullumi imailiurniaqtugut"—tarijaaliurtulimaat qaujimattiarniarmata pilirijariaqaqtaminit.

Sanaqatigijat tamarmittiaq tukisiumattiaraangata qanuq piliriniaqtaminik, turaagarijaq tikinnasuklugu ajurnannginniqsausuuq. Apirijaulauqsimagama tarrijausiuqtuqaqtillugu ikajuqujaullunga, kikkuummarilaurninginnik uqarumanaga, kisiani aulaningat ajjiunngittummarialuulauqsimangmat, uvagulli atuqpattaktinnit. Uqallaqatigiittianginniq akaunngimmat, akiraqtuqatigiilirnaqtuq, ammalu iqqanaijaqtigittiarunniirnaqtuq, pinguqtinut, ajjiliurijinullu. Akiraqtuqtuqaraangat nalunasuungunnittuq ajjiliuqtautillugit. Piuniqpaanguvuq parnaktiasimaluni, aaqqittiaqsimavagiirlunili uqallaqatigiittiaqattarluni kisiani sivumuttiarnartmat.

LM: Turaagarijasili-nangminiq uvvaluunniit tamassi- asijjiqsimaliqpaat?

time I make a film, I think I am lucky that we received funding to make a film. Might be the last time, because who knows? I do not know the future.

I think it is very interesting that we wrote this script for *Tia and Piujuq*. Finding ourselves in Igloolik this summer is a real treat. Working together, it is Lucy's directorial debut. Her daughter is in it. I'm producing. I think it is pretty meaningful that we're still doing it, we're able to work together. It is different than when you're doing it 10 years ago. Doing it now, in 2017, means something different. It is great that we're still doing it.

Susan wants to be the art director, wow! It's still special that we are still wanting to work together. Madeline's going to be acting as the grandmother. I think it is great and very lucky.

LT: I have learned from my past work through Zacharias, Marie-Hélène, Madeline, Susan—I have learned a lot from them. I will use what I have learned for my upcoming feature *Ababa*,[11] and future works, and pass it on to the younger generation. Being able to communicate—directing actors, cast members, film crews, everyone—to understand the process. I find it rewarding to work daily, starting from the morning, giving direction—"This is what we're doing today"—so that everyone is on the same page.

When everyone understands the total expectations, it makes the goals much easier to achieve. I was asked to work on a film, I will not state specifically, but it was so different as to our working style. When there is no communication, it creates more conflicts and people get caught in between co-workers, crew, and actors. When there is that conflict, it is visible in front of the camera. It is always best to be prepared, planned—and communication is the key.

BM: Have your goals, both individually and collectively, changed?

LT: My goals have evolved, for sure. Once we went to Mexico to meet other Indigenous women filmmakers. We showed our films, as well as seeing theirs. At that time, I think we were more focused on documentaries. While today we

....

11. *Ababa* was the working title for *Tia and Piujuq*.

LT: Turaagakka aaqqigiaqsimajut, nalunangilaq. Miksikumualauqsimagatta asinnginnik nunaqaqaaqsimajunit katiqatiqariaqtuqluta. Tarrijausiavut takuqqutigillugit, taikkualu sanasimajangit tarrijarillugit. Taissumani suliniqsanit tarrijausiuqpalauratta. Ullumili pinnguavigjuarniksanik turraaqqujikalauqtugut, kisiani, matuinngainnaujarniaqtuq ajjiginngittunik tarrijausiuriniq sanavaktattinnik. Asinnginnik unikkaanik saqqittijumagama suli. Tusaqtaujariaqaqtunik innaqutivut nungulaunnginninginik. Taikkua ajjiliurumajakka nipiliurumajakka.

LM: Kisunigli suli unikkaalaungilatit?

LT: Sulittiaqtumit uqaruma taissumani *Atanarjuatmit* ilaujariuqlunga tarrijausiurnirkkut, isumalauqsimanngittiaqtunga taimaak akuniutigijumik kajusilaariaqsaq: arraagunik avatinik. Manna suli pimmariugijara, taissumanitut, ammalu kajusiinnarumallunga ajungittaraangama. Unikkaarumanajaqpunga qanuq qiturnngiuriaqarnirmit Inuit piqqusingit maliglugit, taissumanitut Inuit atuqpalauqtangit aturlugit. Imaak surlu, uqqaujjauvalauqsimagatta numaasuksuujaqujaunata akuniluaraaluk, asittinnik uqausiqaluariaqsarluunniit, asittinniglu isumarlugiaqarnata. Tamakkua uqausituqait aksualuk aturniqarmata makkungniqsaujunut, taikua qiturngiuliriiingmata. Ilangit qiturngaminik isumakkiutitivalirmata.

Anaanagijaujuq nutaqqaminut aakkaarunnangittiaqtuq sunalimaanit, uqalluni "Paningma pijumatuaqpagu pitinniaqtara." Taimaak qiturngaata sivuniksanganik isumanngittiaqtuq. Tanna nutaraq isumakkiulualiruni, aksualuk piujunniituinnarialik. Nalunanngimmat, isumattianngikkuni, taimailiuqtaunikut sivuniksaminik pijunnangitaalungminik pijunnarasugiqattalaaqtuit. Tanna uqausiujariaqattiaqmat. Taissumani atuqtauvalauqtut nutaqqait miksaanut maliktauvalauqtut qaujimajaujariaqarmata ilitaukkanniriaqarmata. Taimmagli tarrijausiurniruma, arnaq angullu uqausiqarajaqput qanuq nutaqqanik piruqsailunik piulaangungmangaat, qanuq akaunngittunit iliqqusiqaqunagu pijarialiit, piungittunigluunnit taissumanititut. Taimaittumik tarrijausiurumalaattiaqtunga.

M-EK: Aamai nalujunga. Uvaguulunuqai tarrijausiulaaliqpuguk!

are exploring the feature film genre, but the door will always be open to differing styles of presenting our work. I still want to present other stories. Some that have to be heard before we lose our Elders. These I wish to record.

BM: What stories have you yet to tell?

LT: To be completely honest, when I first started film, with *Atanarjuat*, I never thought I'd continue this far: to 20 years. So it is still as important as when I started, and I'd like to continue when I have spare time. I would like to tell a story of how to raise a child according to Inuit beliefs, in the way Inuit would bring up a child. For example, we were told not to be downhearted for long periods of time, or to gossip, or to think badly of others. These types of teachings would be beneficial for the younger generation who are, of course, bearing children. Some of them are spoiling their children.

A mother not refusing a child anything—saying, "My daughter wants, so I will get." This is not thinking of the child's future. When that child will become too demanding, it could have major negative consequences. It is clear that there is no consideration, that the type of action taken at the moment will translate into unrealistic expectations in future. This is an important topic to bring forward. Past traditional child-rearing practices need to be revisited and relearned. If I were to present this in film format, there would be a woman and a man discussing proper parenting skills, how to prevent undesirable or negative habits in the manner of past traditions. This is one theme I would like to visit in a future project.

M-HC: I don't know. Maybe one we'll make together!

Stephen Agluvak Puskas

Stephen Agluvak Puskas was born and raised in Yellowknife, Northwest Territories. His family is originally from the Whale Cove area in the Kivalliq Region of Nunavut. After studying art and media at Sheridan College in Oakville, Ontario, he worked as the Media Officer for the departments of Environment, Natural Resources, and Industry, Tourism & Investment for the Northwest Territories. In 2008 he moved to Montreal, where he has worked as a freelance artist, media producer, and educator with a specific emphasis on representations of Inuit in media. I conducted this interview with Stephen in English on June 1, 2017, in Montreal.

MARK DAVID TURNER (MDT): How do you understand the historical Inuit experience with film?

STEPHEN AGLUVAK PUSKAS (SAP): This might be difficult to determine now, because I think that a lot of the first Inuit that experienced film have passed on. I don't think Inuit experiences with film were something anyone really cared to document. It seemed there was much more documentation about what the film-maker thinks is the Inuit experience, not the Inuit experience itself. And also, documentation of this kind of romanticized version of Inuit experience before the Europeans came; not documenting this experience of being in contact with the Europeans and the experience of having so much change happening in a very short period of time. With the exception of a few—I think Isuma, they do have some films about that—but that's only really happened in the past 20 years or so. Whereas Inuit in film has been happening for about 90 to 95 years. So it's only been more recently that there's been some documentation about that, when it comes to Inuit experience in film.

From what I've seen—from my perspective as an Inuk with mixed heritage—I think it was very practical, very much like it was still coming from this system of trade. And you didn't think much of it, after that. I think a lot of Inuit and Inuit culture is much more practical and functional, or utilitarian, in that sense. I think for a lot of people it can be very difficult to look outside your own world and see how others might perceive you. So, many people didn't think anything of it when someone came up and said, "I've got food" or "I've got money" and "All you have to do is do this in front of a camera." For a long time, people have been coming North and doing that as well. "I've got money, you just have to give me some fur." Or, "You've got some old toys kicking around, I want to trade you for that." I don't think many people second-guessed these transactions. There was no oversight on these transactions. And often there was no money. I think there's been a number of incidents where filmmakers have gone up North and they have been able to make films without having to contribute to the community. My *anaanatsiaq*[1] experienced this when a film crew told her what to do in front of the camera for *Angotee – Story of an Eskimo Boy*.

MDT: When do you think that film began to really play a significant role in Inuit Nunangat, and why?

SAP: I'm not quite sure when that happened but I can see why that would happen. It's probably because of a lot of Inuit—not just Inuit, but people in general—started noticing that things were changing very quickly up North. I remember reading newspaper articles from the '60s and '70s about how ethnographers were afraid that Inuit culture was disappearing so quickly and rapidly and that there wasn't going to be any Inuit left very soon. So there was a scramble with ethnographers to go up North and record as much as they could and get as much material culture before the culture died out, in their eyes. I think it was during that time you had people, like James Houston, who were going up North and teaching Inuit different

....
1. Grandmother.

art forms, different art practices, like printmaking. It was probably around that time these new mediums were coming in and people started to take notice and say, "Maybe there is value or importance in using these mediums to record our culture, record our stories."

MDT: What do you see as being some of the impediments to the development of filmmaking in Inuit Nunangat?

SAP: One of the difficulties is location. Shipping things up North and just shipping things down south, it's very expensive. For a very long time, it was much more expensive to produce films and videos. The tools of production were not as accessible to the mainstream population as they are today. Cameras were big, heavy, and expensive and you would have to send film to get processed. If you're living very far from processing centres, it could take a very long time to get that done. I remember some people talking about still cameras: mailing their film out and then the photos came back a year later. It was very commonplace. There is a history of federal and provincial governments not really placing much importance on or interest in Inuit culture and art. These governments tend to see these things as economic development projects. There wasn't really a lot of support for a very long time for Inuit telling their own stories. There is also the issue of education. The quality of education that's offered up North is very different than what is offered down south. There is no university in Inuit Nunangat.

MDT: What about exhibition access?

SAP: There are a lot of films about Inuit that Inuit don't see, Inuit don't watch. I just got an email from an editor to comment on *Living with Giants*, a film that the community of Inukjuak had apparently seen before it was widely distributed. Although the community was given the opportunity to watch the film, there was a critical piece of context missing here. For the community, the film explored the loss of a young person and would likely have been seen as a memorial. However, for outside audiences, the film was seen as representative of social problems stereotypical to Inuit Nunangat. This film was not a story about an individual for this audience. From what I saw with public discourse, the film prompted a discussion of what it's like to be Inuk. I think that's quite common with just minority representation in general. You have a story about an individual—and if they're not White, and if they're not from the mainstream culture, then they become the mascot for whatever community they're from.

MDT: How would you describe the state of media literacy among Inuit right now?

SAP: I think there are more Inuit who are becoming literate in film—how to read a film—and about filmmaking. But I think there is still a long ways to go in terms of Inuit being in control of our own representation and in telling our own stories. With a lot of organizations, like Youth Fusion in Quebec, for example, that go up North and offer educational programs to kids, there's still a problem with educators dumbing down material to appeal to the lowest common denominator to improve educational success rates. This is seen in *Qallunaat! Why White People Are Funny*, where Inuit laugh looking at scientific educational material aimed at Inuit students that dumbs down the content to the point of absurdity. A lot of educators are still facing the problem of trying to get youth involved and committed to their education. It seems like a lot of educators are still sacrificing quality and content over trying to get students engaged. Along with Youth Fusion, Wapikoni Mobile will go into Indigenous communities and teach film, among other things. But these organizations basically parachute into a community, they stay there for a few weeks, and then leave. That's not enough time to learn the nuances of film production—like editing—or a lot of film theory or history. It's also not enough time to build long-term relationships. It's only enough time to give a very basic understanding of many practical things, like how to use a camera, how to use a microphone, the basics of storytelling. From the educational material that I have seen with these organizations, it really falls short in providing an in-depth understanding of film. But there are still a number of Inuit out there who specialize in Inuit film.

MDT: Do you think that kind of community-based literacy is important to have?

SAP: It's very important to have at least someone in the community who is knowledgeable about storytelling, about film, because it's very much a part of culture. It's becoming a part of our culture, not just Inuit but Canada as a whole, especially since a lot of these films are reaching a larger audience than other forms of fine art that Inuit make—in the sense that you're going to see Inuit material culture in an art gallery or in a museum. As opposed to these films, which you can watch at home on your computer, or on TV, you can watch them at the theatre. Film, television, and new media can have a lot more reach into the greater public than an art piece does.

When it comes to that—to the community and having the literacy in the community—that's very important because this is the message that is being sent to a wider audience and that is representing us and representing the communities. It's really important that we have a say as Inuit, and as community members, over how these media represent us.

MDT: What do you think is the legacy of that ethnographic tendency, of southern filmmakers representing Inuit culture on film?

SAP: It's a legacy of mis-educating an audience, mis-educating the greater public. It's a legacy of propaganda from the Quebec and Canadian governments, exerting nationalism, trying to create a sense of national pride by using symbols that are not their own. As part of this legacy, there's also a tendency to exert Arctic sovereignty, to define Inuit as a part of Canada, and our land as part of Canada. It's created a legacy of Inuit being used for the purposes of provincial and federal governments, while at the same time mis-educating the greater public about Inuit culture, history, and society while creating and perpetuating stereotypes about Inuit.

There's a general distrust with ethnographers, there's a general distrust with outsiders coming in and taking things. There's a long history of outsiders who come in and take things, then leave. A lot of people in the communities are tired of that, tired of people coming in taking what they want and leaving and never seeing them again. I think one Inuk told me about how they don't like anthropologists because they take our stories then go down south and use them to build a career and a name for themselves—while this exchange doesn't benefit the Inuit who were involved. These continued experiences have made a lot of Inuit bitter about outsiders who come North looking for material.

MDT: Can you broadly describe the contemporary relationship between Inuit and film?

SAP: It's a diverse relationship. For example, there's Alethea Arnaquq-Baril, there is Isuma with Zacharias Kunuk. Their relationship with film is very different, as filmmakers, compared to many non-Inuit filmmakers or Inuit who work in front of the camera. Then there are many Inuit exposed to southern filmmakers who go up North to make films. There is a bit of a bit of a clash between the two because a lot of southern filmmakers have access to a lot more money and resources compared to Inuit filmmakers in the North.

In the past year, there was a funding agency that gave their entire budget to Québécois filmmakers for two films set in Inuit Nunangat, but nothing to Inuit filmmakers. The two films were *Two Lovers and a Bear* and *Iqaluit*, the movie. Then they had to go and tell Inuit filmmakers living in Nunavut, "Sorry we have no money for you. We ran out of our budget." That is a big problem. Some of these organizations don't do the greatest job representing Inuit and they don't have Inuit representing Inuit. [They are] making decisions that are not in our best interests, such as funding films about us that are not being told by us, as opposed to funding Inuit films. I think the reason why this happened was because southern filmmakers have a lot more clout, and they also have a lot more reach.

There's also a history of institutionalized racism in some organizations. For example, some funding organizations do not recognize Inuit as audience members. When it comes to funding film projects, funders count ticket sales and seats as indicators of success, which informs their decision of funding a film or not. So a film that was made up North, whose main audience is up North, wouldn't be considered for funding. But if there's a film made from the south and it's intended for the south and they already have great relationships at film festivals, then it's a lot easier for them to obtain funding.

There's also institutionalized racism in funding organizations like SODEC,[2] a Quebec cultural funder. They have a yearly budget of roughly $60 million, however they've given no money to the Inuit and Cree region in Quebec from 2010 to 2016. There are similar situations with the Canada Council for the Arts, as well as provincial arts councils. As far as I know, the Canada Council for the Arts did not fund any Indigenous art up until 1985. And with organizations like the Quebec Arts Council, only in 2017 did they specifically allocate funds towards Indigenous artists. By comparison, the British Columbia Arts Council has allocated budget for Indigenous artists for about 20 years. That's a very big difference: it's been very difficult to actually get funding to create artwork as Indigenous artists in Quebec and other parts of Canada.

MDT: How do you think that difficulty of accessing funding affects production?

SAP: Basically, the films don't get made. Someone may have an idea for a film, but it's probably not going to get green-lit—or if it does, it's going to be very low technical quality because they usually don't have the access to resources like professional equipment. It's something that people may do in their free time, so they don't get to devote the majority of their waking life to their own projects. If that's the case, you can have lower quality productions that are more difficult to get into film festivals and get to audiences. And at the same time, funders might not be as keen to support you if you're not making high-quality productions. This was my experience with *Ukiuktaqtumi*. I had a budget of $330 to make a short film and a provincial arts council wouldn't respond to my emails looking for funding opportunities.

MDT: How does this funding situation affect the training of Inuit filmmakers? Right now, there seems to be a proliferation of Inuit filmmakers.

SAP: I think there is a proliferation of Inuit filmmakers in spite of the lack of resources in education and funding. Filmmaking equipment is an information technology that has become democratized. It's much easier now to make a video,

....

2. Société de développement des entreprises culturelles.

compared to any other time in our history to make a film. It was a luxury to have a cellphone 20 years ago; it was practically unheard of to have a cellphone up North. It's a lot more commonplace now and we have HD cameras with the capability to shoot video on our phones. It's become a lot easier for Inuit to access this type of equipment at a much more affordable price.

MDT: Do you consider the ability to represent oneself and one's culture a basic human right?

SAP: Yes, I do. I was reading about this last night: it's a basic human right for self-representation in the Justice system. There is a similar basic human right in another system of our society, so I don't see why that cannot be applied to other systems in our society. Why is it a basic human right to be able to represent myself in the Justice system but not in arts and culture?

MDT: What do you think happens if one is not able to represent oneself in arts and culture?

SAP: I think what happens is that it opens the door to have others telling stories on our own behalf and without our permission, without our consent, without our knowledge. Especially in a social structure where minorities don't have access to the same resources, platforms, and opportunities as non-minority storytellers or filmmakers have. Yet at the same time, there's a great demand for Inuit stories specifically. Many non-Inuit and non-Indigenous storytellers have noticed and exploited this demand. In the capitalist society that we live in, where culture is a commodity that people can buy and sell, Inuit culture is sold by non-Inuit storytellers who share none of their profit and ultimately none of the liability for these stories.

MDT: How would you define an ethical filmmaking practice, as it pertains to Qallunaat working in any community in Inuit Nunangat?

SAP: I think the ethical thing for them to do is to teach filmmaking, to be a mentor and a teacher to Inuit artists, and work with Inuit. If you're going to make a story about Inuit, you actually work with Inuit on it. Inuit should be co-producers at the very least. They should get to have a say in the creative process, as well, and the decision-making process.

When it comes to collaboration, it's not enough to just hear from a filmmaker, "We collaborated with Inuit, we had them consult with us." That doesn't address the power relationship between the filmmaker and the Inuit involved. Consultation could just be the filmmaker, after they've made all their decisions, showing the finished film to an Inuk for their stamp of approval. The Inuk doesn't know what was left on the cutting room floor. They don't really know what the film could have been. All they get to see is the finished piece after all the decisions have been made. I don't think that's an ethical way of consulting because in that scenario the non-Indigenous filmmaker has already made all the creative decisions.

Let's say you made a film here in Montreal about Montrealers, and you get some random Montrealer off the street to approve the film. Does that mean that the filmmaker can go to the rest of the world and say, "I got approval by Montrealers?" The random Montrealer says, "That looks great." But is that person educated or knowledgeable about film and representation? Do they realize that some of the things that were shown in that film could be damaging? I don't think it's enough to have that type of consultation or collaboration with Inuit. It really has to be much more of a balanced power relationship between Inuit and non-Inuit film-makers. I think the most ethical thing to do is to get Inuit to make stories about ourselves, to tell our own stories, and for non-Inuit filmmakers to be there to help us overcome obstacles. Non-Inuit filmmakers should be self-conscious about their capacity to influence our stories.

MDT: How do you envision true collaboration and true partnership?

SAP: We can see an ethical collaborative relationship with Arnait films and with productions like *Sol*. Marie-Hélène Cousineau is a Québécoise filmmaker who co-directed *Sol* with an Inuk filmmaker—that is a more equal partnership in terms of decision-making. I know Marie-Hélène has spent many years living up North, not just travelling north to film. She has shown a personal investment in the community. She has built relationships with Inuit storytellers, as well as with the rest of the community. That is also a very important part of collaboration. Once you are able to build an honest and sincere relationship with the community, you'll start to realize the responsibility you have in representing that community. Once you accept responsibility, as a non-Indigenous filmmaker, you start to realize the consequences of your actions for communities.

MDT: Do you see a trend toward more ethical filmmaking practices across Inuit Nunangat?

SAP: I think in Nunavut there's a lot more tendency to working towards ethical filmmaking practices, because I think the film industry in Nunavut is a lot more developed than in Nunavik. I think the Nunavik government—or just Nunavik in general and in Quebec—it seems like the big push for economic development in Nunavik is about resource extraction, is about manual labour. It's about government, it's about providing basic level services, offering mental health services and education and stuff like that. I don't think Nunavik is quite there yet, in terms of their economy, to be able to start developing more specialized areas of arts and culture. Whereas I think Nunavut is a bit more ahead in their development of that area.

So, when it comes to Inuit Nunangat, I think Nunavut is a lot more ahead when it comes to developing ethical filmmaking practices and an ethical filmmaking community and institutions—except for the Nunavut Film Commission—but compared to Nunavik. Nunatsiavut, I don't know as much. I think the Inuvialuit have noticed and have acknowledged an importance with film and video. With that film I made, *Ukiuktaqtumi*, I was in contact with some Inuvialuit cultural centres and the work I saw that they did I thought was very ethical.

Nunavummiut have noticed a need, have thought of it as important, have put more thought and work into developing their film community. And because of that, they have more educated, more film-literate members of their community. If you don't develop that, then you have people who are not literate in film, who are not knowledgeable, or who do not have expertise in that. And that leaves them very open to be exploited, to just go along with an outsider who comes in and says, "Oh, well, can you just do this for me in front of the camera?"

MDT: Do you think that there's a model for what represents ethical filmmaking practices with Inuit?

SAP: Arnait and Isuma provide models for ethical filmmaking practices. With films like Isuma's *Atanarjuat*, where Inuit were actually learning old sewing methods just to make authentic props and costumes for the film. Not just Inuit being in charge of the production and the decision-making process, but also going back and learning, or re-learning, cultural practices so that they could have an authentic portrayal of Inuit pre-contact culture in the film. Even though Arnait's *Sol* was very heavy and intense, and Marie-Hélène was very conflicted about making that film, she ultimately decided to be involved in that project because people in the community wanted to tell that story. She wasn't pushing people to tell that story, people were pushing her.

MDT: How might Qallunaat filmmakers and their Inuit collaborators alert their audience to the fact that what they are watching is a genuine collaboration?

SAP: I remember having a discussion with other curators about authenticity when I worked at the Canadian Museum of History. On one particular project, direction was given to the curatorial team that the content had to be authentic, which meant we spent a lot of time discussing authenticity. We had a debate about what constitutes authentic representation of the boat artefact. It's the exact same boat as it was when it was first made, it looks exactly the same, but over the years a piece of wood gets replaced by another piece of wood, and so on. Eventually none of the original materials of the boat remain but its shape and form remain the same.

The same thing can happen with a film. You can look at every movie or film that's made about Inuit by non-Inuit and see what's been replaced. Of course, it's not black and white. I think of it more as a sliding scale, where there has to be a checklist of authenticity. In terms of an artefact of material culture, does the object have the same shape and form as the original object had when it was created? Did the object come from that time period where those objects were commonly used? Was the object made from the same material as the original?

Or was it made by the people that would make those objects? Was the object used for its intended purpose, or was it made for a museum exhibit? Those are all different levels of authenticity. You can use those as a checklist. One object in an exhibit might not check every box, however the curator can include other objects that check other boxes. Taken as a whole, the curator is able to present something that meets a threshold of authenticity. The same can be applied with film: you can have a checklist of how you can make a more authentic film. If you can't check off a certain box, then you need to ensure that you check off others.

MDT: What is on the checklist?

SAP: For Inuit film: have Inuit filmmakers, have an Inuit production crew. Have Inuit in front of the camera and behind. But it's not just that. It would be really great to have Inuit producers, as well, and Inuit funders. That's a huge problem right now, films about Inuit are largely made by non-Inuit producers. Inuit have to apply to get our films funded by non-Inuit institutions—and the problem with that is that these non-Inuit institutions often have evaluation criteria that don't align with Inuit values. Some of those institutions have a history of racism. It's essential to have Inuit producers, funders, directors, storytellers, production crew, actors, scriptwriters. You have to have a good explanation if you don't have any Inuit in your crew. Why can't you find Inuit crew members? If you can't find Inuit crew members, you could at least provide training opportunities for us. I think another important part of the checklist is to make sure that when a production leaves a community, that community is more capable of making its own films than it was before the production arrived.

MDT: What role might Inuit filmmakers play in ensuring ethical filmmaking practices are being actually applied in Inuit Nunangat and with Inuit communities?

SAP: Our role is to promote literacy in our representation in media and promote our rights and responsibilities. That happens in other industries that we enter, where we don't know our rights. That's when it becomes very easy for us to get exploited and be tokenized.

I think someone like Alethea has taken on a lot of responsibility—and she's not an Inuit representative in this sense: no one elected her. That doesn't invalidate what she has to say in any way. She is speaking for herself and she speaks very eloquently about what she believes. It is a huge responsibility to have to speak up about Inuit misrepresentation and cultural appropriation. You're opening yourself up to the public eye and being scrutinized by strangers you don't know. That is a very heavy responsibility.

Inuit filmmakers shouldn't be solely responsible for advocacy and education. That's putting a lot of responsibility on the artist for things that do not include making art. Are Qallunaat artists responsible for advocacy and education in this way? Some are. Many non-Indigenous artists don't need to think about the responsibility of educating other artists or advocating for the arts. They just do what they do. They make art and work on their own career and focus on their craft. It is a responsibility to represent community, but it's not a responsibility that I would want to push on any filmmaker or any artist because you do get a lot of stress from that. I think it's much better to have an Inuk be involved with the education and the advocacy work. But I don't think it should be expected to be included in the job.

MDT: How might we treat films that are explicitly unethical toward Inuit? Is it simply an issue of censoring them or is there something that can be learned from, or done with, these films?

SAP: It would depend on the film. The concept of censorship has a different meaning and a different history to different cultures. Here in Quebec, for example, a lot of people are against censorship because of the history of the provincial government and the Catholic Church censoring media from the Quebec public. A lot of Québécois are really against the idea of censorship because they have been on the receiving end of a powerful institution deciding what they get to see, read, and hear. But you have to take power dynamics into account. If you have a marginalized group of people being poorly portrayed or misrepresented in a film and they say, "We don't agree with the way we're being represented in this film," and the producers don't listen to their feedback or refuse to collaborate, then that is also a form of censorship.

I've had this talk with others about how some of these problem films could be used in a beneficial way. When I watched Dominic Gagnon's film *of the North*, for example, I did not think of how it can be beneficial at all to be shown, especially in the context that it was shown in. The film was made from stolen footage from online streaming sites, purportedly by Inuit and about Inuit. It depicted images of naked women and children without their knowledge or consent. If you're going to publicly screen a film that misrepresents Inuit, you have to provide an awful lot of context and educational material to counteract the misinformation and negative portrayals in that film. You need to provide a space for discussion about why that film misrepresents Inuit and invite Inuit to be able to speak. If you don't have those types of things in place, then maybe the film should not be shown. Films like this do a lot more damage than good. They perpetuate institutionalized racism.

In 2016, I was invited by what was then known as Rendez-vous Québec Cinéma to host their screening of *of the North*. I told them how the film was already screened at Cinéma du Parc, in Montreal, and about Inuit experiencing homelessness who live nearby. I expressed concern about how audience members saw those Inuit when walking out of the theatre after watching that film. I don't think it was positive. It prompted me to think about the systemic racism in Quebec's healthcare system, where Indigenous patients are being denied healthcare because of implicit bias and medical professionals harbouring racial prejudices against Indigenous people. There's a story about a First Nations patient dying from a stroke, which was easily preventable, but they could not get medical help they needed because doctors and nurses thought that he was drunk and told him he just needed to sober up. I think that's how films like *of the North* really hurt us: people in public watch them and they carry these stereotypes and prejudices with them. They define how they interact with us as Inuit.

MDT: What roles might film critics and film criticism play in counteracting the effects of problem films like *of the North*?

SAP: A lot of film critics need to be educated about Indigenous people in general, about histories, culture, identity. A lot of non-Indigenous film critics need to be in contact with Indigenous people, talk with Indigenous people, as well, so that they can get a better understanding of where Indigenous people come from and our perspectives. There needs to be Indigenous film critics, too. We need diverse voices, diverse opinions. In the case of *of the North*, with the exception of one person, every other film critic or writer who wrote in support of *of the North* was White and from Quebec or France. That represents a very homogenous set of voices with an established platform. One race, one language, one culture, all saying the same thing in unison.

There was another side of this public debate made up of a diverse group of voices. It wasn't just Inuit, it was non-Inuit and First Nations who spoke up against the film. There should be more space in film criticism for these diverse voices and to have some form of intercultural exchange. It's not good enough to have a diverse set of opinions when you have one set of opinions being much louder, better funded, with broader reach. It's not good enough. There's this narrative here in Canada that we live in a multicultural society. But you can have racial segregation and inequality in a multicultural society.

MDT: How would you characterize responses to your efforts to educate the public on ethical film practices with Inuit and the difficulties of a film like *of the North*?

SAP: Sometimes the responses leave me feeling like my efforts are futile. I'll speak about it if I'm given the opportunity to, but it takes a lot of emotional energy to do so. Oftentimes, I don't feel like I want to speak about it. However, I feel a duty to speak about these things. After *of the North* was first screened as part of the Rencontre International Documentaire de Montréal in 2015, someone sent a link [to] the film and invited me to talk about it on a radio show. I had a strong reaction to it. I was traumatized, in part because I had attended the Nunalijjuaq Film Screening series the week before, which focused upon giving Inuit opportunities to tell their own stories with media. *of the North* was the opposite of this.

After I watched *of the North*, I felt—as an Inuk with a background in film production and anthropology—that I've got a responsibility to say something. It wasn't something that I really wanted to do, it was something that I felt like I had to do. I remember supporters of the film were saying, "We are showing this film to start a conversation." I'm not certain who was supposed to be included in this conversation, but Inuit were not invited to a majority of these screenings. If there was a conversation, then I felt like I was being coerced into having it. If *of the North* was meant to start a conversation, it was starting a conversation in bad faith. You cannot start a meaningful conversation with Inuit by showing a racist film against Inuit.

I felt like I was on the defence every time I was solicited to speak about the film. And I felt coerced by the supporters who were so insistent on screening the film. I spoke about it a lot, and every time I knew that I was going to speak about it, I had to spend a lot of time researching and formulating my ideas. When talking about the film in the media, I quickly realized that I often only had a short amount of time to say what I wanted to say, even though it was a very complex issue. How can I distill these issues of racism and misrepresentation into a five- or ten-minute response? There's this history to put this film into context and similar films into context. How can I make people understand that this film is a symptom of these larger structural problems in Inuit representation and the difficulties we face because of the Eurocentric climate of film production in Quebec and Canada? This is a history that many people don't know about and do not have an opportunity to be educated about. How do you speak to these things in five to ten minutes? I felt like I was on the losing side of this debate because I was going up against people from Antitube, Rendez-vous Québec Cinéma, Cinémathèque Québécoise, Productions Réalisations Indépendantes de Montréal, Vidéographe, Conseil des Arts et des Lettres du Québec, SODEC, as well as people from government-funded institutions who are getting paid to support a racist film. I was not being paid to engage with them. I was advocating during my free time. This was not my job. I felt like I was going up against a very well-tuned propaganda machine. This is their work, this is what they're getting paid for, and they're being paid with public money to oppress marginalized voices and promote racist propaganda. I tried to do the best that I could in that situation. I don't know how successful it was. The film is still being shown. What can you do when someone's not going to listen, and is not willing to try?

I think I was able to educate some people with my efforts. A few strangers approached me earlier this year and thanked me for the public talks that I gave. But at the same time it seems like, here, that there's an inner circle of Quebec cinefiles—of this "higher-class" culture—that do not want to talk with other people other than themselves. The unfortunate thing is, a lot of these people in this inner circle are the decision-makers, the funders, the people who hand out public funds, and the people who get to spend it.

MDT: What do you see as being the most significant impediments in your advocacy work?

SAP: I think one of the biggest things that I've butted up against is bigotry. When a person's sense of belief is stronger than their ability to rationalize or to think logically. I think that's a problem because there has been a long history of nation building in Quebec through the work of the public education system. Creating that belief system is an important part of nation building, but it also suppresses minorities. I know other Québécois nationalists who have told me that they believe in self-determination for Quebec, but they don't like the direction of Quebec nationalism. So it's not the case with all nationalists. I think that one of the main obstacles that I'm up against is wilful ignorance. It's unfortunate that many of the people who display wilful ignorance are the people who hold power in many public institutions, like the ones I mentioned before. There's a lot of Quebec film organizations here who are not inclusive of minority communities and who support people from their own circles. That's one of the biggest obstacles. That, and trying to get the government to change their funding and ethical practices.

MDT: So, what's the next step?

SAP: I was just chosen as an Indigenous Youth Leader for the Senate of Canada. So the next step is to keep talking about these issues whenever and wherever I have an opportunity. I feel like I've made that commitment, I've taken on the responsibility. I'm not a spokesperson for Inuit, but as a citizen in our society I have a duty to participate in this country's democracy. I want to get more people involved in the conversation but also in action. I would also like to try to get more funders involved and aware about these issues, so that they can make better decisions in the future. I am trying to reach out to those organizations, even though it seems very futile right now. Recently, I spoke with Professor Bruno Cornellier[3] who published an article about *of the North* and he said he sees things are changing.

I think younger generations are going to be a lot more knowledgeable and a lot more sensitive about these issues. You can see the change of conversation in classrooms. Another important step is to bring up these issues of ethics and representation in colleges, high schools, and universities. Another thing I want to see in secondary and post-secondary schools is education around ethical representation of Indigenous Peoples. There are arts and communication programs in post-secondary schools where non-Indigenous graduates go on to create works that exploit Indigenous people. This is something that needs to be addressed in post-secondary institutions. There are established ethical standards in social science disciplines like anthropology and sociology, so why aren't there ethical standards in the arts and humanities?

MDT: Can you describe the process of making your film *Ukuiktaqtumi*?

MDT: I remember it was you, in the Inuit Studies Conference, who approached me about making that film. First we talked about the idea of responding to *of the North*. This response would be exhibited at the Inuit Studies Conference. There was a lot of flexibility on what I could do with such a response. I began by looking at videos on YouTube and social media. I already had some videos by Inuit that I wanted to incorporate in this response. Then I started reaching out to the creators of these videos, telling them about my project, why I'm doing it, and what I hoped would come out of it. I think the *why* was very important for many of the people I approached. Some of the Inuit I approached were directly affected by *of the North*. I thought it would be very important to include these Inuit in this response. I asked for permission and consent to use their videos. And I asked them what videos they would like me to use. I did not want to be the only decision-maker in this film. I wanted everyone to have an opportunity to choose what they wanted to include. The great thing was that many Inuit trusted me and almost everybody told me I can use whatever they had posted online. But I always went back to them

3. Associate Professor of Cultural Studies in the Department of English at the University of Winnipeg.

and told them which videos I wanted to use and requested their permission. Only then did I put together my film.

One of the major obstacles was that most of these Inuit live up North and have very bad broadband connections, very slow internet speeds. I could not send them regular rough edits of the film because they wouldn't be able to easily stream them. But I would upload a private YouTube video and send them the link so only they could watch the rough cuts and give feedback. The feedback that I got was all positive, everyone liked it, and they knew where the film was going to be screened. I also submitted the film to Presence Autochtone and I planned on informing everyone who contributed footage when it was going to be shown elsewhere, if it was being shown elsewhere, and for what reasons. I think that's very important to keep in touch with the contributors and let them know when the film is being shown.

MDT: How did that consent process structure your own editing work?

SAP: I didn't get to go through YouTube and pick whatever videos I wanted. I restricted myself to the videos I received permission to use. It wasn't a restriction in a negative sense, it was one that was ethical. If anything, this guided the decision-making process about what kind of videos I wanted to use.

MDT: Did it force your hand in terms of the story that you ended up telling?

SAP: It forced my hand, I think, in some moments. Not all moments. I remember when I was invited to talk with non-Indigenous filmmakers at Rencontres Internationales du Documentaire de Montréal who were producing documentaries about Indigenous Peoples. One person commented, "You don't have ownership. You don't have creative control. You don't have power over your own film." My response was along the lines of, "You're sharing their power with someone else." Sure, I did not have as much control over what I made in the film, or what I included in the film. But I don't think of that as me losing control. I think of it as sharing some of that control with the people who helped me make the film. It is much more about sharing power instead of losing it.

MDT: As a working process, do you think that what you did with that film is something that people can learn from? Is this a model?

SAP: I think so, particularly when it comes to the issue of collaboration and how I communicated with the people who made the videos. Building the trust was an incredibly important aspect. But building trust is not the be-all and end-all. I've met non-Indigenous filmmakers who built a trusting relationship with their subjects but still did unethical things. Therefore, it's not just about building trust, it's about being transparent and being sincere as well. You need to do what you say you're going to do and hold yourself accountable to the values of the community. You need to be completely transparent about your intentions—because it's one thing to build trust with the community, but you're going to break that trust if you say one thing and do another. That's not being sincere.

MDT: How did you go about ensuring transparency in making *Ukiuktaqtumi*?

SAP: Consistent and transparent communication is important. I think it was very easy for my film because it was built into the approach. I explained to the contributors that *Ukiuktaqtumi* is a response to very negative portrayals of Inuit and I want to make a film as a counterbalance. Some of the portrayals in my film may not seem that positive. For example, the film covers social issues in the last five minutes, but in a way that, I think, this was empowering for Inuit. There is a healthy way to talk about social issues. You can't talk about alcoholism or other issues like suicide without giving a counter-argument, without giving context. There is also an issue of perspective. I've noticed a lot of non-Indigenous storytellers or filmmakers tend to take a deficit-based approach when telling these stories. In other words, they portray Inuit as helpless. Many storytellers don't realize that the work that they're doing compounds the social issues they are trying to address. You have to have a good understanding of the subject matter in order to provide the proper context.

When it came to addressing social issues in my film, it came from a position of strength and resilience. It's a very different approach to what I see in other forms of media, where outsiders come into a community and try to address social issues without any understanding or context. Often, outsiders situate themselves as saviours in a community that apparently can't solve its own problems. That's a very common approach in media like journalism and film.

MDT: What stories would you like to be told through film now?

SAP: I'd like to see stories about Inuit in the future. We already have so many about us in the past. I'd like to see stories about Inuit succeeding today, that younger generations can look up to and see as role models. I'd like to see Inuit explore different genres of storytelling: science fiction, romance, comedy, horror. I want us to break out of the box that we've been placed in—of documentary, news, and historical drama that portray us as an endangered species—and explore new possibilities and new worlds where we thrive. Stories that inspire us and give us hope for the future.

A Checklist for Making Film In and With Inuit Communities

BY STEPHEN AGLUVAK PUSKAS

This checklist is intended for filmmakers, film festivals, film programmers, film funding bodies, film critics, film educators, film artist organizations. It is also intended for broadcasters, educators, audiences, and anyone with a vested interest in the uses of film.

We are at a crossroads regarding what constitutes acceptable practice for filmmaking in and with Inuit communities. For too long, film production and exhibition apparatuses have been able to tell and circulate Inuit stories without sufficient guidance and inclusion from Inuit communities. The process of *meaningful engagement* is neither complex nor restrictive. On the contrary, media produced by way of meaningful engagement will be richer and more vibrant than the alternative.

This is not to advocate for Inuit films solely produced by and for Inuit and excluding non-Inuit. There is a place for non-Inuit in Inuit film productions. However, there is an intrinsic and inherent responsibility related to telling stories that are not that of the storyteller. It is imperative that the film production and exhibition apparatuses that operate within Canada understand that different cultures share, view, and interpret stories differently. These stories and these systems are not incompatible, but they require a better understanding of the cultures from where these stories come. Sometimes this understanding includes acknowledging and working through ignorance, along with the will to include and adapt to different practices.

For communities in Inuit Nunangat, acknowledging difference begins with acknowledging geographical distance. These communities are far more geographically removed from southern Canada when compared to many First Nations communities. For Inuit communities outside of Inuit Nunangat, acknowledging differences begins with acknowledging cultural differences. Both create obstacles to the presence and visibility of Inuit among non-Inuit communities in Canada.

An understanding of the history of relations between Inuit and non-Inuit in Canada is also important for non-Inuit storytellers who want to tell Inuit stories. There is a long history of outsiders in other fields who have taken Inuit stories and material culture to their own ends. These relationships often disproportionately benefited the outsiders. Numerous attempts have been made to correct this imbalanced relationship, however more work needs to be done to reach an equilibrium.

To achieve this equilibrium, I make the following proposals to ensure a more ethical, balanced, and inclusive set of production and exhibition practices. These are proposals to be implemented by funders, producers, programmers, and educators. They are not meant to serve as abstract criteria by which they assess the work of others, but as criteria to assess and guide themselves.

For film producers:

- Require documentation of uncoerced, unmanipulated, free, prior, and informed consent from Inuit partners
- Actively involve Inuit in creative decision-making processes
- Work with Inuit as equals
- Incorporate Inuktitut as a working language and storytelling language within film
- Include or train Inuit producers
- Hire or train Inuit directors
- Include Inuit film professionals in pre-production, production, and post-production teams
- Hire Inuit cultural consultants to provide guidance in Inuit storytelling
- Provide educational opportunities to ensure accessibility to film for Inuit entering the industry (for example, mentorships, production assistants)
- Contribute to building a more ethical film community for themselves, to

encourage their peers in their understanding of the benefit of ethical cross-cultural collaboration

For film funders:

- Actively involve Inuit in your institutions and your creative decision-making processes
- Hire Inuit in judging capacities for public funding bodies
- Require uncoerced, unmanipulated, free, prior, and informed consent from Inuit partners
- Allocate a set amount of funds for Inuit-led productions
- Communicate clear and consistent ethical standards for film productions and respond to violation of these ethical standards with consistent and appropriate disciplinary action

For film programmers:

- Hire Inuit programmers and curators
- Include Inuit on boards of directors and other decision-making bodies
- Build relationships with communities regularly represented in film productions
- Recognize Inuit communities as viewing audiences
- Program film screenings in Inuit communities

For film educators, writers, and communicators:

- Hire Inuit film educators, writers, and communicators
- Encourage writing of, reflection on, and discussion of Inuit filmmaking in non-ethnographic terms
- Champion discussion of Inuit filmmaking in public forums with Inuit speakers, particularly in the context of ethical discussions
- Include Inuit-authored literature as part of curricula

Producers, funders, programmers, and educators have an obligation to meaningfully engage with Inuit and Inuit communities. This is the work of cross-cultural collaboration, not one-way dialogue. As a baseline, it is recommended that each of these groups:

- Refer to Inuit cultural resource materials, including freely accessible documents such as *The Inuit Way: A Guide to Inuit Culture* and *Guidelines for Working with Inuit Elders*[1]
- Engage with Inuit cultural organizations and Inuit communities
- Recognize and honour the tenets of the 2011 "Declaration on Indigenous Cinema"[2]

These recommendations are not a panacea for ensuring ethical filmmaking practices with and for Inuit communities. It is understood that there are certain challenges that have no direct solutions, but this does not mean work should not be attempted in these areas. The challenges include:

- Working with Southern Inuit communities, in particular in places such as Edmonton, Ottawa, and Montreal, where many Inuit from across Inuit Nunangat live together. There are representative organizations for these populations at various stages of development. There are also many informal networks for Southern Inuit on social media.
- Inuit organizations' ability to oversee and critique Inuit representations. Many of our institutions are not set up to integrate into film production and exhibition apparatuses. Many of our institutions do not maintain permanent spaces to screen films for our community. Do not expect us to do either of these things, and do not expect us to rubber stamp anything.
- Seeking assistance from Inuit filmmakers. We are limited in number and we [need to] work, as well. We are neither ambassadors, consultants, nor interpreters.

....
1. Owlijoot, *Guidelines.*
2. Simma, "Declaration."

This statement was written June 1 and 2, 2017, in Montreal, and reflects the circumstances of this historical moment, defined in part by the Canada 150 celebrations, discussions of cultural appropriation, and a current tendency toward unethical filmmaking practices by non-Inuit that harm Inuit communities and mislead non-Inuit communities about Inuit issues. This statement should be revisited and revised with the Inuit film community as the work of cross-cultural collaboration continues, and as Inuit see ourselves reflected within production and exhibition practices.

asinnajaq

asinnajaq (also known as Isabella Rose Weetaluktuk) is a visual artist, filmmaker, and writer living in Montreal. Born in Kuujjuaq, Nunavik, and raised in Montreal, she studied visual arts at NSCAD University in Halifax, Nova Scotia. asinnajaq was mentored by the National Film Board of Canada throughout 2015 and 2016. During this period, she produced the short documentary *Three Thousand*, which was nominated for Best Short Documentary at the 2018 Canadian Screen Awards. This interview was conducted in English at the National Film Board of Canada offices in Montreal on February 15, 2017. The interviewers were her father, filmmaker Jobie Weetaluktuk, and her producer at the NFB, Kat Baulu.

JOBIE WEETALUKTUK (JW): Actually, our interview is called a conversation. So we'll keep it more like that. You're Isabella?

ISABELLA ROSE WEETALUKTUK (IRW): Yes.

JW: Can you describe yourself a little bit?

IRW: Isabella, I live in Montreal, and I'm Inuk. What else?

JW: Yeah, I know you identify yourself as Inuk and so do your brothers, but you also have a White Qallunaaq mother.

IRW: Um-hum.

JW: Yes, and is either ever a question for you, or never a question?

IRW: How would it be a question?

JW: When people ask you—obviously you look like Inuit, like Inuk—but for some people, some people might say, "Do you speak Inuktitut?" So that's how it becomes a question, like a self-question.

IRW: Well, usually children think that I'm not Inuk just because I can't speak Inuktitut. So the children will say that I'm Qallunaat.

JW: Yeah, but sometimes, some of them, it's not kind of an accusing question—

IRW: No, it's not.

JW: —or a statement?

IRW: They are just trying to understand who you are.

JW: Yes. Can you describe what part of Inuit Nunangat you come from?

IRW: Well, my family is from Inukjuak in Nunavik on the coast of Hudson's Bay, James Bay, at the top of James Bay. My family before me, they would live depending on the seasons in different places: usually in the region all the way until the bottom of James Bay and up the coast.

JW: Now, you have seen much of the Inuit Nunangat.

IRW: Yeah, I have had the opportunity to see a lot of it from a boat and I got to see all along the sides of Baffin Island, the fjords, and in the Torngat Mountains. I got to camp there and have picnics there. I also got to go through the Northwest Passage and Beechey Island—I saw that, and I saw lots of different places and old food caches and old Thule dwellings and lots of stuff like that.

JW: When you were on this cruise ship, right?

IRW: Yes, on a cruise ship.

JW: You must have learned a lot about Inuit, too?

IRW: Yeah, I did. That was a really lucky thing, because even though I grew up in Montreal—that was as soon as I graduated. I didn't even go to my high school graduation because I was working on that ship and immediately I just got to start learning a lot more about Inuit, about Inuit culture historically and presently. That was a very incredible opportunity.

JW: Yes, you met some Inuit, right?

IRW: Yeah, I did.

JW: Not just Inuit but also people who are interested in—

IRW: Yeah, there's some people that still try and email me from Germany and other places that are interested and try and keep in touch with me.

JW: Regarding the North?

IRW: Yes.

JW: Or Inuit?

IRW: Yeah.

JW: So, aside from your tour with the cruise boat, you made some lasting friends.

IRW: Yeah.

JW: Tell me a little bit about Montreal and some Inuit you know from Montreal.

IRW: Well, when I was a kid, we used to go to the gatherings to have dinner, but we stopped going and then I haven't lived here for a few years. But now I'm very happy and very lucky to be meeting more Inuit living in the city. First of all, in the summer we started a new film festival that's just for Inuit films and to try and get Inuit to come all together. I got to meet a lot more urban Inuit at that event. Now, in the summer, I also did *Saturviit*[1] women's leadership training, and at that training we hatched our plan that we would have amauti sewing classes. Now I have a sewing group that I get to spend time with and that's where I've met a lot more Inuit, while doing that.

JW: You said you made an amauti, which is what?

IRW: Oh, that's a woman's jacket that you hold a baby in.

JW: Yes, are there any other things that relate to—or [do] not relate to—Inuit, that you've made?

IRW: Yeah, sure, lots of things. I like to sew shirts and I've sewn jackets and *pualok* mittens and my new bag I just finished.

JW: Can you describe the bag a little bit?

IRW: It's one side sealskin and the other side's just normal leather. What about it?

JW: Does it have any relation to Inuit?

IRW: Yeah, my mom sent me a picture of a bag that my aunt made and I used that style to make my bag.

....
1. The Inuit Women's Association of Nunavik.

JW: Can you talk a little bit about how you trained to be an artist or do artistic things?

IRW: Yeah, well, I don't know why at the beginning, but I remember always wanting to make things. I think I have always been doing that. For my training, even though I always had the desire, I really did practise to try and make myself good at it by going to, first, a craft college. At the craft college I went to, I learned how to do pottery and fibre arts and all of these kinds of very hands-on things. Then, when I finished that, I went to university to study film. That is where I really watched tons and tons of films, studied films, made many short films, and I just got a chance to learn a lot and spend a lot of time thinking about—just a lot about film. Like, "What makes it successful?" or "What can you communicate in a film?" Things like that.

JW: Can you describe a little bit which learning institute you trained in?

IRW: Yeah, I went to the Nova Scotia College of Art and Design University, and they have specifically a film academy that I went to.

JW: This university has some, what do you call those people who graduate from—

IRW: Alumni?

JW: Yeah, who are all of Inuit ancestry?

IRW: Oh, Tanya—Tanya Tagaq. I think Heather Igloliorte, I think she went there, too. Or, at least maybe her brother. Anyways, what I heard was that that school, for some reason, has a very successful time getting Inuit to go there, even though they never ever tried to get Inuit to go there. They've had tons of amazing artists that went there.

JW: Aside from—well, what else do you do as an artist? You sew right? Do you make designs in clothing and stuff?

IRW: Yeah, I do sewing. I do linocut printmaking. I do painting. I do other kinds of prints, too—I do films. Yeah, I like to make films a lot. I used to make music a lot. I don't do it as much now. And sometimes I just dance around like crazy.

JW: But there's also things that you do, you were involved with a group at Concordia.

IRW: Oh, yeah, I did an installation with beads. That's another thing. I do beadwork also. Recently I had an installation—it's up right now—and that's beadwork that I made.

JW: Also, the bicycle thing that you did with a friend?

IRW: We have a bicycle group. In the summer, we bicycle.

JW: It's just people, right? Is it—

IRW: It's Indigenous women.

JW: Indigenous women. Is it driven, in part, because of your identity or identification with Inuit?

IRW: Yeah, of course, absolutely. Well, I think that one thing that really—I said to my cousin when I was visiting her, because I was collecting lots of things from the tundra that I could use to decorate my bicycle—as a joke—I told her, "Every time I get on my bike I'm going to yell '*Inujunga!*'" And she told me to be careful because there were people here that would want to hurt me because of that. And so that's, even more, why I want to do that.

JW: And you see Inuit in Montreal?

IRW: Yeah, and I smile at them, and now—because before when I just had plain clothes, people could just walk by—but now, because I have my own parka that

I've made and my mitts and everything, Inuit always recognize me and want to say hi and we always smile.

JW: Now what does *Inujunga* mean?

IRW: "I am Inuk."

JW: Yes. Well, it's an important statement for you, yes?

IRW: Um-hum.

JW: Yes, but why is it an unsafe thing to say in some circles or in the public?

IRW: Um-hum. Well, I think that sometimes Inuit get hurt just because they're Inuk and that's the only reason.

JW: But you also know that Inuit are very well known for some things. Can you describe, for example, some of the things you've seen that are celebrated?

IRW: Yeah, like throat singing. We're very proud of throat singing. Of our sewing. Women, they're proud of their amautis. Our sewing group—everyone's so happy to be able to do that. And carving and drawing and everything artistic, it's absolutely celebrated by Inuit and non-Inuit alike. Our art is something we can be very proud of.

JW: Can you describe some of the things you work in media, like the things you have done or been associated with regarding work in media?

IRW: Well, one time I helped on this film call *Timuti*—you made it and I helped you with it. That's one thing I did. I recently made a short film that we showed at Christina Parker Gallery in St. John's, Newfoundland, and that was a part of iNuit Blanche. That short film that I made was with archives and animation, family photos, and other video footage I took in the summer. In that film, it was all about what's so beautiful about being Inuk and living on the tundra and all of that landscape. That film was really just about all of that beautiful stuff and why I love it so much.

JW: Do you go to film festivals or festivals related to—

IRW: Yeah, I do. For the past few years I've been going to mostly Hot Docs and imagineNATIVE and I go and see the films there and see what other people are making.

JW: Yes, and Hot Docs, and—they're both in Toronto—

IRW: Toronto, yes.

JW: Do you ever meet Inuit or First Nations or any other Nations there?

IRW: Um-hum. Yeah, I do. I went to—where did I go? I went to Hot Docs, just so I could see Alethea's film premiere.

JW: When you talk to people, are they Inuit curious? Curious about Inuit?

IRW: Most people, if I talk to them, usually they're curious. I think right now, right now, yeah.

JW: Then what led you to work in film in particular?

IRW: I really like films. I remember when I was in high school and I had a film project, I would go like crazy and make it much more crazy than it had to be. The first project I remember I made was stop-motion animation, and it was with flowers growing and a storm. That was really fun and I liked making it a lot. Then, I remember, me and my best friend went to see an Andy Warhol exhibit here in Montreal, and after that we saw that you and my mom got me a video camera. And me and my friend we would just hang out and make weird videos, like we saw in the Andy Warhol exhibit. That was really funny. I really enjoyed that and spending time doing that. I made lots of other things just in high school, and I always like doing art. Then I think at that point I knew I'd enjoy working in film, but I didn't set it as a goal. Then eventually, when I was at that craft school, I did a little video class and they told me that I should go to film school. All of the teachers told me I should go to NSCAD and I didn't really feel like living in Fredericton anymore, so I did it and I moved to Halifax to go study film.

What I really like about it, and why I'm inspired to work in film, is because of the capacity to inspire someone to have revelations about themselves or about the world, and really create feeling. I always really liked reading but I never was confident in the way that I could write, and I never pursued anything in writing far enough to kind of create the world I would want to. But in film, I think I've had an easier time and it's come more naturally for me. That's why I like it, because I like the possibility to really create a feeling and really be able to communicate it well to other people.

JW: Can you talk about what it means to be an Inuk? You're Inuk, but you live outside of the territory. I know you talked a little bit about some of the communities—not just Montreal, but the Inuit Nunangat, the bigger Inuit community. At this point in history, what does it mean to be Inuit anymore?

IRW: Well, I find for me, what it means to be Inuk and to live outside of Inuit Nunangat, at least for me personally, it means that I think more about what it means to be Inuk and what makes you that. It usually comes down to community and who you surround yourself with and being a part of something.

JW: Um-hum. How do you, after that—like, through your work or through a project—how do you promote or explain?

IRW: Well, I think the way that I'm trying to promote being Inuk, it's by trying to make a space in a world where other Inuit can feel proud of themselves, that's all.

JW: Even today where we have things like YouTube that anybody can use, or even Facebook, things like that. There are some parts of the world which are shut off even from those things, but Inuit can have presences there—but are they participating?

IRW: Sometimes. I'm very surprised. There are some Inuit that have YouTube channels and if you see their view count it's like mind-blowing how many people watch those. There's a father-daughter that sing together. It's very beautiful and they have lots of people watching them. I don't think there's a huge number, but there are Inuit that participate like that on the internet. I mean, the internet is a huge place for Inuit to spend time—on Twitter and Facebook and everything, there's a huge presence.

JW: It's a big question, and maybe it's vague, but what is the role for an Inuk artist?

IRW: I think, well, first of all, everyone's role is different because everyone has their own desires of what they want to manifest in the world. The role of the artist would be different for each person depending on what they are trying to pursue. But personally, I think it's really about pride and understanding. So that I can be proud of myself and that other people can try and find their own understanding.

JW: Is that different? When you think about making something or media something or writing for Inuit versus Qallunaat societies, is there a distinction?

IRW: Well, I think that whenever you're authoring something you do have to pay attention to who you are talking to. I think that it does change—what you might include changes—but you describe things differently. For example, if this was just for Inuit, what we are talking about, then when I say "amauti" I wouldn't have to explain what it is because everyone would know. But then if you're thinking about a different audience then that's when you have to explain what it is. I think, yeah, it makes a difference.

JW: Even in things you have, like ulus or pualoks or things like these, which are traditional or cultural things, is that interesting for you?

IRW: Yeah, it's interesting. I love having those things.

JW: What in particular?

IRW: Well, what I don't have but I would really go crazy if I had it, would be an ivory comb.

JW: Yes.

IRW: You said you would get me one and you haven't—

JW: Well, I haven't found any ivory, that's all.

IRW: Yeah, ulu. Like cutting with ulu, it feels nice. Cutting—I love cutting skin, like dried sealskin or treated. I love cutting that with ulu. It feels great. I guess what's nice about all those objects is feeling a connection. That's what you feel. It's really beautiful because time is a great expanse, and when you use objects like that, I call it time travelling. I'm time travelling each time that I use ulu, because then I'm connected with everyone before me and everyone to come after me that uses that similar object.

JW: Do you ever go up North?

IRW: Yeah, I do lots and see my cousins and go on the boat and walk on the snow. Right now, I try and go for two months every year—once in the winter, and once in the summer and pick berries. I need to have Labrador tea, I pick a lot of it and dry it, so I can have it all year. Spend time with my family. My cousins—and everyone—has babies and I have to go and make them all fall in love with me before I leave and break all their hearts. Yeah, it's the fun part. Just kidding.

JW: Being brought up mostly in Montreal—how do you feel about hunting?

IRW: Yeah, I think hunting is great. I didn't always. Well, I didn't always eat meat but I think I never really had any problem with hunting. It's definitely growing up here, and everything, changed that relationship and now I think it's great and I think that's a great way to spend time and to—I don't know, a great thing to do.

JW: You enjoy those—

IRW: Hunting?

JW: Oh yeah, yeah.

IRW: I enjoy everything that my uncle gives me from when he goes hunting. I've been eating *nikku* almost every day now for a month. It's like a dream.

JW: Nikku is?

IRW: Dried caribou.

JW: That some people send you?

IRW: No, I make it.

JW: You've learned how to make it in Montreal?

IRW: Yes.

JW: Thanks to who?

IRW: Yes, you don't have to fish for any kind of compliment. Yes, you helped me to make nikku and now I can make it for myself.

JW: Yes.

IRW: But I don't know why you never taught me earlier.

JW: It was bothersome. Just kidding you. Can you tell me a little about your experience in film and what happens when you make a film? What happens? How do people react? The audience or whatever?

IRW: The last film that I made that was short, that we showed at iNuit Blanche, it was called *Lucky*. When I showed it, some—no one said anything mean to me at all, which was very nice of them. And the nice things that people did say, was that—especially Inuit—they said to me that, "That film felt like home." I noticed my mom's friend, she kept coming back to watch it again and again and again, and that was nice, too.

What I know is that we just don't get to see that kind of thing often enough. To hear someone articulate something and spend the time to make something makes you pay attention and appreciate it. Even if it's simple things, like simple landscapes and children smiling, nothing too complicated. If someone took the time and the care and is trying to illustrate something like that, you really feel it. That's why people had something nice to say, that it felt like home. I think it's important to get to see that sometimes, and to see that it's beautiful. You can be there every day and look around and see that it's beautiful, but you see beauty differently when someone takes the time to watch it and rearticulate it.

JW: When you make a film, do you use archival anything?

IRW: Right now I've been using archives a lot. At this stage, yes. Archives and animation is what I've been doing lately.

JW: Just as straight archives? You just take a digital copy of that and then just repost it or incorporate it into your film? Or do you do anything with it? Like mix?

IRW: Mix. Some of it is straight but lots of it is treated. To change it a little bit, sure.

JW: You've seen a lot of archives.

IRW: Yeah, I have.

JW: Which go back a long time?

IRW: Yeah, I think 1920 may be the earliest.

JW: Since they were mostly made by non-Inuit at the time, is that ever an issue for you or are you just grateful to have those things?

IRW: I'm grateful to have them. You can tell the difference when you watch it. The interesting thing, looking through them, is that you can see a difference in the way the Inuit are acting towards the camera. That's a really interesting thing to see. I guess one thing I'm concerned about with the archives is whether all of those people that were captured in those moments are okay with having themselves captured. I never know—did the person filming ever ask or say what it would be for? It can be concerning. But most of the footage is okay and there's nothing worrying about it and it's probably okay anyways for people to see it.

JW: Do you ever think, when you look at archives, how Inuit felt at the time? They were probably more deferential to and more intimidated by White people, for instance. Do you ever think that is reflected in the film?

IRW: Yeah, I think that it all comes across, either subtly or in any way, depending on what the feeling is. But you can always tell something about who is behind the camera. You can definitely tell, absolutely. There is this really beautiful footage that's all shot by Inuit for Inuit. I think it was for a television program. And in those images, it's like completely different than anything I've watched in the archives here. You can tell intention. What are the images for? Even if they're not edited all together, you can tell what that image was made for, what was its purpose—most of the time you can really tell.

JW: Now, is that training or is that just intuitive?

IRW: I guess it's intuitive.

JW: Some Inuit films or media portrayals of Inuit, or even writing, are not always friendly to Inuit.

IRW: A lot of the times they are not. That's something that I have a hard time with because I am very sensitive. To feel something mean-hearted—some of it is very mean-hearted. I sometimes can just read a line or just see a clip and then know I can't watch that, it's going to hurt me too much. I have to really pay attention, so I don't hurt myself with exposing too much to that stuff.

JW: But even then, you'll help some of your friends defend Inuit in discussion groups?

IRW: It's important that we try and understand other people and that they also are taking the time to try and understand us. I think what we are trying to do is just get everyone to be more sensitive and pay more attention and not jump to conclusions too fast, because—especially in Canada—there is a lot of history that's happened here that hasn't been properly taught. And a lot of citizens that have gone to university and are supposed to be intelligent have been driven away from knowing proper history, and that because of that it's hurting Inuit and other Indigenous people.

JW: But not just in film, also—

IRW: Everywhere.

JW: Like in social media, there is always some groups of people who take offence with who Inuit are, just because—based on their traditions: they're hunters, they fish, or kill seals.

IRW: What about that?

JW: Have you ever been involved in those discussions?

IRW: Like, if hunting is okay?

JW: Yeah.

IRW: Well, I don't think I have been up to now, really, but I wear sealskin all the time, every day. I guess my position is clear, but I haven't really been involved in any of those conversations, not yet.

JW: Based on what we've seen happen, also, scary. How has your home community—

IRW: Inukjuak.

JW: You identify Inukjuak as your home community?

IRW: Yeah, it's like all those people I love, they live there.

JW: How it has it helped shape your work as an artist?

IRW: It shapes it by the fact that what I want to think about is, whatever I do, would my family there be okay with it? Would they be proud of it? And only to do things that I think that they are going to be proud of. That's how it shapes me. That whatever I want to do, I want it to be good for them.

JW: Are any of your family artists, or were?

IRW: We had carvers for a long time. Maybe great-great-uncles were carvers? My grandfather, too, sometimes, and my grandmother—she made baskets, lots of beautiful baskets. My father, well, he was a filmmaker—he hasn't made one lately, though.

JW: Have they ever seen your work, your home community? And how do they receive it?

IRW: I've shown my short film to my close relatives and they all really loved it. One of my cousins asked me why did it ever end, and that it should have been longer. Then my little niece told me that I should make a new one every time I come to see her. I say that's positive reviews.

JW: How do you identify with the community of Inuit filmmakers or young artists? What kind of relationship do you have with them?

IRW: Just a part of that community.

JW: Um-hum.

IRW: It's like, people—we check in with each other. Well, there's been a lot going on in the past year that we've needed to lean on each other for. We kind of scheme together and make plans together and talk about events that we're going through.

JW: Is it kind of a cohesive group? Or is it isolated communities or small groups?

IRW: I think it's pretty cohesive. Maybe we don't all live in the same place, but it's pretty cohesive because it's a very specific group of people.

JW: What do you want to achieve? Do you have a goal that you want to achieve when you do media work or art? Do you have a singular idea?

IRW: For Inuit to be able to understand themselves better and to be able to be happy with themselves. Then, outside of that, to be able to have outsiders have a place that they can understand more, too. But first of all—for Inuit.

JW: Yes. We were talking about archives before—you work with archival stuff?

IRW: Yeah.

JW: Do you know if your relationship to archival stuff is different? Like for a Qallunaaq person? Do you ever get an insight or an idea that I'm relating to this differently than other people here?

IRW: Yeah, I think—well, in one way it's hard to ever know that. But in another way, because anyone that's Inuk that's on the screen feels more part of me than it could ever feel for someone that's not Inuk. In that kind of way, it's different. Whenever I'm seeing one of those images, even if it's another person, even if they're from another region than I'm from.

One image that I really love is icing the bottom of a *qamutiik*[2] and that kind of action and that kind of thing that happens. That's a lot closer to my being than it would be for someone that's not Inuk, you know what I mean? In a way, all of those images—somehow, they're a part of me. I really automatically love all of those people, in the world that they're in. And the kind of respect— the kind of deference—I have to have for it, because it's a part of me, is maybe different than an outsider looking in.

JW: Part of your lineages—you have a Qallunaaq mother—the media is full of works by White people, do you feel the same affinity—

IRW: To what, media?

JW: To what is Qallunaaq-focused?

IRW: I find I don't usually listen to the news. I read newspapers because, usually, I find that whatever they are trying to talk about, they're not ever thinking about me. I think it might be changing right now, but especially in the past 10 years up to now, I'd say, maybe it's changing. But I always had the feeling that whatever they are talking about they are not even considering me in the equation. There's just too much of an emotional toll to listen to that news, because of the way that they are talking, the language they're using. They're not even considering my own person for a second.

....
2. A sled drawn by dogs or snowmobile.

JW: What about the archives itself? When you go up North, it's hard to find anything like that, and any body of work that is related to, well, to anything.

IRW: What was hard about it was because, in a perfect world, I would have wanted all of the footage to come from Inukjuak or from Nunavik, at least. I mean, there's a lot of footage, but there's not a lot in specific places. The film that I'm working on right now, there's no way that I could make it in just one location, it has to be a pan-Arctic film and not just focus on one location, one People.

JW: To be accessible to more communities, as you're saying? To more Inuit especially?

IRW: It's just that it wouldn't have been possible. In this film I have kids playing with dogs, and people in igloos, and a teacher teaching, and all of this stuff that I couldn't find all of those images happening in just one location.

JW: Now, with the experience you have had to date, what drew you to film? When you explain it to people, like your family or your friends or people you work with, how do you describe it?

IRW: What I'm doing?

JW: Yeah, or your relationship to it, or why it's important to you. How do you explain it to people?

IRW: I don't know if I ever really have to explain that. You just kind of have to explain the project you're working on at that moment.

JW: Your personal experiences, have they shaped your work?

IRW: Yeah, everything that happened shapes it somehow. Even if it's just going to a science museum or if it's positive or negative, every moment collapses onto each other and can change the way that you react or behave to something. So, yes, and not in any kind of exact way—but I think everything influences each other. That's just a personal philosophy.

JW: For film art or visual art—is there, for you, any distinction?

IRW: No.

JW: No?

IRW: No, there is just whatever I do, and there's just the best way to act on that idea. Either it's film or either it's installation or whatever, whatever. It's just you have an idea and there's the best way to act on it.

JW: Do you have any other heroes who work in media, anywhere in the world, any tradition, Inuit or not Inuit, that you get inspired from?

IRW: I'm inspired by lots of things. I really like all old cinema. I really like something that just makes you feel, that's all. I don't know, I can't think of any exact people or anything. I'm very inspired by this book or that movie or lots of things in the world that are really beautiful. Lots of very talented people that have made things.

JW: People you work with?

IRW: People I've worked with. You, of course—you're a great inspiration.

JW: Thank-you, Isabella, for talking about your experiences and ideas about media and filmmaking.

KAT BAULU (KB): Bella, I'd like your recommendation on three films you feel every Qallunaaq should see in order to get a little bit of the essence of Inuit spirit and culture.

IRW: Okay. *The Journals of Knud Rasmussen*, *Timuti*, and maybe *Angry Inuk*. Those are three good ones.

KB: Unpack those a little bit for us. You curate lots of film. Why do you think that those are important for people to see?

IRW: Okay, in *The Journals of Knud Rasmussen* you get to see the point in time in which Christianity is beginning to prevail over Shamanism. You get to see the snow, the igloos, travelling, kind of imaginative spirituality, and that gives a very good foundation for understanding how difficult those big decisions were at that time. That's not a decision just for yourself, you don't just make that decision for yourself. That decision has repercussions all the way down the line and forever in the future as long as Inuit exist. That's a very big deal, but you get to learn that and at the same time get an idea about what's it like in an igloo and all of that kind of stuff. That's why I think that film is important.

Then with *Timuti*, you get to see some more delicate and specific things about tradition, and how tradition can manifest itself today. It's beautiful to know about all the important things and the love that you give to a baby surrounding their naming. Because I know the intention around the film, which was that it's about how much you want all of the world for that baby and how much you have to prepare and give to them. It takes a lot of thought. That's why I think that's important. You also get to see the difficulties that surround family, life, and other people wanting things for you. For example, a pregnancy when maybe you don't, you're not ready for it, or so on. And all of that's also informed by the adoption of Christianity.

Then finally, I think *Angry Inuk*, it's important and gets you to understand today. Because it's talking a lot about cultural prejudice and about trying to be proud of yourself when there are lots of things that are masked as good things that are really working against you and are detrimental to you.

KB: Okay, thanks for that. I wonder if you can tell us a little bit about your experience to date being a woman filmmaker? How much does your gender shape the type of films that you make? How do collaborators react to that? How do you notice it in your practice?

IRW: Because I don't know any other way of being, then I'm not really sure about all of the way that it shapes it. But I think that I do have a sensitivity and I don't know if it would be different if I were a man—but maybe? That mostly it's kind of understated. Well, I do think that, from what I understand, that being a woman sometimes makes people feel less like that they belong anywhere or just deserve anything, outright. I guess that makes me work harder. To feel like I know something about myself. Even if I earned something, then I can still keep working. Even if I already earned it, I still feel like I have to deserve it. I keep working and working and working. Maybe that's shaped by my gender, too—I'm not sure.

KB: That's hopeful. When you get an idea for a project, whether it's a film project or a different kind of art project, at what point do ethical considerations come in for you?

IRW: Right away. You think about if you're being respectful and if that's your place, and think about yourself and what you're doing, right away. As soon as you have the idea, because you can't pursue an idea that isn't—First of all, maybe, it's not even your place to talk about it, to begin with. Or maybe, right away, you have to think about it because, okay—I'm going to do this thing, but there would be a best practice. And you have to know that right away. If I want to make a film that's about Inuit and Mohawk, right away I'm going to find someone that's Mohawk. "Oh, is this okay?" "Will you help me?" And, "Can we do it together?" But you can't do that at the end, you have to do it right at the beginning. So, right away, you have to try and challenge yourself. You don't have to know everything, but you have to challenge yourself to try and think about these things.

KB: In the process of making your last few projects, what are some of the best practices that have helped you, in terms of exactly what you talked about—being respectful? What are some of the concrete actions that you've taken, if you look at the projects that you've made so far?

IRW: Well, first I would want to say that, the first thing I listen to it is my gut. And also because, in myself, I know that if I have that feeling in my gut, there's nothing that's going to take it away. I have to fix the problem and there's no other choice. Or I'll just feel sick, and sick, and sick. In *Three Thousand*, I just try and take care. What I've done is just try and talk to many people and not just leave it to myself to decide anything. Ultimately, I leave it to myself to decide things, but I have given the space and opportunity for many other voices to contribute if they feel like doing that. Whether it's someone that's over for dinner and I just slip a quick question in, or if I invite someone directly into the project to comment on all of it, there are many different levels at which I've asked Inuit primarily to give input on what they think about my ideas. I think that it's including community that will help you be on the best path.

KB: What advice would you give to other young artists coming up, around best ethical practices?

IRW: That it takes soul-searching, and you have to allow yourself to be vulnerable to yourself and know your own weaknesses as best as you can, so that you can get other people to help you. That's just the advice. In certain art practices, you can have the luxury of keeping everything to yourself, but film takes so much time, and so much energy, and so many things are happening in it that I think it's very good to try and include many people. Even if it's just for this little piece of input or whatever. I think that it can be very helpful—and it helps me, at least, to make better work.

KB: How would you explain the balance between receiving input and consultation?

IRW: I think that it's a lot easier to request input from people when you trust yourself and know what you want to see. That also depends on what you're asking of people. If I already have a paradigm set which is, let's say, "I'm going to do a painting of people." Then I asked for input, but I don't ask for input like "What shape should the people be? And where should I be placed on the paper?" But I'm asking a different kind of input that doesn't necessarily affect the way, the certain way I'm going to make it.

KB: Your dad is Jobie Weetaluktuk, and he is an accomplished award-winning filmmaker—

IRW: Yeah.

KB: Has his practice influenced your practice?

IRW: Yeah. Well, I think that I learned a lot from him. One of the things that I learned from him that does influence my practice is about leaving space for the people you're collaborating with. That, definitely, is something very concrete that I learned from him, from seeing how he works with other people. I don't know if I would have gotten there alone or if I can only do that because I've seen him do it. But I think that it's an important thing to be able to trust and give space to the people that you're collaborating with. Because that helps you be stronger, because those people that you're collaborating with have done hours and hours of sound recording, or editing, or picture editing, or whatever, and I've only done a small amount. I can tell them what I want to see and then they'll have greater ideas and know lots more things I don't know. That's why we have teams to work with, and that's why we have to trust them.

KB: My last question is this, how important is language in your art practice?

IRW: Language is important because the different languages deliver ideas and information differently.

KB: I wonder if you can elaborate on that a little bit? Would you ever make a film—just because you speak English, French, and Inuktitut—you're learning—

IRW: I'm trying, I'm learning Inuktitut.

KB: Would you ever make a film just in one language? What would your reasons be? For example, maybe, tell us a little bit about the film you're making right now? How are you approaching it language-wise? What's the relevance?

IRW: Well, the thing with that, some people like reading subtitles but I don't like reading them. I like to watch a lot of films that I have to read subtitles, but then I'm always frustrated with missing the image. Right now, the film that I'm making has voice-overs in three different languages so that you don't have to read subtitles. So that you can just concentrate on receiving the information through the images and the audio, and not have to read because that also activates different parts of your brain and you experience film differently. You could make a film just in one language and do subtitles I guess, but that's not what I chose to do this time.

KB: Okay, thank-you very much, Bella.

IRW: Yeah. Thank-you.

Inuk Silis Høegh

Inuk Silis Høegh is a filmmaker and visual artist. He was born and raised in Qaqortoq in the south of Kalaallit Nunaat. After moving to Nuuk in the mid-1990s, Inuk left for Bristol, England, to study film and television production, then returned to Nuuk to work alongside the first generation of Greenlandic filmmakers. In the early 2000s he left once again, this time for Copenhagen to study at the Royal Danish Academy of Fine Arts. He now lives and works in Nuuk. I conducted this interview with Inuk in English on November 14, 2017, via Skype. He was in Nuuk and I was in Nain, Nunatsiavut.

MARK DAVID TURNER (MDT): What were your early experiences with art?

INUK SILIS HØEGH (ISH): I come from a family of artists. My mother is a painter and sculptor and my father is a photographer and writer. When I was a kid and young, it was always around me, but I definitely didn't want to be an artist because I didn't want to be like my parents. So I never thought of it as something that would be for me. It was quite late, actually, that I started, myself, to think that "Ah." I didn't want to kind of analyze films that I was doing. I was in university at one point. Then I was always analyzing films—and then all of a sudden, I found out that I wanted to do it.

I got into a film school in University of Bristol in '96 and then I started to buckle up in the taxis, taking taxis, because I didn't want to die before I came to Bristol. All of a sudden there was something that really mattered to me. And I found out that I've been bored for many years. I didn't know any better. I thought,

"Okay this is life." But it's always been around me in that way and my parents have never told me to be an artist or never, in that way, directly tried to teach me anything. But there were always artists, also, when we had artists coming from other towns or from abroad to our little town. They would always come to visit because that was kind of like the artist home of Qaqortoq, with my parents. There would always be this run of people and exciting people around us, but I didn't think that it would influence me. I'm pretty sure that it's there somewhere and it also made me to what I am today, as working with art.

MDT: How did you train as a filmmaker?

ISH: The University of Bristol had a film and TV production MA. And it was based on making films, and 80 percent practical. They were one of the last places that I could find, also, that had 16 mm film. A lot of them were going on to video, of course, because it's cheaper. And actually, I chose that one because they were kind of still keeping it and that really just attracted me somehow. Because I was, like, "real film" kind of thing.

That was not so specialized in different directions in film, but I really knew that I wanted to be a cinematographer for some reason. I was going a lot in that direction and filming the short films we were doing in the course. So that was what I was thinking I wanted to do and what I was aiming for. It was really like a crash course, with students from all over the world. It was really, really inspiring and also kind of tough to redefine yourself. It was a tough year, but it was great.

I came out and then I went back to Greenland and Kenneth Rasmussen, Kunuk Platoú, and Karsten Heilmann, and I were kind of four geeks and friends that wanted to make film and we wanted to make a film together. I wanted to film it but there was no story and there was no one to direct. We were two cinematographers, one editor, and one kind of—I don't know what the last one was. I had a story I had just written some night, and I was inspired. And this became what we wanted to do. So that became, as a director, my first short film. In Greenland, you have to be an octopus. You have to be a lot more versatile, I guess, and more flexible. Because there's not a lot of specialized people. I ended up directing and writing from there, even though I really wanted to do something else. I feel like a lot of the things that I get involved in are not so controlled—like me having a vision: "I want to go there." Or maybe I had a vision and then I bump into something and I have to go there. But then again, maybe I also like that, too.

MDT: I think that is part of being an artist in the North, isn't it? Especially if your interests are varied. It's not the same kind of critical mass of a community and the division of labour that you have anywhere in the south. You inevitably have to do more, and if you're interested in a lot of things, you have to acquire more skills in order to realize those things.

ISH: I get myself into a lot of trouble all the time because I'm so interested in different things. So, for film training, it was mostly there in Bristol that year. It gave me a lot. Then, of course, after that, I feel the productions that you get involved in after that, all of them teach you lessons along the way. Even if you're filming or if you're directing or if you're even being a camera assistant or doing sound, or whatever, on stuff, you just pick up things. I think, in some ways, I ended up being a director by chance because there was no one else, actually. Everybody wanted to be a cinematographer. So, that was most of my training.

I think I can't talk about film alone. As you've seen, I do a lot of visual art as well. So later on, I found out that making films is super stressful and I was always kind of being warned by how stressful it is, to have to take all these decisions and then the cloud comes. It's not so good for my kind of temperament. I'm kind of an introvert. Then you have to be kind of the centre of a whole lot of people to direct and be on, spot on, at all times with this team of people. It's really stressful.

At some point I got really interested in fine arts because I knew, watching also my mom and my dad, that I could just make it with my hands from here to here, instead of from here—to working with a lot of people and working with a lot of things that I don't think I'm very good at, like asking something of other people. So all of a sudden I thought, "Ah, I'd like to try to make some fine art, just me." And like *Emil i Lönneberga*, if you've ever heard of him—an Astrid Lindgren story from Scandinavia.[1] It's about a boy that is very naughty

....
1. A series of 12 children's novels published between 1963 and 1997, set in Småland, Sweden. Emil, a child, is the title character.

in Sweden. He's always very naughty and then his father punishes him by sending him out to the shed, locks the shed, and then he sits in there and he carves little wooden figures because he's just bored. I felt I'd like to be him. I'd like to sit in a little shed by myself and just carve, or something. So, that's why I ended up doing and participating in some exhibitions here in Greenland and ended up applying for the Art Academy in Copenhagen. That was maybe seven or eight years after I came out of film school. I kind of thought, "Okay, I got into the Art Academy and now I've really found my proper self. This is where I belong. And now I'm sorted and everything's going to be fine now." But then when I came out of Art Academy, then, of course, I started making film again. So I'm as confused as ever.

MDT: How do you define yourself as an artist now?

ISH: I've started to be able to be okay with saying that I'm a filmmaker and artist. I don't think I like still saying I'm an artist. Then people are always going to ask what kind of artist? Then you're going to start explaining. Filmmaker. People understand that, kind of. And then artist. Okay, yeah, it's something. So I do that now. I don't think I see myself as more of one or the other. But lately, people in Greenland know me mostly for my films, because *SUMÉ* got so hugely shown and popular here. I'm kind of the guy that makes films but, "Oh, didn't you also make art sometimes?"

But as we were discussing before, you have to be an octopus, even in films. But then, I have this thing that I think I also get tired of making a film, if I'm making a film. Then, after that, I want to make art—and then [I] probably get mixed up in a film soon anyway. It's a kind of a hate-love relationship with film because I really, really love film. It's the most amazing media. But it's tough, I think. It's tough to do it. I'm not doing justice to the art, but I still really, really like to do art. But I think film is such a powerful medium and I feel that some of it comes really easy to me, in terms of wanting to tell a story in pictures—like one picture after the other. If this picture is here and this picture comes afterwards, then what happens? I like the telling of story in pictures. It also comes out in my art sometimes, doing projects—that I'm telling a story.

I've never been able to mix. I started with film and then I went into art, and I've never been able to make art films. I couldn't mix it. I wanted to do something that was opposite, or kind of opposite, of living pictures. Moving pictures in sculpture. Something still that you can walk around and stare and it's not on a screen, flickering. So, I was kind of going there. My latest project is a film art installation—land-art thing. I enjoy thinking that I'm using some of the acquired skills from film and it's not like being wasted by me going into a corner and carving a piece of something. That I'm actually combining skills, I hope.

MDT: Do you prefer solitary over collaborative art-making?

ISH: Yeah, it's like two opposites kind of pulling, I think. Because I really enjoy the solitude and working, just me and my hands. Or, nowadays, it's like going out in nature and doing something on the spot and being completely alone in a huge landscape. I really enjoy that. But at the same time, I think my strongest projects are ones where I meet someone that's completely different than me. There's some sort of spark that happens, when a round thing and a square meet, or two opposites meet. It's a lot of hard work for me but it's very, very rewarding.

As much as I enjoy solitude and working by myself, then also sometimes you miss somebody to play ball with, kind of. Sometimes it feels like playing football alone. You kind of need someone to kick it back to you and not just, like, a wall. I feel like the solitude can be seen as like when you're a kid, you go to your mom for safety and for comfort and just for a hug. Then when you get it, you know you can run out into the world and be free and hurt yourself and run back and cry to mom when you need it. But I kind of need both. I enjoy both. It's most hard work to make collaborations and you also get a lot of joy, of not feeling alone. But it's also really hard work. I don't think working in solitude is as hard work for some reason. It's not a clear answer but it's because I need both.

MDT: Are you attracted to certain types of artists to collaborate with?

ISH: No, I don't think I purposely think about what type, that it has to be an opposite. No, I think that I look for someone that thinks alike. But then, the best things happen when I find someone that doesn't think like me, because I think I'm always looking for this kind of feeling of safety. If you work with someone and you think alike, you say, "Ah look at this, this is a good idea!" "Yes, this is a good idea!" And if you agree: yes, everything is good. But, actually, you need somebody sometimes to say, "No, I think this idea is better" or "Maybe if we did this?" and you can disagree. And then you kind of push yourself somewhere else to understand things in another way, and then the whole thing becomes better.

MDT: What concerns define your art practice?

ISH: It's felt like it's quite by chance that I get pushed a bit in this direction, and then this direction. But I've kind of noticed that I like to work with things that are a bit also, in my art, kind of opposites: like people and things that don't belong together. How can I describe it? I was making these sculptures and I liked the idea of working with wood put together with plastic, because it doesn't really mix. Wood is so organic and it's been here forever and it's a living material and it breathes. Then plastic doesn't breathe. It's cold and it's fast and it's mouldable. The materials themselves—being kind of opposites, or from different time periods, or different kind of places—it makes it exciting to see what they do together.

I think, in some ways, I always try to put something in the things I do that doesn't belong together. Sometimes it succeeds. I don't think I'm the most daring artist. For me it's like, can you put words in a bottle? It's like this question. I think it's also funny. Maybe there's a little bit of humour that needs to be there, too. It's like the red speaker in the *SUMÉ* film, like in a straight-up documentary. Maybe it's not directly humour, but what's that red speaker doing there?

I also think of it as like, in some films, you have a red suitcase. Maybe we don't know what's in it but you always want to see if they exchange this suitcase and somebody picks it up in secrecy and walks off with it in secrecy, then you want to know what's in it. It's not necessarily important what's in it, but it creates some sort of action, some sort of a visual thing that drives something forward even if it's standing still.

MDT: It's the *Pulp Fiction* briefcase.

ISH: Yeah, the *Pulp Fiction* one. Or in David Lynch's film where they have this little box where we never know what's in it, with a key you put in? You kind of never know. But, of course, in this documentary it had to have some sort of link to Sumé, and it's their red speaker that they used to have. I think the idea always comes before the media. And that's also one of the ways that I choose my partners to work with. If I need somebody that's good at something—like in my last project I'm working with a sound artist because I've actually lost most of my hearing now. So it's also, like, kind of a necessity. But also to realize, as I was saying, we have to be octopuses in Greenland because there are not that many people—but it's also good not to think that you can be an expert on every media. So why not work together with someone and see what comes back? You know, it's more scary. But it also it has big rewards if we handle it right, I think.

MDT: How would you describe the historical Inuit experience with media and film in Greenland?

ISH: I'm going back to when we were the four film geeks that wanted to make the first Greenlandic short film. I think we kind of looked back in time and said: in 1934, there was *Palos Brudefærd* (*The Wedding of Palo*). You've probably heard about it. It's like a fiction film from the east coast of Greenland by a Danish director. But actually, four Greenlanders worked on that film. Knud Rasmussen was one of them. That's kind of what we were looking up to. "Okay, we know that that film—these Greenlanders, they were co-directing it." It's about, really, the old days in Greenland. How life was and how it really says a lot about the old Greenlandic culture and it has really beautiful faces and scenery. It's all in black and white and then it has these two Greenlandic—I don't think it says "co-director" in the credits, but we just know that they were really a big influence on the film. So, for us, that was one of the first Greenlandic films even though it was a Danish director. The reason why I'm mentioning it is because there were really no directors and no real fiction film. There were some documentaries made in the '70s, '80s.

I think that I'd like to look at it also from the point of, when we are making *SUMÉ*—which is by some also seen as the first kind of really ambitious documentary, a feature-length documentary from Greenland, seen from our perspective—then the footage in that, from the '70s, is what we found. We thought we struck gold when we found out we could use this footage of the Super 8 [mm]. There was no sound and all this, but we have to remember that there were not many cameras in Greenland. Even young people couldn't afford to go around filming or even taking photographs that had to be chemically processed and all this.

So that's the history of Greenlandic film. Of course, it's a lot to do with cameras and being able to afford it and being able to process it and all this. These Super 8 films from the '70s we got from people around in Greenland. It was really, I think, the first generation that could film themselves. So in some ways, some of it started there in the '70s, I think. But now, today, with smartphones, I see around on Facebook and Instagram and all these places, people—of course it's exploding with creativity. People are filming each other and editing things together and making small things, visual things, all the time. I can imagine it can be the same in other Inuit areas.

It's hard. I mean—the camera freezes when it's minus 20, anyway. But *The Wedding of Palo* and then, years later, some say that my first short film is one of the first short films in Greenland. Only in 2009 came what most people think is the first feature film from Greenland: *Nuummioq*. And then, there's been a few feature films coming out after that. It's really only in the very last years that I feel that you can start talking about film. It's not an industry, of course. It's something that started rolling in the last six or seven years. It's due to the cheap cameras. But also, they have actual film funds in the Greenlandic government that you can apply for. Even though it's not much per year, it did help some people to take the jump and become independent and try to live off making little productions. It can be mostly paid work for companies, other companies. That started a lot.

But then I want to mention about the community together with Nunavut, Nunavik, everyone. I don't think there really is [a community]. But Zacharias Kunuk's film, *The Fast Runner*, when it came here, I just remember I was seeing it with a friend and we were really kind of blown back by it. And he said—and I think that's true for me as well—that we learned more about our own culture from that film than we ever learned in school. I mean, if you think about it, that's quite crazy. Or cool. Whichever way you want to put it. In that way we were very inspired by Zacharias Kunuk. Not that we want to film from the old days. I don't think that there's really anyone that tries that in Greenland now. But just to say that—"Fuck, we can make a film. We can just go out there and make a film"—you know? It had kind of that feeling to it.

This year there's a fantasy film coming out in Greenland,[2] which I think is like a big leap. There's this one guy, Marc Fussing Rosbach. He's really, really super talented in terms of his language—his film language—and he makes the music, films it, acts in it, and makes the visual effects. It's really heavy in visual effects. It's his first film and it's pretty amazing if you think about it. He's still got something to work on with the story and the editing and compressing it. But he's going to be big if he wants to. It's a guy from north Greenland that just kind of— "Oh, we recorded this film in one and a half months with my friends." And it's a pretty amazing film. It's a fantasy film and it's got some humour and it's really kind of Hollywood-inspired. There's something going on now that I think is really exciting in Greenland with the very young kids.

MDT: I find it interesting that you do not mention Kalaallit Nunaata Radioa (KNR).[3] Have they had any effect on the development of Greenland's film culture?

ISH: I think there's a strong divide. What they're doing—they're very set in a TV kind of way, or even radio way, of doing things. All the people that were making radio, when they started deciding that they wanted to make TV (also for KNR)— it was radio people starting. They still kind of had the same ways of doing things, which were not visually very exciting, or not taking very many chances, or not being very personal in their way that they express themselves. It's still a little bit like that, but there's something happening, as well. There's a new generation coming aboard in there, now. So hopefully something is going to happen. But I don't think we ever felt very inspired by what KNR was doing. I mean, we wanted it to change. We wanted to kind of, like, take the institution and shake it because it wasn't very

....

2. *Akornatsinniitut – Tarratta Nunaanni* (*Among Us – In the Land of Our Shadows*), 2018.

3. Greenlandic Broadcasting Corporation.

creative. But, also, they didn't try to make fiction. It's been standing still for quite a lot of years.

Of course, for showing films—to some extent, yes, people could see films on KNR. But I think for us, it was more exciting to go and show a film in the community house and to take a projector and show it there. And also, that's what some of the filmmakers were doing when they had this, like a couple of horror movies coming out in the last five or six years. Tumit Production was one of the first production companies that actually succeeded in doing completely their own thing: travelling on the coast, going to the community houses, putting up a projector, and showing the films and taking an entrance [fee]. And they actually made money for it, that they could invest in their next film. It was so inspiring. And that's also something that inspired us when we were doing the *SUMÉ* film: that we went on a tour on the coast with a projector. [We] wanted it to be like a real seat in a cinema, because there's no cinemas in Greenland except for two or three cinemas in three of the big cities. So we did that, as it was inspired by Tumit but also inspired by Sumé [the band], that went on a tour on the coast and we thought that was a nice homage to Sumé that we also went on a tour with their film.

We should think that KNR could have a really big influence and I'm sure they probably have on people out there on the coast that can't get to the cinemas. And I know that they watch KNR a lot. And, of course, we want our films to be seen everywhere, so we also want it shown on KNR in the end, to get it out to everyone.

But I think this is also interesting: in Greenland—because we still don't have any roads and it's a very, very large, big country with a lot of small communities—we use the TV and use the internet. In one of my later projects, now, that I'm working on—this land-film installation I was speaking about—we want to make an edition that comes out in the newspapers as a poster, so that it can be accessed by people that can't come to the exhibition because of travel. I'm trying to think it in. It's really interesting.

But I think, of course, KNR must have a big influence. I would like to think of TV and internet, of course, as some, like, big table that you can put things on that everyone can see around the whole country. I'm sure it does that to some degree. But on the filmmakers that mostly are independent, they—KNR—have not had a big influence. Except now that they broadcast a lot of old reruns of old, old shows from the, like—even the Danish radio made or films like TV broadcasts—from the '80s and '90s. They broadcast those and it's quite fun to see sometimes, just to see the way people were speaking or how our country was looking at that time. I mean, it's only now that we are building a treasure chest of images because we didn't have much cameras before.

When I was a kid, we went to the cinema in the community house and they would show Danish films. And then every 20 minutes they would turn off, and the screen would become blue, and then a voice in Greenlandic would tell the audience what's going to happen in the next 20 minutes. So you would already know, when you saw the film, and you would understand what was going on, if you couldn't understand Danish. To some degree, this is still what we're dealing with. Until recently, KNR was basically the Danish television, just reprogrammed. Then there would be occasionally a Greenlandic show put in. Now they changed it so it's only Greenlandic. So other things are going to happen.

MDT: What impediments are there toward the development of film practice in Greenland?

ISH: I was just thinking of one thing that—it's mostly as a documentary filmmaker and even TV—that I feel can be a problem. Maybe it's also a bit of my weakness. How do you get people to open up their houses or their hearts or themselves to a filmmaker from their own country when we're only fifty thousand people? I feel that people are very self-aware about—when you come to them and you want to film—they're very self-aware of how the film is going to be perceived by the people. Like you're going to meet them on the street and say hello to them the next day. I feel it's a problem because you have to work hard to make them open, to really have them not think about this private fear and to open up themselves and be exposed. You can imagine: if you live in a community with three hundred people or even three thousand, that everybody knows everybody. So they're going to know something about you when this documentary comes out, if it's about you.

I don't know how to deal with it. I've seen some TV programs or documentaries done by foreigners that come to Greenland and where I sometimes I feel like, "Whoa they've got a lot of access." I imagine it can be because, if you have a total stranger coming in, and so it's: "I don't know where it's going to be shown. Maybe in Germany, somewhere far away." Then you're more relaxed because "they don't know me and I'm not going to meet them on the street tomorrow." And that makes people relaxed sometimes and forget that they might be shown in Greenland, actually. So, this thing of us being only fifty thousand, in terms of doing documentaries, sometimes I feel you need to work around that. Maybe we should get filmmakers from Nunavut and Nunavik and wherever else to come here and we should go there to make films.

This is also totally kind of my own fears, probably. Having the fears of asking too much of people or maybe I even take their fears on me. So, of course, it should be able to be worked around. But I just feel that there's not a lot of documentaries in Greenland happening where I really feel that they're kind of under the skin of people. I think they have to feel that the filmmaker is on their side, or something. And I also sometimes feel that it's so cautious here in Greenland. It might, as well, be me that needs to work around it.

But more obstacles working with film here is also the transportation, I think. In all the film productions, it's the biggest post on the budget. Travelling to Greenland is so expensive. But that's just another reason I think it's important to do it. Because if we can't travel to each other, then we can hopefully see films about each other.

MDT: How would you describe the state of film and media literacy in Greenland?

ISH: That's a hard question but I just feel that, as I said, with the smartphones now, it's just making a revolution. Everyone, of course, has a smartphone and the internet is picking up speed in Greenland, so everyone is on Facebook, everyone is on Instagram, everyone is posting about themselves and filming and doing it with funny things on the internet. In that way, I think the literacy is really picking up now. But as I said—before, in the '70s, young people couldn't afford cameras. It's what we realized, when making the film about Sumé. We were looking at the still images of that band and we ended up finding five or ten or something, because the young people couldn't [take photos]. Maybe very, very few of them had a camera, but then it had to be developed and all this. So it's very young. Using pictures is still a very young way of expressing yourself. But with the smartphones, it's like "Boosh!" It comes with the camera, somehow. Now you can actually film. You can afford filming. So I suppose I feel that it's really happening now.

And as I said, in TV there was radio people starting. And I think that they probably made an obstacle themselves, by having radio people making TV. So they kind of just needed to wait for them to be retired, for the young people—that think more, from the start, in pictures—to start making TV and making film in Greenland. And it's happening now.

MDT: It's interesting how challenging it can be to bring an oral culture into a visual medium.

ISH: But that's another funny thing. It's always a tradition here in Greenland that you keep the radio on. We also used to have it home in Qaqortoq. The radio would just always be on, even if you're not listening. And the same thing is also happening after that with TV, that people keep it on. They don't even have the sound on. They turned down the sound and they don't watch it. So, yeah, it's strange. But I think it's interesting. I haven't really been able to work it out: how, if we see images differently, then how do we do it? But I've been thinking lately that we don't have any trees here. And if you think about it, out in nature, there's not many vertical things. So I was thinking, because I'm working with land art now, that what I'm always looking for is something vertical. Because, yeah, it's a long story. But then I was thinking: everything is weighed down somehow, and there's no haze because the air is so dry, so you could just see 20 miles, you know? You have to be different. And even when you make sculpture, then the way that we see things—because we see contours, the way we see animals, very far away— you can just see the whole thing.

Yeah, I don't know where I'm going with it, but we see the images from Europe and you have a lot of trees in the background and you have a lot of the middle ground and all this. It's different. I don't know what to say with it. It's not a finished sentence. I'm only starting it for myself, I think, to try to think about what I, as a Greenlandic artist, go out in my own nature and sometimes look for. That I think is that cool image. Then I realize, sometimes, that I can't have something disturbing, [some] damage in the foreground, because there is nothing. Yeah, it's a different way of maybe of building an image

MDT: Do you see filmmaking in Greenland as being integrated into a larger film-making practice or industry that spans all Inuit lands?

ISH: No, unfortunately we don't have that much contact. And I think Zacharias's *Fast Runner,* I think a lot of people saw it here but still I think we're mostly influenced here by American films and by European films. I think it ties mostly together with, generally, that we don't have that much contact, because it's only online or on the few planes to Canada and Alaska. Too much lack of contact. So, I haven't thought about our film community here being a part of others in the Inuit countries that much.

But we certainly want it to happen, you know. We should be able to work more together or be inspired by each other. I'm not sure exactly how we're going to make it happen more. We had this first Nuuk International Film Festival just a few weeks ago and we invited Zacharias Kunuk and Natar [Ungalaaq]. But they couldn't come, in the end, because things went wrong. I hope it happens more and I also think we should be able to learn from each other. But it's just so far away. It's a shame. I mean, because the way out of Greenland is mostly through Denmark. That's where all the planes go if you go abroad. And that's where all the television comes from. It's become a little bit of a window to the world, even though it's like pretty far away, as well. I hope in the future it's going to happen more.

But as I said, certainly we were inspired by *The Fast Runner in* some ways, learning about our own culture. I think that's very, very important. Especially in the Inuit world, I think film is even more important than in other places, than in bigger countries, because we have all this cultural invasion coming through TV, internet. Even what we eat is flown in or shipped in and we eat it. We eat butter and maybe most of us haven't seen a cow, ever. And in the same way, I think, of course, all the American films or whatever we watch, we can use it as human beings but also it's good for us to see something that's made by ourselves and about our own hearts and what's happening right outside our window. It's something else. I think it's a part of the diet, of the cultural diet, that we need more of. Some vitamins are missing. I think that's just more important in a small culture like ours, that we make our own stuff.

MDT: I like that idea.

ISH: I do think it's a cultural diet. I mean, there's good things in the diet that we get from abroad. And, of course, us people—we are more alike than we are different from each other. Like, even whatever culture we are from, us humans. But then there's also specificities.

MDT: What is the relationship between your work as a film artist and your work as a plastic artist?

ISH: Yeah, I think we touched a little bit upon it: that I liked the meeting of opposites. Of course, I also start projects out of my own curiosity for things. I think I would stop doing it if I didn't think—hope—that for my art or film that somebody would see it and would start some thoughts, ask some questions. Not like a joke that you have the point and then you can laugh and then you can go on in your life. But maybe a riddle. Something that I could make in some small way people see things from a slightly different angle than they would have. It's not activism. But I don't think I could do things without also thinking that it matters that people see it and think about it. It doesn't matter if it's film or if it's art. It interests me some ways that it can reach out to somebody walking on the street and just maybe even make them stop for a second and think about things. Yeah, I'd like to do that. But I know I don't have any answers, I also just ask questions.

But I've been thinking that working with film and then working back with art, that it's two totally different things. I've learned something from working with one thing that I've taken to the other. And I think that, from working with sculpture, I learned for film that—say we're editing something and it's a piece of time. Then, if you edit one part—really, really small part of it—it's like a piece of sculpture and you're carving something, and you really, really work on a little detail on this side and then you turn it around and you work on the other side.

And then when you come back to that detail the next time, then in proportion to what you've done on the other side it might be all wrong, so you've wasted the time. So, it's good to keep on turning the sculpture. Just making it a little bit, turning it, making the other side. And it's the same thing when you're editing. I feel that instead of getting lost in some details, it's trying—working—more as a sculptor in the editing, trying things and not finishing it and then come back to it with fresh eyes when you've been around the rest of the film. So this kind of way of working, I think, I'm learning from one medium to the other.

MDT: Do you think that you think about film more, now, as having texture?

ISH: Maybe not texture, but maybe form. Like a shape. Like a plus and minus. Or like a concave, like in or out. So that if you're watching a film and you're seeing it as an object then—I mean not just telling a tale or something. But if you blow up one scene and make it really strong, when you have the next scene, or if you have somewhere else in the film, you have to think about how it influences the whole film and that scene might not even fit in the film if it sticks out too much. So then you're back to square one. I think these kind of proportions—I think I've learned from sculpture and vice versa, kind of moulding. It's maybe, as we were talking about making films from words, then I'm just kind of maybe learning something from working it more like from the stomach than planning it too much. Because I started in film, I started making art by planning the whole thing: like it has to have a script, the sculpture had to have a script. And then that got me into a lot of trouble because then you're not really taking good chances, I think. It's not the way to do it. So it took me a long time, when I went to art school, to get rid of my film thinking and just start from another point. And then I think I could take that way of working—I took it back into film. I wouldn't script as closely and have as much control. I dared to lose control of it more when I came back to film again.

MDT: What role does space play in your work as an artist?

ISH: I'm kind of interested in an art object or a film like not having it separate from where it's done or where it's shown. But I kind of like to think of the place that it's

124 | Inuit Takugatsaliuᑲatiget / On Inuit Cinema

being shown or made as a part of the experience. Making a fiction story or making a documentary is a little bit something else, but at the same time, as I told you, us going on a tour showing the film in community houses about Sumé in the '70s going on a tour playing in the community houses—that meant a lot to me. Then when we showed the films in the community houses, I felt that it somehow fit it so well. It has this kind of community spirit and this is what the film is about, like us, you know? So, I enjoy these things.

But also, in the art that I'm doing—going on a location out in nature and doing something and photographing it on the spot and taking it down again and it doesn't exist physically any more except in photographs. I kind of like that, as well. The idea that you could actually exhibit the photograph of a sculpture that you've done out in nature in the same spot, but it doesn't exist anymore. There's some strange things that happen with time and space there that I also think is interesting. I can't give you a very precise answer to that, except that I think I'm getting more and more interested in the space.

I'm working with a land-art piece now, that we film. I'm doing small invasions in nature with a colour that I pour into water or something and then I follow the green colour going down the ice cap, like melting water but it's becoming green so we're following that. Then it's going to be like four big screens that you can walk in between, and you're surrounded by this kind of nature place in four films. But I also would like to see what happens if you put those four screens out in nature, or in the city. The relationships with where you watch the film are interesting, I think. I don't know whether I can get any closer to it. I'm getting gradually more interested in it, let me say it that way.

I had one teacher in—or like, one artist that we met in—Art Academy in Copenhagen called Thomas Demand. He's a German artist. But he would do photographs of a scene, like a diner or something. And it would look like a photograph of a diner but actually he recreated the whole diner in cardboard exactly so it would look like it was this diner but there was something wrong about the image, it looked strange. And if you looked closely you could see that it's cardboard. I like the idea of that. This is maybe a detour but maybe it can help us. He would be inspired by a newspaper photograph of an event that happened—like a murder had taken place in that diner and there was just a photograph of the diner. And so it would be like the thought of folding down the newspaper and folding up this scene in [the] paper, taking a photograph of it, and kind of unfolding it again, even though it looked almost exactly like the original. It was like folded down and folded up. And I kind of like this. There's something strange happening there. Strange kind of loop: like it can be false and tell something about the truth that's maybe more real than the truth, kind of feel to it.

MDT: Do you now find that story is taking a back seat to this interest in space and fidelity to space?

ISH: No, because I think what I'm doing is telling a story about something that happened in time and space. Like they say, did the tree fall in the forest if you didn't see it? It's kind of the same thing that I'm doing—such a small change in a place in time and space. And five minutes after, you wouldn't be able to see that it had happened. I think I'm still really interested in story. But I'm also interested in, if something happened in an instant and you show that moment, you show that same space that it happened. I like the thread that it is, that it could happen again in five minutes. It's a possibility. I'm thinking it's still very much a story, but I'm also hopefully pushing myself a little bit more out, taking a chance that I'm not the one that's completely controlling the situation. Or—what happens if I pour out some paint in some water. What's going to happen? What does it even do if it's not there in five minutes?

MDT: I keep coming back to the image of the guitar amplifier in *SUMÉ*. You can tease out a much larger narrative about that thing in that space.

ISH: Remember, I like to think about it as: the red speaker was the visual, the music was how it would echo against the surroundings. So, it's kind of also a bit about space.

MDT: Are there different reactions to your work between home audience and Inuit abroad?

ISH: We've shown it at Toronto. But in Greenland, I know some more because we, of course, we went around and showed it. I was afraid, when the film would come out, that our interests in what happened in the '70s, like the revolution of our parents, that it wouldn't matter to the young people of today because maybe they'll just say, "Oh. So what? What happened, it was a long time ago." But that was the thing that made the most impression on me when we showed the film to young people in Greenland, people from gymnasium, high school kids. They would really sit and after the film and we were discussing it with them and they were going, "Yeah. But we want, we need to do something as well, we need to—What can we do?" kind of this spirit. It was kind of, a little bit revolutionary spirit that was kind of getting to them. So that was a really, really big reward for us to see that it could inspire in some ways.

I'm aware that, like right after you've seen the film, you're kind of really in the mood and I don't know what happens next. But I think in Greenland, the way that they received the *SUMÉ* film was just like over the top of what we expected. It was like 16 pages in the newspaper that was only about the film, and like a special something in the newspapers. I think it was ten thousand people that saw it in the cinemas and there's only cinemas in the three towns. And then we went around and showed it. So I think some people saw it many times. But I also believe that people would see their parents or grandparents on the screen. So you'd also go see a film and it's kind of a family film about your own country. So, I think it was really nice to see how much it mattered to people.

Also, we got reactions that some people were afraid that it would spark like a nationalistic feeling of hatred to the Danes and all this. And I'm not sure I'm finished with what I think about it, because I think there's a lot of division within us and whose fault it is and all this and I'm not sure what position the *SUMÉ* film has in it. But I mean, they were very critical of what the authorities did, and in today's Greenland. It's a lot of pointing fingers at the Danes. And all people from Nuuk, from the capital—we're like the Danes of Greenland now because we're the ones ruling the whole country and it's become like a class fight. But I don't know the reaction of the other Inuit parts. Unfortunately, it's not been spread so much. I tried sending it to the co-ops and it's been in some festivals in Canada and Alaska, but I really wish it would come out maybe more widely or something. I was in Iqaluit for this conference, Inuugatta, it's one and a half years ago. And I showed *SUMÉ* at a high school in Iqaluit. And those kids didn't seem really to care much. It was weird. They were—I think there was something, a language barrier or something. I'm not sure. So, yeah. I'm not really sure about the other Inuit areas, whether it makes any mark.

I tried pushing it to the cinema in Iqaluit, but I think they were kind of like—they're just used to getting in the Hollywood blockbusters. So it wasn't really like, "Oh no, I don't think so." I think it's also a matter of—I don't know, their structures, maybe. I think my producer on the film tried to speak to Isuma about what could we do? Could we work together on distributing? I'm not sure how it ended up, whether—what they talked about? It would be nice with better distribution between our countries in terms of the Inuit films.

MDT: In a 2015 interview for *First American Art Magazine* you state, "culture doesn't survive unless it evolves."[4] What kinds of change do you think that artists should be responsible for making and how are the arts central to helping cultural change in general?

ISH: Yeah, I think we started discussing this a little bit when we were saying this with the cultural invasion. I feel that because there's so much foreign culture coming in, then our role as artists and filmmakers becomes that much more important—or just the fact that you even air Greenlandic or Inuit film in the community. It just leaves such a great amount because there's so little of it, because it's a good thing, but it also gives us more responsibility. I think I made that comment because I think the perception of art in Greenland, I know from a lot of people, is that if it's Greenlandic art, the art should be a nice sunset over the mountains or it should be symbols of our own ancestors or something. And we also need that, but I know in Greenland that we don't recognize enough that a lot of the mixed culture, with a lot of things that we do in daily life, is: that's Greenlandic culture and that's Inuit culture. Art in Greenland I know could reflect more of that. Like horses, people have these blinkers on, so they can't really see that everybody

....
4. Winifield, p. 67.

around us are signs of our culture and how we are as human beings today. And it's important to show that as artists, and to question it. I think it's also—together with this cultural invasion—that, of course, we need to be open to the world and to develop and stay. For our culture to survive, we need to adapt. Just to say that—we need to keep moving also to stay alive. For the culture to stay alive. Otherwise, I think we're going to—it's going to be a foul smell if it's old, closed, hermetically closed. We're going to die.

MDT: What role do you think art plays in facilitating social and cultural change?

ISH: I think generally that where other means of communication end, then art has a place. So it's really just an open kind of space, also, to express feelings and questions that wouldn't be able to be expressed any other way, I think. And we need that. I think especially when we talk about Inuit culture, Inuit identity, that we're trying to still define ourselves constantly and to find ourselves again, that we're talking about, or find ourselves in the world today. Then I think that art could have a bigger role in it than it has today. It's not just a matter of funding. But it's also a matter of the artists being more courageous and also us being, maybe, better at organizing ourselves in some ways and having self-confidence.

MDT: So, do you think that the documentary arts have a particular role in facilitating that kind of change?

ISH: Yeah. I mean it's not one way has more value than the other, but a documentary can be a more direct mirror to what's happening around us, or what has happened. So it's really important. I think it speaks more, very directly, about the reality around us. Whereas other forms of films can speak more indirectly. It will stay as a document of the reality for many years to come. I know that fiction can do it as well, in some sort. But documentary in that way is more direct.

I think that we are kind of the first generation, we found out, that can make archival films for real about our past. Because in the '60s they started filming a little bit with Super 8s and stuff, but before we don't really have images recorded by our own people that much. So I think that's really, in some ways, exciting.

Because things are changing so fast for the Inuit anywhere, then that's something to do with your documentary question, as well. Then documentary also becomes more important because it's a time document. Even what happened 30, 40, 50 years ago, it's such a big leap that it's gold to be able to have documentaries from different times. I don't think I can milk any more out of my brain now. I also think I've said what I wanted about it.

MDT: Do you find that there's resistance to the change that you're interested in, in your work?

ISH: I'm not an activist so I don't work towards a specific change, but if there's a resistance—like the project with *Why We Fight*, and all this *Melting Barricades*—where we made a military, a fictional military for Greenland and we invade the world. I think people loved it but also there's a resistance. I think we wanted to kind of open a discussion about values. If we want to be independent as a nation and as people, everybody's talking about how to get that piece of paper or that key and let's do it. But nobody's talking about, "What are we going to put onto that ship, or whatever we can call it, that we want to steer into the future?" What are our values? And I think there was a resistance to talk about the really important issues. I'm only talking about locally in Greenland, I don't know if it's the same. But because it hurts and because there's no black-and-white solutions, then it's so easy to talk about all the things that don't matter as much.

I think that is some sort of resistance that's even in myself, you know? That it's so much easier to carry on what I did yesterday than the change that we really need. And now, of course, I'm talking politically. Something needs to happen and it's not happening and I'm not sure. As much as I say that we need to do it, I'm just as much an accomplice, a usual suspect. So, like, to say the *SUMÉ* film is about a revolution. And if they say that—someone said that—every generation needs a revolution, then if the last one was in the '70s, then now it's almost 40 years later. This is the next generation—so where's the revolution? So I think there's also a bit of truth in Nirvana, even if it was in the '90s, we are so far behind in Greenland that it's coming here now. Our generation is just kind of waiting to be entertained or waiting for something to happen and we're not really doing anything. That's why, I think, our interest for what happened in the '70s, our parents' generation revolution, is so interesting to us and makes us want to do something. But then when we've just slept on it and then next day nothing happens—I think the whole Inuit People, we are kind of a little bit stuck, you know? It's like frozen in time, a little bit. But it just seems like something is building up. I keep saying it, in the last years: "Something is building up. Something is going to happen." And nothing has happened yet. I hope that something explodes soon.

OKâlaKatiget Society

Incorporated in 1982, the OKâlaKatiget Society (OK Society) is a radio and television broadcaster and producer in Nain, Nunatsiavut. OKâlaKatiget translates as "people that talk or communicate with each other." Its mandate is to preserve and promote the language and culture of the Inuit within northern Labrador. It is the only broadcasting service that provides programming in Inuttitut/Inuttut. Despite its remarkable output in print, radio, television, and film, the work of the OK Society remains under-represented outside of Nunatsiavut. These interviews focus primarily on OK's work in film and television.

Fran Williams

Fran Williams was born and raised in Hopedale, Nunatsiavut, NL. Trained as a nurse, Fran practised in several Labrador communities before serving two terms as the president of the Labrador Inuit Association, the precursor to the Nunatsiavut Government. After her time in government, she took on the role of Program Director for the OKâlaKatiget Society and went on to serve as its Executive Director. Fran worked with the OKâlaKatiget Society for 25 years. I conducted this interview with her in English on February 24 and 26, 2015, at her home in Nain.

MARK DAVID TURNER (MDT): How did you come to work with the OKâlaKatiget Society?

FRAN WILLIAMS (FW): I really didn't know what I was getting into, after nursing and all that, learning how to be a politician, and all the other things I dealt with before then. I had no clue about technical equipment or anything like that. All I knew, when I accepted the position back in 1972 or '73, when LIA[1] had an annual general meeting in Makkovik, they said they would like to have their own Native communication system. So someone was hired to look into that and find funds to set up their own Inuktitut[2] broadcaster. They wanted to hear Inuktitut on the radio. Mainly it was radio at first.

So from there, in 1982, it was incorporated under the laws of the province. They already had a training program going on, albeit a very small office with an administrator and a trainer for both radio and television, I think it was. As Program Director, I helped or devised what kind of program should we offer to the audiences and arranged training for the producers, so that they could report and operate the equipment that was needed to do that. And reporting to the board of directors on how we were proceeding and also helping. If we had to submit a budget, we did it together—to determine how much money we would need for radio programming or TV training, you know, whatever.

....

1. Labrador Inuit Association.

2. Throughout this interview, Fran Williams and I use the enduring term "Inuktitut" to refer to Inuit languages in Canada.

MDT: That seems like a lot of work for one position.

FW: I think they felt it was important that whoever got this should also speak Inuktitut. Because this was the first time our people were hearing news or information in their own language. There was an administrator, but like we worked together. It was such a small operation at the time I joined it. You know, it was necessary to work together to expand our funding, expand our program, you know, and all that stuff.

MDT: Can you walk me through the first 10 years, then, from this annual general meeting in 1972 up until the 1982 training program?

FW: I don't really know. All I know is that I saw in the LIA minutes that they wanted a communication system of their own and in their own language. I'm not too certain about how they worked to achieving it. But in 1982 they had gotten as far as getting a board of directors and naming the Society and having a broadcast plan and things like that, so that they could get funding from the Secretary of State. And at that time, it was just one of the 13 Native communications across the country. There's one for Labrador Inuit, and one in Quebec, one in Baffin area, one in Ontario—Wawatay. There was another one in Manitoba, you know, in all the provinces across Canada. The Native Communications Society, as we were called, and was funded to broadcast. Some only in radio.

MDT: Was the OKâlaKatiget Society ever officially a part of the LIA? I don't understand the relationship between the two at the outset.

FW: No, it wasn't a part of LIA. It was an organization on its own with its own board of directors and own funding source. Except that it was supported by LIA, and in the earlier days we used to have a director who was from LIA. I'm not sure if they have that anymore, but up to kind of recently, there used to be a board member who represented LIA. Now I don't think it has happened since it became Nunatsiavut.

MDT: Was the publication of *kinatuinamot illengajuk*[3] a part of OK's operations from the beginning?

FW: No.

MDT: What happened there?

FW: I can't remember the date, but I know in 1985 we moved into the old school, where we set up a radio department, a television department, administration upstairs. That was in 1985 we moved into that place, and then we were approached by LIA if we could take over the print. And we added print to our, to the Society, and put them upstairs with administration, while we had radio and TV downstairs. I can't remember the exact year, but it was after we moved into the old boarding school that it happened. They asked if we could take over from LIA and of course we did, because there was just no room in the basement of that little daycare centre where we were situated before.

MDT: So it started as the newsletter for the LIA?

FW: Yeah, it was a newsletter for the Labrador Inuit. Like it says, "To whom it may concern."

MDT: But then it turned into something that focused on the North Coast more generally?

FW: Yeah. It covered stories from all communities that LIA represented. But I'm not sure, I thought that was the case, too, when it was operated by LIA, representing Labrador Inuit wherever they may live. Who was the first editor of *ki*? I think it was Amos Dicker. I know Amos Dicker originally was involved with *ki* and William Kalleo and Rosina Kalleo, too—she's Holwell now, of course— would know a lot more about the beginnings of *ki*. So was Christine Dicker, who's

....

3. "To whom it may concern" or "something for everyone."

now Christine Goodwin, I think, were the original ones that worked with the newsletter.

MDT: Let's go back then, a little bit, to what OKâlaKatiget was like when you became Program Director. You said that there was a board in place. Money had been secured for a training program. Were there any full-time employees other than yourself, at that point?

FW: Oh yeah, there was a lot more employees before I joined it. The Inuit Broadcasting Corporation set up a training program for radio trainees and television trainees. Who were the original ones? I know Mary Andersen was an original radio person, I think Martin Jararuse. They had hired one person, tried to get one person, from each community: from Rigolet, Makkovik, Postville, Hopedale, and Nain—and they had those. They hired from each town. There were more from Nain because it was situated here, and there was an administrator and a trainer. There was no special staff at that time, like bookkeepers and other positions that are available now. They had very old equipment, of course. In the radio department, by that time, there was a local radio station here in Nain and some other towns. They used to air their—radio, at least, used to air—their little 10-minute piece that they had produced on the local radio station.

After OKâlaKatiget was officially formed in 1982, some of them were already in place, but I can't say for sure which ones. But I know Nain was, because we were using their local station to air our little pieces. I'm not sure if Hopedale had one? Maybe it did? But after that I know that OKâlaKatiget was able to get money from Secretary of State to buy equipment for all the local radio stations. And our Executive Director, Pat Nagle, installed equipment in those communities. And we had an agreement with the local radio stations that, once we got on air, that they would air our programming on their feed.

MDT: Where did the first batch of equipment come from, for OK?

FW: From somewhere. I'm not sure, it might have come from the Inuit—what was it called? The ICSL.[4] They were like a subsidiary of IBC, but they were in television. Pat Nagle would be able to answer that question. They were probably from Nova Scotia somewhere, where they have—I can't honestly say where we got the equipment from, but it was from a place where you could—but I think it was in Atlantic Canada we got it from.

MDT: How did the relationship between OK and the Inuit Broadcasting Corporation start?

FW: They had a relationship already before I joined them. I got on stream with them in 1984. Some of the real—the people who really had something to do with setting up OKâlaKatiget and funding and all of that—one of them was a communications person for LIA, Randy Sweetnam. But he's passed away now. Kendall Lougheed, who lives in Ottawa. Tom Axtell, I think he lives in Garthby right now. Dorothy Kidd, she's working at a university in San Francisco now. Those are the people that were there when I got employment with OKâlaKatiget Society.

MDT: So it was a bustling place when you came in?

FW: Yeah. There was four in radio and four in television, I think, that were being trained. They were training for one year because in 1985 we had a big graduation do for them after a year of training in either radio or TV.

MDT: Do you remember who the first people were in television?

FW: From Nain, I know it was Mary Andersen and Maude White, I think she's passed away. From Hopedale was Jonas Karpik, I think he's passed away. From Postville, it was Brenda Manak, she's now Brenda Colbourne. She works with NG[5] right now in Postville. From Makkovik, it was John Jararuse, I think. And from Rigolet it was somebody Allen.

....

4. Inuit Communications Systems Limited.

5. Nunatsiavut Government.

MDT: Was there equipment for video production?

FW: Yeah. There was video equipment even in that little basement. It was crowded, but it had both radio and video equipment. Although it was very sparse. There was more radio equipment than TV equipment. Any equipment they had was used mainly for training. They had a camera and an editing machine: the sparsest equipment needed to put a program together.

MDT: Did everybody go home after the training?

FW: No, they stayed. They stayed and progressed as television producers to make programming.

MDT: When the training program was finished, was that when the idea for the *Labradorimiut* television series was developed?

FW: Well, the idea was there after the training program but I don't know exactly when it was chosen to be called *Labradorimiut*. I really can't remember when the first TV show aired, but I know the first ones that were aired by the television department were aired on *Qaggiq* program of Inuit Broadcasting Corporation. They gave a 10-minute time slot to air the TV production of *Labradorimiut* on their airtime. It wasn't until 1985 that we really got a good television production centre and equipment, after we moved into the old school and it had its own department space. And you're getting trainers on a regular basis and producing on a regular basis.

MDT: Did anything else change in 1985?

FW: We had a lot more space. It was still four people in television production and usually a trainer all the time. We hired different trainers. The thing that changed, I guess, was the number of hours of production, from a 10-minute piece. I mean, it gradually increased.

MDT: Why did that change?

FW: We had more access to airing. Especially when Television Northern Canada [TVNC]—the Inuit had their own transponder, so they were able to air more programming because it was dedicated to Inuit, Inuktitut television.

MDT: How long were you doing that for, those 10-minute segments?

FW: Once we got TVNC, the transponder, we were able to show half-hour television programming on TVNC, like all the other Inuit areas, and the Cree.

MDT: Did you have to physically send tapes to IBC for them to broadcast?

FW: Yeah, we had to mail them. Send them by mail to them. If they wanted to interview me about something important, they could get my picture. I don't know how that happened. I don't know what it's called even. We had no services like that then.

MDT: What was the OKâlaKatiget Society's relationship to TVNC?

FW: We just supported it. I think IBC did most of the work to get money for that system to air Inuktitut programming. The rest of us—like Taqramiut Nipingat and OKâlaKatiget and ICSL in western Arctic—we all supported. But IBC did most of the work, I think, on it and we just supported it.

We used to have meetings when it was called the National Aboriginal Communications Society. That was before APTN.[6] Prior to that it was NACS[7] and all the 13 Native communications societies across the country who'd attend an annual general meeting, wherever it might be, and talk about our own broadcasting systems, whether it be in radio or in TV. On a national level, sometimes they would award a best story in TV or a best story in radio and things like that. And OKâlaKatiget got quite a few awards from NACS for doing exceptional Inuktitut programming in TV and radio. So, yes, we used to meet with NACS, who was our national body representing all of us 13 Native communications

....

6. Aboriginal Peoples Television Network.

7. National Aboriginal Communications Society.

across the country. And it was very helpful at the time, because we used to meet—and there were pretty good concerns from each communications group whether they were Inuit, or Cree, or Ojibwe, or whatever—and have a good discussion. And now with APTN, it seems they never aired any French programming, like APTN does now. We weren't limited to the production, what you showed on TV. Today it has to be between the youth and the Elders and nothing aired on issues that are affecting the people in northern Labrador. So, that has changed a lot.

MDT: Did you have more creative control under NACS?

FW: Not us, as an organization, but yeah, it was a lot more representation of Inuktitut programming when it was TVNC. Now, with APTN, it's a lot less.

I found that with NACS, they gave more recognition to the good work that the different communication societies did, for the kind of programming that they did, for the language it was done in, and that sort of thing. You used to get awards for the best Inuktitut documentary, or the best Inuktitut radio show, or something like that. Or for best technical work. So it was encouraging to all of us 13 communications across the country, to have recognition of some kind for the work that we did.

MDT: Did the OKâlaKatiget Society aim to do more audio-visual programming beyond *Labradorimiut*?

FW: We were always aiming for more hours, whether it was on TVNC or APTN. In the later years, like in the mid-'90s to early 2000s, when a funding program like Canada Manpower kind of left—up to that time we were always getting trainers to come in, because our staff was always changing, either in radio or TV, so that they got at least the basics of journalism training and things like that. But after the training funds ran out, and our funding from NNBAP,[8] Secretary of State, or Canadian Heritage came down by a lot, we were starting to struggle.

....

8. Northern Native Broadcast Access Program.

So we had to limit a lot of things that we were used to before, when we used to get a lot more money in the earlier times than we did like in the mid-'90s. In the mid-'90s, I know that Gerry Weiner was Secretary of State and we had a wiener roast on the ice, protesting the cuts to all the Native communication groups. In those earlier days, the Secretaries of State were very understanding and positive about the work that all of us were doing across the country and supported it for funding. So it was really good, we could even get money for buildings. So that was good in those days, but now it's down by at least two-thirds of what we used to get back in the 1980s.

MDT: How did those cutbacks affect production?

FW: Well, it certainly changed. What we always used to say, when we first started TV production, is that quality of the work that counts, not quantity. So, when all our funding started being cut it certainly affected the quality of the programming that we were doing, because we didn't have the resources anymore or the money to do it like we used to before. It was starting to be rushed. So, yes, it changed the quality of the work that we did.

MDT: If you go back and watch those episodes of *Labradorimiut*, just before and during that period, do you see a quality difference?

FW: Oh yeah, even in the camera work or the story development, because they have trainers at that time that showed them how to do a story properly. How to do camera work properly. And how to put it all together properly as a show. But the most important thing is, there are not many producers in the television department that are speakers. They're young but they speak it, but they have—it's blah—they have no emotion. I realize it's because of the time constraints. Like you have, say you have 90 seconds to say a lot of things in English in that little time slot. In Inuktitut you really got to rush and rush and rush to say it in time, and you sacrifice the feelings to get the information on. You know what I mean?

To me, our language is very important. So if we're doing production, radio is okay because they have good speakers in Inuktitut that can get more inflection and more feeling to what they're recording. But I feel that in TV, lately, they've never had someone who was a totally good speaker in Inuktitut and they're unable to come across on TV with feelings about what they're saying, because they weren't really that fluent. They just have to get it out and get it out as fast as possible. But you can do it. If you're a more experienced speaker in Inuktitut, you can do it.

MDT: The mandate of OKâlaKatiget is to preserve and promote and protect Labrador Inuit culture and language. Did you ever find the work difficult to square with that mandate?

FW: We always knew what our mandate was. For the first time, people could hear news and information and entertainment in their own language. And one of the most important mandates was that we, through our programming, we were keeping the language alive through our programming, our culture alive through programming, our values alive through programming, so that our future generations could see it and hear it. One of the very important things is that, on television, people in the different communities, when we started broadcasting regular programming on TVNC, they were always happy to see someone who was a relative. It connected them from community to community, seeing people in the programming who were their relatives or their friends. So, that was an important way of connecting the communities. When we started, there was only one Inuk show on Tuesdays in 19-something. We decided we needed to do more Inuktitut programming on radio. So everything was in Inuktitut, no English. Then we had a call from an audience member in Makkovik saying, "We'd like to hear the weather report in English, because we listen to your station every day and we like to know what the weather is going to be for going off to our cabin." So from that you can say, all right they listen to our radio programs, and they watch our television shows, and they contribute to the content, as well. It was interesting that they wanted to hear the weather report on our only Inuktitut programming, that was an extra bonus, I felt.

In the start, a lot of people didn't have cable or even they couldn't access our radio programming, because when we started production first in radio, before TV, we could only be heard in Nain and Hopedale and not in the other towns, that was radio. Then with television, when we started television production, we used to make VHS copies of our programming to send to all the communities so that they could see it.

MDT: How did that work? Did you send them to individuals or was there a place where everybody could come together and watch them?

FW: To our board members in each community usually. Or to a school or something.

MDT: How long did that last?

FW: It lasted quite a while, until we finally got in television, when we were able to be seen by all towns at the same time. I can't remember when that happened, but I think probably Lorne Burry knows more about that than I do. I'm trying to get the years together now. I know it was sometime in mid-'80s or even '89 by the time we got everybody seeing our television programs at the same time, on TVNC, I think.

MDT: Who came up with the idea to share the tapes that way?

FW: It wasn't a matter of who decided, it was a matter of providing it. We knew they wanted to see the programming and, "Yeah, this is a way we can do it." So, we all had video ability to watch the programming. They could use it at home or they could use it in a public place. So that was how we started off, really, with the other communities who couldn't see our television programming. And the Labrador East Integrated School Board through Sarah Townley, afterwards, copied almost every program that OKâlaKatiget produced. So that was a big help when our building burned down, because they had copies there.

MDT: What other kind of audio-visual programming did the OKâlaKatiget Society do?

FW: I remember, I don't know what year it was, I think it must have been mid-'90s or late '90s, that we were sending our programming to be aired on through Halifax on ASN.[9] And that we also produced Inuktitut copies of, must have been NFB I suppose, on Africans doing similar things like Inuit did, doing Inuktitut versions of their culture, of different countries' culture.

MDT: You were dubbing into Inuktitut?

FW: Yeah, we were dubbing the programs that were provided us and making it into Inuktitut and showing it on air, on our time slot.

MDT: In the late 1990s, you worked with Nigel Markham to do the two films around the Hebron relocations, *Forever in Our Hearts* and *Without Consent*.

FW: Nigel was very helpful in accessing funds from Telefilm Canada. And Telefilm Canada said they were very anxious to fund us because they had never funded anyone in Labrador before, when we applied to them for monies to do the Hebron relocation thing with the help of Nigel. Yes, it was a lot of administrative work, but at the same time it was great to have a camera-person like Nigel doing work with our television department, and it was a wonderful production.

MDT: That was the first time you got Telefilm funding?

FW: Yeah, that was the first time they ever funded us.

MDT: Were there any other television shows?

FW: It was all *Labradorimiut*. We got Sid Dicker, who always introduced the show with his own song, "Labradorimiut." That's why it's called *Labradorimiut*. We had an agreement that we would use his song every time we introduced our show. Except that the name changed to *Tamânevugut* for the TV production and the whole focus was changed in programming. It was no longer representing all the people, all the stories from the communities. It was only representing Elders and

....
9. Atlantic Satellite Network.

youth. And the same thing, same old things, drum playing and all that. As far as I'm concerned now, the TV shows are no longer inclusive of life of the Inuit in our communities. It only represents a certain group, not everyone. It's not inclusive, I feel, of the issues that are important to the Inuit in all the communities anymore. It's great to have Elders and youth mixing together, but our original mandate wasn't that. APTN insists on that for television programming. But that's not our original mandate of why we were formed in the first place.

MDT: Can we go back to your work with the OKâlaKatiget Society? When did you make the shift from Program Director to Executive Director?

FW: Well, right after May of 1984, after I finished my second term as president of LIA, I was encouraged to apply for the Program Director position with OKâlaKatiget Society. And I think it was Ken Lougheed, if I remember correctly, encouraged me to apply. I did. And I got it. It was in the very early beginnings of OKâlaKatiget. I really didn't know anything about radio and TV communications. Remember, I trained as a nurse. I knew how to help sick people and help them get well and that kind of thing, but I certainly didn't know anything about equipment used in radio production, or television production, or about journalism, or anything. Although I did watch news all the time before then. It was a lot like being president of LIA—I learned a lot. And when I look back on my life now, I wish I had worked with OKâlaKatiget Society before I became president of LIA, because I got to know more about communicating with the people and those OKâlaKatiget represented, which I didn't do very well, when I look back now, as president. So, it would have been a great help to me if I had worked with OKâlaKatiget before.

But anyway, getting into a totally new field of communications, technical stuff and how to train our people to become journalists like everybody else you see on the news, it was a whole new thing for the radio producers and the television producers. But the fact that they did have trainers all the time in those earlier days instilled the pride of being someone who was in the different—or learning to be—in a different career. And an exciting one, because in the earlier days it's like breaking news. We were taught that way. Today, it seems to be not a career for them anymore but an 8:30 to 4:30 job and a paycheque every week.

When we had trainers—the way I was taught, too, a lot by the trainers—we were taught that news doesn't stop at a certain hour. That news is happening right in front of your eyes in the town. You have to think beyond the four walls that you're working in, and that there's always not just two sides, but three sides to a story. And that you have to check those out, all sides. The fact that you're related to—well, that was an exception, I guess, if we had to report on our own relatives if they were going to jail or something like that. But don't become biased in your news story about people you know, and things like that. Those were the things I learned as a Program Director. And where to look for money to improve our organization.

But as an executive director I found it much more difficult, because you had to understand about money, financing, accounting, accounting for your funds, and all that stuff. I have no idea, to date. I depended totally on my bookkeeper. Although we all planned that this is how much we'll need in operations, either office equipment, or radio equipment, or TV equipment, and things like that. I find for older people, money and accounting for money is not important to them. First of all, most people don't have money anyway to account for. So when I got into that position of trying to learn as much as possible about all the lines on a yearly basis—all the lines that say "this is this"—and trying to ask the auditors every year for as much help to understand the accounting system. But in other areas, the people said I was getting people involved, more of a people person, knowing how to deal with difficult situations with staff, or whatever. And getting stories from everybody, all the communities. And getting the producers to—whether they were in TV or whatever—to ask the right questions. Then I often did voice-overs for TV, like TV depended a lot on radio people to do voice-overs for them, and things like that. Rather than an administrator, I was more productive with people and getting them to work. That's what I found different between my Program Director and my Executive Director job.

MDT: What other kinds of difficulties did you face?

FW: One of the difficulties that I really had was in hiring. Because usually it was myself, the senior producer in radio, the senior producer in television, and the administrator, were on the hiring committee. Whether it was for radio production or television production or for administrative work. And every time that a position became available, whether it was in any area within the Society, we used to have so many applications, all the people looking for work. And then we take that—we didn't do this thing where we [say], "Okay, we won't interview you anymore." But we took time to interview them all just to hear their responses to our questions. Most times, a lot of them had no experience with Inuktitut. That was a big thing lacking.

And then, in the later years when we interviewed people, they had good knowledge of Inuktitut, but others thought they didn't have a good social experience, so to speak. I always fought for, at times, fought for Inuktitut-speaking people, to give them a chance to see if they'd work out, rather than just ruling them out because they had a social problem or something. I think that worked out in a number of cases but not all cases. And over the years, because I was with them for 25 years, it was the same people applying all the time when a job came open. And I felt so bad that we kept rejecting them year after year after year, sort of thing. But we did give a few of them a chance, because I felt that they needed to work, to have a job to make their lives better. That's what I found difficult.

MDT: With the stories that they would look for and seek out, was there a different set of concerns for Inuktitut speakers?

FW: Oh yeah, there was all different—one of the questions that we would ask was, "What story would you go after today?" And depending on how they answered it, you could tell whether they listened. If they were, say, aware of what was going on, not just in Nain but in other communities.

Yeah, looking back on it, I think so. Some of them were more concerned about knowing the technological part of production. And if there were Inuktitut speakers, I think they had put more value on the culture and language aspects and how the environment and the animals and everything that we cherish or use for generations. I think they understood that part more if they spoke Inuktitut, because they were able to communicate with Elders who talked about these kinds of things in their own language.

MDT: That's an interesting point.

FW: I know that if they spoke Inuktitut, or weren't really speakers but they wanted to learn more Inuktitut, they were more open, too, to doing stories that were about what was happening in the towns. But if we hired someone who didn't speak Inuktitut, a lot of them understood why we were going after stories of people and what was happening, the issues that were important to Inuit in all the communities. They understood that. But there were others who were more interested in technology, the technological part of production, than culture or language. And they were important, too, because we needed them to produce good-quality camera work and things like that. I guess, over the long run, we used to have a good mixture of both. But quite often in the television department they needed help with voice-overs a lot, from myself and others who spoke it fluently. But that was okay. We helped each other out. They helped us. The TV crew helped the radio crew, the radio helped the TV crew.

MDT: Did you see radio as being the core of what the OKâlaKatiget Society did? Or did radio and TV inform each other?

FW: Only in the sense that radio was immediate, it gave the news as it was happening. Whereas in television, usually, you did stories that had already happened, or was happening at the moment but shown much later. But that was the way it was. We couldn't cover something that was happening immediately in television. Like before, on someone who was lost or something, and show it the same date type of thing, only in that sense. And in television, we found that people were so happy to see people they knew, because a lot of them lived in different communities after relocation, they would see people they hadn't seen for a long time on TV. That was a big thing for the audience in other communities. They enjoyed it so much, seeing people they knew and people who were their friends and people who lived in other communities. Moreso than the story being told, quite often sometimes, I think. Just to see relatives and their friends that they hadn't seen for a long time.

The difference between radio and television—I guess ultimately, radio was: you got in contact with people by telephone. With television, you had to go where events were happening, rather than getting—well they couldn't do their stories on telephone, so they had to travel to other communities to get their stories because that was the only way they could do their productions, was to travel to communities and film it and things like that.

MDT: With such an emphasis on people, it makes sense why there are relatively few shots of the communities.

FW: They weren't concerned about that, really. They were concerned about getting right into the people who were involved in the story. Getting an establishing shot of the town, maybe they did at times but very rarely. Shooting an event and having people tell the stories about the event that was happening, or whatever, was more important than getting establishing shots of the town they were in.

Because it's such a new form of a career, in a small Inuit town or community, it was always more about, in television, more about happy events, people you knew, rather than the story itself. Now I find with CBC, *Here and Now*, they do too much coverage on the courts, for example. But the Inuktitut program I've seen from IBC or other Native communication groups, like Taggamiut Nipingat Inc. and ICSL and OKâlaKatiget, it was all more important about covering an event, or something happening that was important to the people living in that town, and usually a good story and not a sad story.

MDT: Do you think that the other Inuit broadcasters had the same central focus on people?

FW: Yeah. But one thing I haven't mentioned is that, in other Inuit areas like IBC and Taggamiut and ICSL in the western Arctic, their programming was only in Inuktitut all the time, with no English, really, until later. I always wished we were able to do that same thing, just Inuktitut programming, which would make it a lot easier for our producers. But our mandate (because it wasn't just Inuktitut, we also had English speakers in our membership) was that it be in both languages. So that's what we had to go by. If it was an Inuk show, it had to also be an English version. If it was English—oh yeah, we used to do just an English version *and* an Inuktitut version before. Now it's just one show with subtitles.

MDT: Was that the policy right from the beginning, programming in both English and Inuktitut?

FW: Oh yeah, both, with radio programming—because not all our membership or audience spoke Inuktitut. It was both English and Inuktitut.

MDT: Were there ever any plans for OKâlaKatiget to do other types of production than documentary?

FW: It was always about the present, what's happening at a certain time. We had bad enough times trying to do ads on radio, leave alone TV. When it's money-making, they pay well (as for radio anyway), but we never even had time for it on TV, like you see today. But if Air Labrador wanted to do an ad on radio, they say crazy things—that it's very hard to translate into Inuktitut. Like what I'm dealing with that translation now: "The heartbeat of our land." You know, you can say it a lot better than that in Inuktitut, because Inuit just dealt with things that happened. Nothing glorified or nothing like that. It's hard to find words that glorify. Or, in English, to translate things like "soaring in the air" or—you just say "flying." There's so many English words that you can use, but there's only one way you can describe it in Inuktitut. And you usually have to do it in a sentence, not one word, so people will understand what you're talking about. But it's fun. It was a great experience.

It was funny having a wiener roast for Gerry Weiner. It was fun to give David Crombie a baseball cap from OKâlaKatiget. We never ever had a minister of our funding source come to Nain or OKâlaKatiget, but we used to have [a] regional liaison committee in the earlier days, from CBC, Department of Communications—used to be Canada Manpower, one time. Used to be five different departments, federal departments, and we always used to get together every so many months to, I guess really—it was almost something like an audience survey, to see how you're doing, to see how you're getting along, to see the work you were supposed to do in a certain time period and that. That was a big help. Because we needed a lot of—well, CBC was a big assistance to us in equipment, setting up equipment, and coming here if something went wrong and fixing it, and helping us with budget and things. So was the Canada Manpower—they always had money for training. And Department of Communications. They always were helpful, too, because in the earlier days we had HF radio and VHF radio testing, to see which was better if you were out on the land. We used to have our own equipment from Department of Communications. It was HF. So that people out on the land could communicate with the town and things like that.

MDT: That was part of your early operations?

FW: It was an experiment that they were doing up here and OKâlaKatiget was the organization to help them. And they provided the trail radio equipment and we looked after them to see who used them.

MDT: Who was it that sponsored that program?

FW: The Department of Communications in Ottawa.

MDT: Is there anything else that you think that's really important for people to know about the history of OKâlaKatiget?

FW: One little thing. I said it's providing programming in our own language. And in both TV and in radio, when we did programming in Inuktitut sometimes—especially if we're talking about weather—sometimes we used the wrong word. And we used to get an immediate reaction from the audience. "This is not how you say it, this is the right way to say it!" So that was really helpful. They didn't criticize us, they were just being helpful.

Sarah Abel

Sarah Abel was born and raised in Hopedale, Nunatsiavut. She is the Senior Television Producer at the OKâlaKatiget Society, where she has worked since 1997 producing dozens of episodes in both the *Labradorimiut* and *Tamânevugut* series. I conducted this interview with Sarah in English on March 29, 2016, at OKâlaKatiget Society studios in Nain.

MARK DAVID TURNER (MDT): How did you start work at OKâlaKatiget Society?

SARAH ABEL (SA): Let's see. I was working, waitressing at the hotel. Well, I moved back to Hopedale for a year-and-a-half. I worked down there waitressing, night watch, stuff like that. But after a year-and-a-half I decided nope, I don't like living there. So, I moved back here and waitressed. And then it was at the protest in Voisey's Bay[1] to stop the construction of the road, I came back, and the job ad was out for TV Producer and I thought, "I'll try," because it was more money. Plus it was a way to try and get my language back, because I kept hearing it all the time. And that was it.

MDT: When was that?

SA: It was September of '97 that I started working here.

MDT: Prior to that, had you had any experience working in like film, television?

SA: Nothing at all.

MDT: What drew you to the ad then?

SA: Well, like I said, I was being honest—I needed the money. I needed work and

....
1. The site of a nickel mine close to the community of Nain.

I needed work that wasn't shift work, because I had my son to raise. So it was a nine-to-five job and so that's kind of what drew me towards it.

MDT: And at that point, what were the duties involved with television production?

SA: It's the same as what it is now: filming, editing, transcribing, the lighting, the interviews, the voice-overs—more or less everything that we do today. Everything was a lot harder because we were filming U-Matic—three-quarter U-Matic— then having to learn how to use editing equipment, and knowing your exact time, and when to press the button. I found it a lot harder.

MDT: Was it on-the-job training?

SA: It was on-the-job. There was no trainers. It was whoever was your supervisor, or whoever was here the longest, trained you. It was, more or less, like you were taught the basics on how to do what you're supposed to do and then everything else you kind of had to catch on by yourself and figure it out. Back then we had internet but we wasn't into using it as much. So it was more or less like trial and error, trying to figure things out.

MDT: Who was your supervisor when you first started?

SA: The late Sarah Obed. I think she was here with us for four years. Then she moved on to employment elsewhere in another community.

MDT: Where did she receive her training?

SA: I think she was one of the lucky ones. Because back then, before the budget cuts and whatever from the federal government, they had full-time trainers here for radio and television. They had someone that lived here year-round and trained radio and television. David Zelcer was a trainer. He worked with CBC. And I don't know who the other—Lorraine Thompson, I think it is? Pat Nagle was here before, from CBC. When he lived here, he worked with OKâlaKatiget.

So that was like, I guess, the mid-'80s on, until I'd say early '90s, they were here. They taught them, like, interview skills and different ways to use the camera, that sort of stuff. Even with the radio department—what kind of audio levels to get, and what kind of background noise to get, and stuff like that.

MDT: Who else was in the television production department when you started?

SA: There was myself, Sarah Obed, her sister Bonna Obed, and Beni Merkeratsuk. There was always four. And I think there was one more, because I think I replaced Bonna because Bonna went to school in St. John's. Sarah, Beni, Bonna finished, I replaced her. Jerry Star had already finished. I can't remember the fourth one, it was so long ago.

MDT: How did you split up the duties then, between the four of you? Were you all producers?

SA: Yep, everyone did the same. It's just—maybe Sarah did more of the online editing, like the fixing whatever problems we might have had. Because everybody had to do the voice-overs. Everybody. You were assigned a show and you went out and filmed it, you transcribed it, you did the interviews, that sort of stuff.

MDT: In terms of the gear that you were using, you mentioned there were three-quarter-inch tapes that you were using back in the day. What kind of cameras were you using?

SA: They were huge. I don't know if they got some upstairs in the storage room, because they got like a mini museum. But they were like, basically, they got a big cord to go to the power pack that you had to lug around. And the power pack was a big belt and it was like maybe 15 pounds. Then you also had to take the deck to put the tape in.

They had a proper edit suite set up, so it was good. They had one for just transferring and one for importing your video and all that. So everything was recorded on three-quarter-inch. There was no zoom recorders or anything. You had to do voice-overs with the big cameras.

MDT: So you'd do all the audio in-camera too?

SA: Um-hum.

MDT: So, you used U-Matic for a while—what was the next move and format?

SA: It went straight to Avid.[2]

MDT: Oh, okay.

SA: In 1999.

MDT: Oh. And that's when you started using, I guess, Betacam and the MiniDV formats?

SA: Um-hum. It was more of the MiniDV. We used Betacam just for exporting the broadcast shows to Beta to ship to APTN.

MDT: Oh, okay, okay. So, when you did that, were you able to transfer all of the old stock footage that you had on U-Matic into those formats? Or what happened with it?

SA: We were starting to, and then the fire. We lost over four thousand tapes of original footage. Footage that was transferred from, and copied from, the Hettasch's videos[3] from 1930s and '40s, prior to relocation, that they had up North. So all that lost, and all the shows that was done since '82. They had it all in categories, so it was easier to find if you wanted to do a show, say, on spring fishing. There would be all this—just one row would be copied from other footage. Maybe all the copies on each tape was just fishing stuff. Another row would be just hunting stuff. And, say, maybe one was just church stuff or holidays, that sort of stuff.

....

2. Avid is a digital non-linear editing system for audio-visual media.

3. A family of Moravian missionaries that worked in northern Labrador for much of the twentieth century.

MDT: So you came on just before the fire?

SA: Um-hum.

SA: Did the production process change after the fire?

SA: I found, after the fire, it seemed like we had to work harder, because we had to build up everything we lost. Then—plus the funding cuts and whatever—our travel was a lot less, to be able to go to out and film in the different communities. So if we planned to shoot now, we have to plan at least three stories in each community to make it worth the while because it's so expensive.

MDT: So before the fire and the funding cuts, you were able to approach each episode as a stand-alone item?

SA: Yeah. It seemed there was more. You had more outdoor shows because people would be going up North, because people would still be fishing. You'd have more footage of any of the festivals that was going on in the different communities. But now, if there's a festival going on in one community, is there going to be enough stuff shot to make two shows? Or is there something else that we could film, so we can have another separate show? Usually you have to send two people, so you can get the two different camera angles, and maybe one is more fluent in the Inuktitut language if you're speaking to a unilingual person.

MDT: Did you also find that your approach changed with the switch to digital platforms?

SA: It seems you could film more, because you could edit more. Whatever you put into the Avid you could use for another show without having to re-digitize or re-import, because you could just take it from another bin. It made it a lot easier in some ways. But then, with the amount of people, you think it would be faster now because we got two Avids. And we got a third stand-alone, which needs to be set up proper again because they didn't do it right the first time. But when one person finishes a show, another person is waiting in line. It seems to, like, slow down the process because there's too much being filmed and too many people are waiting in line for the Avids. Where we all have children. Well, I'm all right now because I don't have any children under a certain age. But with the other two producers, you cannot give them hours like 4:00 to 12:00, or whatever, because they have to be home tending to their kids that are school age. So, it's basically 9:00 to 5:00. I suppose it's different.

I tried to explain to our boss: when it comes to special holidays, it's not like in the city where you got a schedule you can follow. Here it's more relaxed but—you get your work done—but it's not like in the city, where you can put your older kids in daycare or whatever. You can't find childcare here. If there's a church holiday you can't miss it, so that your kids don't lose the traditions. I don't know—it's harder, I guess, in a way.

MDT: How do those issues affect your approach to your work?

SA: I think we look at it more when we do a show. I guess it makes it easier for us to explain, in our shows, to the outside world what our culture is like. Because, where we live it. Instead of, say, Goose Bay—even though Goose Bay is just down the coast. I wouldn't feel comfortable doing a show on something like figure skating because we don't do nothing like that. We don't. Our kids aren't into that kind of thing. Now, if there's a hockey tournament or something, that's something that we could film because our kids are very into that sort of stuff. We try and show it—I guess, the pride of our way of life—and try to do it in our shows and explain it to the outsider. Someone who may not know about Advent, or the different church holidays, or even, like, say fishing. Because to most people outside, it's like a catch-and-release thing. Whereas here, it's something you got to do to eat. I guess, like—I don't know, it's just different.

MDT: Can you describe the process of making a television episode?

SA: Right now, I got three shows on the Avid. It's on the *Piulitsinik* exercise that was held up in the park.[4] That was a joint project between JRCC—the

....
4. Exercise Piulitsinik was a 2015 search and rescue exercise conducted by Joint Task Force Atlantic in the Torngat Mountains National Park.

Search & Rescue Centre out of Halifax—Gander, and the Parks Canada staff at Torngat Mountains National Park. We were invited to go up and film and try to do a show on this exercise, that will show what the Parks Canada staff needs to do, to be able to conduct a good search and rescue, say, if something needed to happen. What the steps are when they have to call Search & Rescue Halifax, and what kind of information they got to get, and who else they got to call, like Grenfell Health for medevac services.

What we do is, we'll get a little pamphlet or something—like this size, I guess—just explaining the project and what they're going to be doing. So we'll go up there and film everything we can. Then we come back and we'll do some interviews, when we figure out what we're filming and who to film and what the project is all about, that sort of stuff. We try and get enough interviews so that it could last more than one show, to explain without having to do so many narrations, I guess. Then we'll come back here, we'll log your tapes or disks or whatever we're using. Then we transcribe everything so that it's on paper, it's in the computer. Then we start doing a script. That's the way I do it, the girls do it differently. Then I will start editing it and then when it fits and it's cut down to the size I want, it looks like it's the way I want it, then I'll hand the script over to a translator. Then they translate it.

While they're translating, then I do the subtitles—because all our shows, where it's in a different language it's got to be subtitled in English, especially for the hard of hearing. Then it comes back. Then you put the voice-overs in and you try and make it match the titles. You may have to cut it down a lot. Then you put in your cutaways to match your titles, so that it's in a different language but your pictures are matching the English. Then you export it to DVD, two copies. Then you transfer it out to Beta for APTN. Then you wipe your media off your Avid, so that you got more space for the next person to get on. So, normally, from start to finish for editing, it usually should take three weeks, from start to finish. But then you have problems. "Okay, we can't find a translator right away"—or we can't find the people to do with the voice-overs or you still need to do another interview just to fill in the gaps.

MDT: How do you select topics for each episode?

SA: Usually we'll call each of the communities to see what kind of activities they have on the go in the next month or two. Then we'll look at, if there's more than one thing on the go during the same week. We got to look at that, too—we can't afford to go back to film something else because we don't have much funding. Then we'll write it down and we'll say, "Okay, last year we did this many shows out of Nain, this many shows out of Hopedale. We need to try and get some stores from this place and this place, so that it's not just two main communities." Then we'll look at—"Okay, is this something what the youth are into, and what they're interested in?" Because our shows are geared towards the youth—aged 13 to 30, I guess.

MDT: Do you plan out the full season?

SA: We write down on the blackboard how many shows we need, and what's being worked on, and what have we filmed, and how many more do we need? Right now, I think we're ahead again for next year's shows. If we could, we'd like to do more stories outdoors, like say off the land, or stuff we know kids are interested in. If we find out that the Elders are taking youth out and we can film them, we'll go.

MDT: So you work on a model in which you are always producing, and as long as you reach your 13-episode cap [you're good]? You don't need to come up with season-long arcs?

SA: Nope.

MDT: Can you talk about the differences in producing *Tamânevugut* and *Labradorimiut*?

SA: *Labradorimiut* was just any style, it was just documentary, magazine, lifestyle, whatever. But now, we're geared towards the youth. I guess it's "youth" and "lifestyle." It's almost like *Labradorimiut*, I think. But to me, it's just like a different name put on it, just to have a show on.

MDT: Do you find it's changed your work, targeting youth?

SA: It's harder. Because, at least with a general audience, you could go and film everything—anything and everything. And be able to do more magazine-style shows, that fits every age group. But now it's hard because, on the coast, Nain got the biggest population, most youth. And it's also got the most activities and programs for youth. Whereas the other communities, they're not as active towards the teenagers, other than volleyball and maybe ball hockey at the gym, sort of thing. Whereas here, the Recreation department will have a lot of stuff on the go for youth. So—and, say, with the DHSD[5] or Going Off, Growing Strong groups, there's more programming for youth. So I find it a lot easier to film here than anywhere else.

MDT: It also seems like there was a broader selection of things that you would cover in *Labradorimiut*.

SA: Like church holidays and stuff like that. We can't cover stuff like that because our shows have to be repeated throughout the year. Christmas shows—we can't do that because it will only be aired at Christmas. So that's not something they would air in June. So if we can only get one airtime or playtime, then it wouldn't be any good.

MDT: Do you have many opportunities to produce for contexts other than APTN?

SA: We might do special projects—what we call them—for, like, Nunatsiavut. What we do is: we film their Assembly sitting and we edit them for their purposes, for their copies. Say if the Torngâsok[6] got videos they want to put voice-overs on. We did the voice-overs for the National Film Board for *Eye of the Storm*, *Till We Meet Again*, *Unitas Fratrum*, there was another—

....

5. Nunatsiavut Government's Department of Health and Social Development.

6. A former branch of the Labrador Inuit Association and Nunatsiavut Government, which performed similar functions to the Nunatsiavut Government's Department of Language, Culture and Tourism.

MDT: *Labrador North.*

SA: Yes, *Labrador North*, that kind of stuff. We've done stuff for Torngâsok, about the seal hunt and how important it is. How the outsiders view it as killing seals and wasting and whatever, whereas we put it out there that everything is used from the seals—the skin, the meat, even the bones for the carvings or whatever. That sort of stuff. Depends on if someone needs a special project done and if we're not too busy.

MDT: Do you approach your work on those special projects differently?

SA: Yep. I find it a lot easier because it's not only something that the youth would be interested in, but it's also like something an older person that may not even get to go off anymore. It'll show them, I guess. It reminds them of what your life is like and how good they got it. That sort of stuff. If that makes sense.

MDT: How do you keep up with your own training?

SA: Google.

MDT: Are you entirely self-taught now? Or do you have people come in for training anymore?

SA: Yeah. We've had a trainer here last winter. That was the first one since—that was the first one that came here since I don't know when, if there was a trainer. I think we had a script-writing trainer, or audio trainer, but it was more for radio. The script-writing trainer was back in the old building before the fire.

I went to St. John's along with Martin Obed and Fran [Williams] for editing *Saputjinik* with Memorial University. That was our first time on an Avid. Then I went to St. John's and I guess I learned how to do typos, subtitles, and that, on an Avid. Because I put the titles on for *Forever in Our Hearts* with NIFCO,[7] but there was no real training. I think it was, maybe, seven years ago we went to St. John's for

....
7. Newfoundland Independent Filmmakers Co-operative

a week-long editing tutorial. It was myself, Olivia, Patrick, and who was the other one? Shirley—no, not Shirley. There was four of us. But it was—when we go for training like that—it's like, where we're all at different levels, one person might have nothing to do because they're already at that level and wanting to learn something else. Then by the time they get to do some training, your time is more or less up. So the stuff I want to learn how to do is learn more camera work. Because you weren't really taught much in that, as well—especially with the new cameras. And the girls would like to learn more tricks for the Avid. Mine was like, you more or less learn it on your own. Or the times I went to St. John's, I learned a few little tricks. And going to school in Stephenville, you're taught a different way of editing. Like for—it's more towards—artsy, what I calls "artsy-fartsy" stuff. Not documentary-style, really. So I don't know, it's different.

MDT: One thing I notice in the OKâlaKatiget Society's work is shot lengths. That's pronounced in something like *A Traditional Seal Hunt in Nunatsiavut*. There are some very long shots there that you would never see in other contexts.

SA: And I find when you got to do that, to [do] it, because when you got to put the Inuktitut in you want your shots to match the Inuktitut. You don't want it to— especially with the title: if it's an English title, there, then you don't want your shot to end while the title is still there. Otherwise, you're trying to focus—"Okay, am I reading the title, or am I looking at two different shots and getting all jumbled?" and that sort of thing. I liked it before, when it was *Labradorimiut* and you didn't need subtitles. Because you kept it in your language. And we used it as a tool to try and get our kids to retain the language. But how are they going to do that if they're reading the titles on the screen?

MDT: That's APTN policy?

SA: For the hard of hearing.

MDT: That's interesting, the relationship between subtitles and shot length. Do subtitles have any other kind of stylistic influence like that?

SA: Not really. I don't know, it all depends. Sometimes you got to change, you got to cheat and change your titles so that—because sometimes the person who is doing the translation, they translate it wrong. So you kind of got to cheat sometimes, and that could make your shot longer. Sometimes we feel: this shot is important to explain something, we don't need a narration or something. Just a shot alone can explain what needs to be done, I guess. I find that with these new shows, you got more dialogue than you did with *Labradorimiut*. You have more audio, like music in the background. And just—seniors' shots, or stuff like that. You don't even see stuff like that much anymore. There's more dialogue, more narrations.

MDT: Do you still continue to work in a mentorship system now? Or is it different with the piecemeal training and the digital systems?

SA: No, it's still the same. It's just: "Okay, whoever comes in first." But, say if I'm busy, then Simone will train the new person in what she can. Then, say, the editing part: I'll show her little shortcuts or whatever. What I usually get them to do is watch a few of the old shows first, just to get an idea of a storyline and how everything flows. Then they're taught how to digitize, and how to do sequence, and how long it's got to be. Then, when they're done their rough cut, I usually go through it. And if I got to, I'll move stuff around. You show them: "Okay, you could have done this, so that this flows with this part," and that. Then, even if I do that, then Morris will watch the end piece and then he could say, "Move this here, move that there." Which could slow us down a lot. And it do.

MDT: Do you still see yourself as a storyteller?

SA: It's changed. It's harder, I find, because before we could go and get the information from anyone and everyone. But now, where it's geared toward youth and you don't have many. Because before, we used to get a lot from seniors, traditional stuff. But now, the youth don't interact with the seniors as much, and the Elders. So they're more in the electronic age, I guess, and there's that big gap. There's a few that still go—not that many—but will go off hunting and fishing to help their families or seniors or Elders. But the majority of them, they'll just get on the ski-doo just to go for a ride.

With the Elders, they give out the information freely. There's no restriction. Whereas the youth now, they're one-word answers or they're not interested in it as much, like the older ones, or even the younger ones. I find the really young ones are really interested in the land and learning stuff or whatever, but the teenagers—they're just more to the technology and electronics. They're not—I guess they're more, too modern, I guess. And then trying to find shows that would interest them or whatever—it's harder to do, I find.

MDT: Do you find that composing images for an Elder's words is a different process?

SA: I find doing a show on an Elder, you could actually use old footage and you could use old photos. But then, with the Elders, with just their expressions or whatever, you didn't really need much. But with youth, you got to use all these graphics and a lot of pictures, or whatever, just to pique their interest, I guess, and keep their interest. It's different. It's harder, and it's harder to find stories geared around youth, for youth. Then we'll get a lot of complaints, like, "It's always Nain or Hopedale." But when we call the communities, they say they don't have anything on the go. So, you can't win.

I just wish there was more opportunities for us to get training. We hear of training opportunities, but it's always funding or we're too busy with other programming or there's only three of us on staff when there usually is four. But then, a lot of times, we can have a lot of down days and just trying to find stuff to do. But then there are other days, or even weeks, that we're just bogged down and busy, busy, busy, and we can't get anything done because one thing is just piling on top of the other. That's what it feels like. If we had opportunities to go for the training—but when you got small children that you can't leave for long periods of time, I guess, it's hard. Maybe we'll go for a week at a time. But then, when you go for a week at a time, you're not learning as much as you should, or you can. Then when you get a trainer here, we got to look at the factor of weather. Because when we had the trainer here before, it was flu season and pneumonia season. So, there were some people not able to make it to training, or their kids were sick and I'm trying to explain to him—because he'd be like:

"Where are you going? It's only, like, 12 o'clock."

I was like, "Yeah, it's lunch time, we got kids to pick up and bring home to feed and bring back."

"Don't you have a babysitter?"

"Our kids are this age—they don't need a babysitter."

But trying to explain to people that come from outside—like, say, it's Easter Week. Well, it was Easter Week and try to explain to him that: "Okay—like for Joanna, it's really hard for her because she's in the choir and she's one of the main radio producers and then she's running back and forth between the church and here." Trying to explain to him, "Okay, this is how we grew up. That church was always a big part." And I don't know—it's just harder.

MDT: Do you find that balance—between work and home life—difficult to maintain?

SA: It's good now, but I found it hard when my son was younger. Being a single parent and then having to travel and finding caregivers and whatever. Then being away from home a lot or even just, even in town, but being away from the house a lot because of work. It caused problems, I guess. Especially in their pre-teens and teenage years, it's hard when you don't have enough time for them or attention. So it's not a job I would recommend to someone that's got a family, or just starting out, or anyone that got small kids, I guess. Because it does take a lot of time away from them. Especially if there's things you got to go outside to film, or even things you got to film at night. Or if there's deadlines, you got to work late, it's hard. You almost need a nine-to-five job. It's still 9:00 to 5:00, but you got to be prepared to do a lot of overtime, which we haven't done lately, thank God.

3. Moments in Inuit Cinema

As contributor Blandina Makkik once pointed out to me, the idea of "key dates" in Inuit cinema does not exactly square with Inuit approaches to history. It is better, she suggests, to consider that "history" as a series of moments whose significance extends beyond any date. This is a useful approach because it allows us to reclaim moments that have been lost in some narratives about Inuit cinema and expand the timeline of others.

In the series of moments that follow, I provide the contemporary name for the territory or region to which subjects are connected. For individuals from Inuit Nunangat, the contemporary Inuit language names of their region and community are given, rather than the historical southern names. For example, Esther Eneutseak's birthplace is given as Nunatsiavut (established in 2004) rather than the Dominion of Newfoundland, and Kenojuak Ashevak's birthplace is listed as Nunavut (established 1999) rather than Northwest Territories.

1901–2. Labrador Inuit in the company of Esther Eneutseak (Nunatsiavut, 1877–1961) are featured in five films shot at the Pan-American Exposition in Buffalo, New York. Three of these films—*Esquimaux Leap-Frog, Esquimaux Village,* and *Esquimaux Game of Snap-the-Whip*—were made by the American film pioneer Edwin S. Porter for the Edison Manufacturing Company. All are available through the Library of Congress. Other films produced during the 1901 Exposition, such as *Esquimaux Dance* and *An Esquimaux Game* (American Mutoscope & Biograph Company) and *The Esquimaux Village* and *Panorama of the Esquimaux Village* (S. Lubin) do not survive.

1911. *Lost in the Arctic* and *The Way of the Eskimo* are released in the United States. Both were directed by William V. Mong (USA) for the Selig Polyscope Company and filmed in Escabana, Michigan. The scenario for *The Way of the Eskimo* was written by Esther Eneutseak's daughter, Nancy Columbia (born Chicago, 1893–1959). Both films starred Simon Aputik (Nunatsiavut, ca. 1861–?) and Zacharias Zad (Nunatsiavut, 1884–1918), who often performed with Eneutseak.

1912. *The Alaska-Siberia Expedition*, also known as *The Carnegie Museum Alaska-Siberian Expedition* (Alaskan-Siberian Motion Pictures), is released in the United States. This is the earliest confirmed ethnographic film made in Inuit Nunaat and may also be the earliest made in either Alaska or Chukotka.

1914. *Grønland 1914 I-III* directed by William Thalbitzer (Denmark, 1873–1958) is released in Denmark. This is the earliest confirmed ethnographic film shot in Kalaallit Nunaat.

1918. The romantic comedy *Das Eskimobaby* is released in Germany. Directed by Heinz Schall (Germany, 1885–1933), the film stars Astra Neilsen (Denmark, 1881–1972) as Ivigtut, an Inuk from Kalaallit Nunaat. The story centres on Ivigtut's courtship of a European polar explorer named Knud Prätorius. This is likely the earliest feature film in which an Inuk is played by a non-Inuk.

1919. *Hudson's Bay Company Centenary Celebrations* is released in Canada and Europe and follows the seasonal east-west route of the Hudson's Bay Company (HBC) ship *Nascopie* through Inuit Nunangat. This was the first of five films depicting HBC operations in Inuit Nunangat to Canadian and European audiences.

Both *Heritage of Adventure* and *Romance of the Far Fur Country* were released in 1920. *Trading into Hudson's Bay* was released in 1930.

1920–22. Robert J. Flaherty (USA, 1884–1951) travels to Nunavik to shoot *Nanook of the North* with Allakariallak (who played Nanook, ?–ca. 1923) and other Nunavimmiut. *Nanook* was released in the United States in 1922. Flaherty was credited as the director, cinematographer, editor, and producer.

1921–27. Knud Rasmussen (Kalaallit Nunaat, 1879–1933) undertakes the Fifth Thule Expedition between 1921 and 1924. Cinematographer Leo Hansen (Denmark, 1888–1962) joined the expedition in 1923 and documented the remainder of the expedition. His footage was compiled under the title *Med Hundeslæde gennem Alaska* (*By Dog Sled Through Alaska*) and released in Denmark in 1927.

1922–52. Ray Mala (born Ray Wise, Alaska, 1906–52) meets Frank E. Kleinschmidt (Germany, 1871–1949), who hires Mala to carry a camera on a scientific expedition to Umqiḷir (Wrangel Island). Joining this trip began a career that put Mala on both sides of the camera. He worked as a camera operator for Knud Rasmussen and on several Hollywood productions, and as a writer and actor.[1] His most recognized role is as Mala in the 1933 film *Eskimo* (see below).

1925–1940s. Commander Donald Baxter MacMillan (USA, 1874–1970) films several expeditions to eastern Inuit Nunangat and Kalaallit Nunaat. In late 1927 or early 1928, he exhibited these films of Inuit in Nain, Nunatsiavut— one of the earliest recorded film exhibitions intended for Inuit.

1931–34. Knud Rasmussen prepares to make the dramatic feature *Palos Brudefærd* (*The Wedding of Palo*) during the Sixth Thule Expedition. The film was shot in east Kalaallit Nunaat, principally around Ammassalik, and Rasmussen is credited with writing it. It was directed Friedrich Dalsheim (Germany, 1895–1936) and released in Denmark in 1934. It is presented in the Tunumiit oraasiat dialect with intertitles.

....
1. Fienup-Riordan, *Freeze Frame*, 64–65.

1932–33. Production for the film *Eskimo* occurs in Tala, Alaska. Directed by W.S. Van Dyke (USA, 1889–1943) and released by Metro-Goldwyn-Mayer in 1933, this is one of the earliest Hollywood films shot within Inuit Nunaat. The film is an adaptation of two books by Peter Freuchen (Denmark, 1886–1957), *Der Eskimo* (1928) and *Die Flucht ins weiße* (1929). An early sound film, *Eskimo* is presented in both English and Inupiaq with English intertitles.

1943. The National Film Board of Canada (NFB) releases *Eskimo Arts and Crafts*, directed by Laura Boulton (USA, 1899–1980). This is the earliest known NFB production from Inuit Nunangat and is part of a trio of films by Boulton that are known as the Baffin Island (Qikiqtaaluk) films. *Arctic Hunters* and *Eskimo Summer* were released in 1944. All three were prepared in English and French versions. Robert Flaherty was credited as a consultant for the series. *Eskimo Arts and Crafts* is also significant because it is likely the first of an ongoing tradition of media to focus on Inuit arts and crafts.

1949–55. The NFB releases four films directed by Douglas Wilkinson (Canada, 1919–2008): *How to Build an Igloo* (1949), *Arctic Saga* (1952), *Land of the Long Day* (1952), and *Angotee – Story of an Eskimo Boy* (1953). All four films were prepared in English and French versions with dialogue presented in voice-over. In *Angotee*, characters are filmed speaking Inuktut, which is never heard. Three films (excluding *Arctic Saga*) were widely distributed across southern Canada. In 1955, Wilkinson published a book, *Land of the Long Day*, about his time and work in Inuit Nunangat.

1950s–2011. James Robert Andersen (Makkovik, Nunatsiavut, 1919–2011) begins shooting home movies some time during the 1950s and continues until his death. Until a 2009 exhibition of his still- and moving-image work at The Rooms Provincial Art Gallery in St. John's, Newfoundland and Labrador, Andersen's films were mainly screened in Makkovik for visiting and local audiences.

1950–97. Jørgen Roos (Denmark, 1922–98) is involved in 20 or so (the exact number is unknown) films about Kalaallit Nunaat, in roles ranging from direction, script, and cinematography to editing and sound. According to Gunnar Iversen's entry on Roos in *Encyclopedia of the Documentary Film*, many of Roos's

Kalaallit Nunaat films have been shown extensively in Denmark and he "has heavily influenced several generations of Danes and contributed to their image of [Kalaallit Nunaat]."[2]

1953–54. Walt Disney releases *The Alaskan Eskimo* in the United States in 1953. It is the first film in a series called *People and Places*. Directed by James Algar (USA, 1912–98), the film won an Oscar for Documentary Short Subject at the 26th Academy Awards in 1954.

1958–63. The NFB releases three films directed by John Feeney (New Zealand, 1922–2006). *The Living Stone* (1958), *Pangnirtung* (1959), and *Eskimo Artist – Kenojuak* (1963). *Pangnirtung* is a profile of the community of the same name, but both *The Living Stone* and *Eskimo Artist – Kenojuak* belong to the Inuit arts and crafts media tradition and helped to establish their international prominence. *The Living Stone* profiles the work of carvers in Kinngait, Nunavut, while *Eskimo Artist – Kenojuak* profiles the life and work of the iconic Inuit artist Kenojuak Ashevak (Nunavut, 1927–2013). Both films were nominated for the Academy Award for Documentary Short Subject.

1963–67. Between 1963 and 1965, anthropologists Asen Balikci (Turkey, 1929–2019), Guy Mary-Rousselière (France, 1913–94), producer-director Quentin Brown (Canada, dates unknown) and Robert Young (Canada, 1924–) visit the Kitikmeot Region of Nunavut to film the *Netsilik Eskimo* series. The series was produced by the American Education Development Center and released in the United States and Canada in 1967. Many of the films were incorporated into *Man: A Course of Study*, which was taught in American public schools during the 1970s. The curriculum also included Flaherty's *Nanook of the North*.

1972–75. The NFB holds workshops in Kinngait in film animation from 1972 to 1974 and Iqaluit in Super 8 live-action from 1974 through 1975. Professor Lorna Roth has suggested that the live-action production unit "transformed into a drama production unit called *Nunatsiakmiut*, which would be later integrated into the Inuit Broadcasting Corporation in 1981."[3]

....

2. Iversen, *Encyclopedia of the Documentary Film*, 1145.

3. Roth, *Something New in the Air*, 105.

1972–77. Representatives from Memorial University of Newfoundland's Extension Service provide means for local production and exhibition with video tape recorders in Nain, Hopedale, and Makkovik (Nunatsiavut). Surviving productions, such as *Labrador Resources Advisory Council* (1976) and *Labrador Land Use Conference* (1977), are pan-Labrador in focus and represent the perspectives of Innu (a distinct Indigenous People). These experiments in regional organization/documentation laid the groundwork for the OKâlaKatiget Society, a Nain-based Inuttitut/Inuttut publisher and radio and television broadcaster.

1972–1988. Sarah Elder (USA, 1939–) and Leonard Kamerling (USA, dates unknown) create several films as part of the Alaska Native Heritage Film Project, distributed by Documentary Educational Resources. As Elder has written, "We wanted to participate in a new kind of filmmaking where we did not determine the representation of minority people, but at the same time, we did not want to relinquish our aesthetic and technical control or our ethnographic concerns. We believed it was possible to have shared authorship, and—even more idealistically— that the villages we worked with would determine their own representation. We called our method 'Community Determined Filmmaking'."[4]

1973. CBC North, the Canadian Broadcasting Corporation's service in northern Canada, begins broadcasting television.

1975–77. The NFB releases three films directed by Mosha Michael (Nunavut, 1948–2009), "one of Canada's first Inuit filmmakers."[5] The NFB also suggests that one of these films, *Natsik Hunting (*1975), is "the first Inuit-directed film produced at the NFB."[6] It was followed by *Asivaqtiin* (*The Hunters*, 1977) and *Qilaluganiatut* (*Whale Hunting*, 1977). Michael was also involved in the cinematography for a 1977 independent film directed by Edward Folger (USA, ?– 2013) called *Nanook Taxi*.

....

4. Elder, "Collaborative Filmmaking," 97–98.
5. "Mosha Michael," National Film Board of Canada.
6. Ibid.

1978–81. The Anik B communications satellite is launched in 1978 by the Government of Canada's Department of Communications, which also allocates $1 million as part of an experimental program for *Project Inukshuk*. *Project Inukshuk* was undertaken by Inuit Tapirisat of Canada (now Inuit Tapiriit Kanatami), to link the communities of Iqaluit, Mittimatalik, Igloolik, Qamani'tuaq, Arviat, and Iqaluktuuttiaq using video communications via the Anik B satellite. In 1981, the Canadian Radio-Television and Telecommunications Commission licensed the incorporated Inuit Broadcasting Corporation to produce and broadcast Inuit language programming.[7]

1982. Kalaallit Nunaata Radioa (Greenlandic Broadcasting Corporation) begins television broadcasting.

1983–2011. The OKâlaKatiget Society begins producing television content in 1983 under the title *Labradorimiut* in Inuttitut/Inuttut. The productions are first broadcast during IBC's *Qaggiq* program, then on Television Northern Canada, and finally on the Aboriginal Peoples Television Network.

1988. The Government of Canada's Department of Communications provides $10 million to establish a new television channel, Television Northern Canada. TVNC's members included the Inuit Broadcasting Corporation, the Inuvialuit Communications Society (Nunavut), Northern Native Broadcasting (Yukon), the OKâlaKatiget Society (Nunatsiavut), Taqramiut Nipingat Incorporated (Nunavik), the Native Communications Society of the Western Northwest Territories, the Government of the Northwest Territories, Yukon College, and the National Aboriginal Communications Society.[8] In 1999, the network re-organized as the Aboriginal Peoples Television Network. At this writing, its operations are continuing.

1989. The American Library of Congress selects *Nanook of the North* as one of the first 25 films to be preserved by the National Film Registry.

....

7. Lorna Roth provides a detailed account of the establishment of the Inuit Broadcasting Corporation (IBC) in *Something New in the Air*, 122–71.

8. See, again, *Something New in the Air*.

1990 (ongoing). Zacharias Kunuk (Nunavut, 1957–), Paul Apak Angilirq (Nunavut, 1954–98), Pauloosie Qulitalik (Nunavut, 1939–2012), and Norman Cohn (USA, 1946–) establish Igloolik Isuma Productions in Igloolik, Nunavut, in 1990. It remains one of the most iconic and prolific Inuit-led media production companies.

1991. *Inuit Art Quarterly* publishes its first feature-length article on an aspect of Inuit cinema: "Zacharias Kunuk: Video Maker and Inuit Historian."

1991 (ongoing). Marie-Hélène Cousineau (Quebec, 1960–), Madeline Ivalu (Nunavut, dates unknown), Susan Avingaq (Nunavut, dates unknown), Carol Kunnuk (Nunavut, dates unknown), and Atuat Akkitirq (Nunavut, 1959–) establish Arnait Video Productions in Igloolik, Nunavut. Their goal is "to value the unique culture and voices of Inuit women and to open discussions with Canadians of all origins."[9]

1995 (ongoing). Nunavut Independent Television Network (NITV) is established in Igloolik, Nunavut. Between 1995 and 2007, NITV broadcast *Nunatinni* (*At Our Place*), a live local news and cultural affairs television show in Igloolik via community cable access. NITV was also a founding partner in the Digital Indigenous Democracy (DID) Project, launched in 2012. According to Norman Cohn and Zacharias Kunuk, the DID "uses local radio, television, multimedia, and social networking tools to insure meaningful community participation in oral Inuktitut in public hearings and in environmental impact and benefits decisions affecting Inuit for generations to come."[10]

1998–2008. In 1998, Igloolik Isuma begins development of *Atanarjuat – The Fast Runner*, directed by Zacharias Kunuk. Released in 2001, the film was a commercial and critical success and received the Caméra d'Or award at the 54th Cannes Film Festival in 2001. It is the first narrative feature film written, directed, and acted entirely in an Inuit language. The first film of the *Fast Runner* trilogy, it was followed by 2006's *The Journals of Knud Rasmussen*, directed by Zacharias Kunuk and Norman Cohn (Igloolik Isuma), and 2008's *Before Tomorrow*, directed by Marie-Hélène Cousineau and Madeline Ivalu (co-produced by Igloolik Isuma and Arnait Video Productions).

....

9. "Arnait Video Productions," accessed July 2, 2021.
10. Cohn and Kunuk, "Our Baffinland," 50.

1999 (ongoing). The Nunavut Film Development Corporation is established by the Government of Nunavut. Its core functions include:

- Deliver the Film, Television and Digital Media Development Fund . . . .
- Promote the growth of Nunavut's current and emerging film, television, and digital media Industry sectors through liaison and public relations activities with Industry associations, the private sector, and key stakeholders.
- Develop strategic plans and priorities to support labour force development and skills training by the film, television, and digital media Industry.
- Collect statistical information for annual reporting of program funding outcomes, including the development of an Industry tracking framework and social impacts/benefits tracking framework, to document and evaluate the development of the film, television, and digital media Industry.
- Operate the Nunavut Film Commission [established in 2003].[11]

2006. *Uksuum Cauyai – Drums of Winter*, **part of the Alaska Native Heritage Film Project, is selected for preservation by the American National Film Registry.** This is the second film about Inuit to be selected for such preservation.

2006–10. The Inuit Broadcasting Corporation and NFB partner in 2006 to deliver the Nunavut Animation Lab. During the first phase of the project, NFB staff held a training workshop for 15 participants from each of Iqaluit, Kinngait, and Pangnirtung. At the end of the workshop, proposals from four participants were selected for further development at the National Screen Institute in Winnipeg, Manitoba, and production at the Banff New Media Institute in Alberta. The four films were released in 2010: *Lumaajuuq* by Alethea Arnaquq-Baril (Nunavut), *Qalupalik* by Ame Papatsie (Nunavut), *The Bear Facts* by Jonathan Wright (Ontario), and *I Am But a Little Woman* by Gyu Oh (unknown).

2008. IsumaTV is launched. Isuma is a collaborative, web-based, multimedia platform for Inuit and Indigenous media-makers and media organizations. The founding program partners included Igloolik Isuma Productions, the Nunavut Independent Television Network (NITV), Arnait Video Productions, Artcirq,

....

11. "Film, Television and Digital Media Development Contribution Policy," 5.

imagineNATIVE Film+Media Arts Festival, Vtape, the Native Communications Society of the NWT, and others.

2008–9. Production begins on *Nuummioq*, directed by Otto Rosing (Kalaallit Nunaat, 1967–) and Torben Bech (Kalaallit Nunaat, dates unknown), in 2008. Released in 2009, the film is Kalaallit Nunaat's first international feature film production.

2012–?. The first Greenland Eyes Film Festival is held in Berlin, Germany, in 2012. It is billed as the largest film festival to focus on Kalaallit Nunaat.[12] In 2014, it toured all of the Nordic countries. In 2015, it travelled to Washington, DC, at the invitation of the Smithsonian Institution. The festival appears to have become dormant in 2015.

2012. FILM.GL is established. It was created in Kalaallit Nunaat to "professionalize the local film industry, create better financing conditions for Greenlandic filmmakers, and raise international awareness on Greenland as a film producing nation."[13]

2012. Tanya Tagaq (Nunavut, 1975–) gives the first performance-response to *Nanook of the North* in 2012, at the Toronto International Film Festival. The event was part of the festival's *First Peoples Cinema: 1500 Nations, One Tradition* retrospective. She went on to give other versions of the performance-response in North America and Europe.

2012. The Inuit Broadcasting Corporation launches its Sanavallianiq Isumagijaujunut – Building for Dreams campaign in 2012 with a goal to build the Nunavut Media Arts Centre in Iqaluit. Opened in 2015, the centre houses both production studios and an Inuit Film and Video Archive.

2015 (ongoing). Ánorâk Films launches Inuiaat Issat (Eyes of the People) with supports from the Government of Kalaallit Nunaat and Sermeq Fonden. Inuiaat Issat is an open-access, online film archive of private Super 8 films from Kalaallit Nunaat made in the 1950s, '60s, and '70s. The footage was collected and digitized during the production of the film *SUMÉ – Mumisitsinerup Nipaa.*

....

12. "About," accessed July 5, 2021.

13. "Home to the Vibrant Film Community in Greenland," accessed July 5, 2021.

2015–17. *of the North* by Dominic Gagnon (Quebec, 1974–) is released in 2015, a catalyst for months of debate. Gagnon drew from over 500 hours of amateur film purportedly made by Inuit and posted to streaming services such as YouTube. Billed as an experimental documentary, its graphic depictions drew swift condemnation from Inuit in Canada and sparked a broad public debate about media ethics that lasted for nearly two years, much of which was covered in the popular press and academic journals. Prominent Inuit voices in that discussion belonged to Alethea Arnaquq-Baril (Nunavut) and Stephen Agluvak Puskas (Northwest Territories).

2017 (ongoing). The Nuuk International Film Festival is established in Nuuk, Kalaallit Nunaat. In 2020, the festival began accepting submissions from anywhere in the world.

2018 (ongoing). The Arctic Indigenous Film Fund is established. Made possible by a partnership that includes the Canada Media Fund, the International Sami Film Institute, the Nunavut Film Development Corporation, FILM.GL, Archy, and the Sundance Film Institute, it exists to:
  - Support development of high-quality Indigenous film/TV productions
  - Support production of high-quality Indigenous film/TV productions
  - Encourage and create new platforms for Arctic co-productions
  - Help produce culturally relevant film
  - Build a network between film institutions, companies, producers, and universities, thereby strengthening business and competitive advantages
  - Organize film and TV education for young Indigenous talents
  - Lead common projects and programs with partners[14]

2019. Isuma represents Canada at the Venice Biennale.

2019. The first issue of *Inuit Art Quarterly* entirely devoted to film is published.

2021. NITV and IsumaTV launch Uvagut TV on January 18, 2021. It is the first television station in Canada devoted exclusively to Inuit languages.

....
14. "Arctic Indigenous Film Fund Announced."

4. Filmography

The following filmography presents a representative selection of 500 film and television productions *about* and *by* Inuit. It is organized according to the year of release. For each item, I have indicated the original title, the media type (film or television), the genre (documentary, narrative, or experimental), the country or countries of production, the director, and the production company, as far as my research could determine. In cases where I could not determine specific credits or none were given in the film itself, the credits are excluded entirely. In more than one entry, neither the director nor production company are listed.

As much as possible, I have consulted original sources (i.e., the films themselves) to compile the information in this Filmography. When the original films were not accessible, I consulted databases, such as those maintained by the National Film Board of Canada, Det Danske Filminstitut, IsumaTV, and secondary textual resources. For all entries I have attempted to keep the information as close to the original source as possible.

The Filmography is presented as a visual essay. All images are frame enlargements from selected films. My belief is that this presentation will give the data meaningful context *and* give some sense of how the look of these films changes over time.

1901 *An Esquimaux Game*
FILM | DOCUMENTARY | USA
American Mutoscope & Biograph Company

Esquimaux Dance
FILM | DOCUMENTARY | USA
American Mutoscope & Biograph Company

Esquimaux Game of Snap-the-Whip
FILM | DOCUMENTARY | USA
Edwin S. Porter, director
Edison Manufacturing Company

Esquimaux Leap-Frog
FILM | DOCUMENTARY | USA
Edwin S. Porter, director
Edison Manufacturing Company

Esquimaux Village
FILM | DOCUMENTARY | USA
Edwin S. Porter, director
Edison Manufacturing Company

The Esquimaux Village
FILM | DOCUMENTARY | USA
S. Lubin

1902 *Panorama of the Esquimaux Village*
FILM | DOCUMENTARY | USA
S. Lubin

1908 *Esquimaux of Labrador*
FILM | DOCUMENTARY | USA
Goodfellow Film Manufacturing Company

1911 *Eskimos in Labrador*
FILM | DOCUMENTARY | USA
Edison Manufacturing Company

Esquimaux Game of Snap-the-Whip, 1901

Lost in the Arctic
FILM | NARRATIVE | USA
William V. Mong, director
Selig Polyscope Company

The Way of the Eskimo
FILM | NARRATIVE | USA
William V. Mong, director
Selig Polyscope Company

1912 *The Alaska-Siberia Expedition*
The Carnegie Museum Alaska-Siberian Expedition
FILM | DOCUMENTARY | USA
Alaskan-Siberian Motion Pictures

1912–1918 *Tip Top of the Earth – Arctic Alaskan Eskimo Educational* (series)
FILM | DOCUMENTARY | USA
William Van Valin, director

1914 *Captain F.E. Kleinschmidt's Arctic Hunt*
FILM | DOCUMENTARY | USA
Frank E. Kleinschmidt, director
Arctic Film Company

Grønland 1914 I-III
FILM | DOCUMENTARY | DENMARK
William Thalbitzer, director

Through Eskimo Land
FILM | DOCUMENTARY | USA
Alfred Ward Birdsall, director

1918 *Das Eskimobaby*
FILM | NARRATIVE | GERMANY
Heinz Schall, director

Grønland 1914 I-III, 1914

Filmography | 185

Levende billeder tagne under den 2. Thule Ekspedition til Grønlands Nordkyst 1917-18
The Second Thule Expedition to Greenland's North Coast
FILM | DOCUMENTARY | DENMARK
Thorild Wulff, director

Life in the Frozen North (series)
FILM | DOCUMENTARY | USA
Donald B. MacMillan, director

1919   *Hudson's Bay Company Centenary Celebrations*
FILM | DOCUMENTARY | CANADA
Hudson's Bay Company

1920   *Heritage of Adventure*
FILM | DOCUMENTARY | CANADA
Hudson's Bay Company

Romance of the Far Fur Country
FILM | DOCUMENTARY | CANADA
Harold M. Wyckoff, director
Hudson's Bay Company

1921   *En Rejse til Grønland*
A Journey to Greenland with the Royal Ship
FILM | DOCUMENTARY | DENMARK

Fotorama - Grønlandsekspeditionen
FILM | DOCUMENTARY | DENMARK
Nordisk Films Kompagni

Kongeparrets Grønlandsrejse
FILM | DOCUMENTARY | DENMARK
Industri-Filmen

1922   *Den store Grønlandsfilm*
FILM | DOCUMENTARY | DENMARK
Eduard Schnedler-Sørensen, director
Fotorama, Nordisk Films Kompagni

Heritage of Adventure, 1920

Nanook of the North
FILM | DOCUMENTARY | USA
Robert J. Flaherty, director

The Eskimo
FILM | DOCUMENTARY | USA
Slim Summerville, director
Fox Films

The Frozen North
FILM | NARRATIVE | USA
Buster Keaton, director
First National Pictures

1923 *Adventures in the Far North*
FILM | DOCUMENTARY | USA

1924 *Teddys sidste Rejse*
FILM | DOCUMENTARY | DENMARK
Kai R. Dahl, director

1925 *Justice of the Far North*
FILM | NARRATIVE | USA
Norman Dawn, director
Columbia Pictures

Kivalina of the Ice Lands
FILM | NARRATIVE | USA
Earl Rossman, director
B.C.R. Productions

1926 *Alaskan Adventures*
FILM | DOCUMENTARY | USA
Jack Robertson, director
John Morton Allen Productions

Les Esquimaux
FILM | DOCUMENTARY | FRANCE
Jean-Baptiste Charcot, director

Mission du Pourquoi pas
FILM | DOCUMENTARY | FRANCE
Jean-Baptiste Charcot, director

1927 *Med Hundeslæde gennem Alaska*
By Dog Sled Through Alaska
FILM | DOCUMENTARY | DENMARK
Leo Hansen, director

Primitive Love
FILM | DOCUMENTARY | USA
Frank E. Kleinschmidt, director

1928 *Grønlandske Skolebørn*
Schoolchildren in Greenland
FILM | DOCUMENTARY | DENMARK
Paul Hansen, director

Milak, der Grönlandjäger
Milak, a Greenland Hunter
FILM | DOCUMENTARY | GERMANY
Georg Asagaroff, Bernhard Villinger,
directors
UFA

1929 *Frozen Justice*
FILM | USA
Allan Dwan, director
Fox Films

1929/ *Vom Spreewald zum Urwald*
1930 FILM | DOCUMENTARY | GERMANY
Friedrich Paulmann, director

1930 *Bob Bartlett's Labrador*
FILM | DOCUMENTARY | ENGLAND
British Pathé

Eskimo
FILM | NARRATIVE | NORWAY, DENMARK
George Schnéevoigt, director
U/Spillefilm

Trading into Hudson's Bay
FILM | DOCUMENTARY | CANADA
Hudson's Bay Company

1931 *Deutsche Grönland-Expedition –
Alfred Wegener*
FILM | DOCUMENTARY | GERMANY
Degeto Filmothek

Inuit, die Nachbarn des Nordpols
FILM | DOCUMENTARY

Paa togt til østgrønland
FILM | DOCUMENTARY | DENMARK

Filmography | 187

1932 *Igloo*
FILM | DOCUMENTARY | USA
Ewing Scott, director
Edward Small Productions

1933 *Eskimo*
FILM | NARRATIVE | USA
W.S. Van Dyke, director
Metro-Goldwyn-Mayer

S.O.S. Eisberg
FILM | NARRATIVE | GERMANY
Arnold Franck, director
Deutsche Universal-Film

1934 *Entstehung von Eisbergen an der Küste Grönlands*
FILM | DOCUMENTARY | GERMANY
Ernst Sorge, Walter Riml, directors
RWU Berlin

Governor's Trip to Eastern Canadian Arctic
FILM | DOCUMENTARY | CANADA
Hudson's Bay Company

La Mission Polaire
FILM | DOCUMENTARY | FRANCE
Jean-Baptiste Charcot, director

Nordpol – Ahoi!
FILM | NARRATIVE | GERMANY
Andrew Marton, director
Deutsche Universal-Film

Palos Brudefærd
The Wedding of Palo
FILM | NARRATIVE | DENMARK
Friedrich Dalsheim, director
Palladium

1935 *Gamle flyvebilleder fra Grønland*
FILM | DOCUMENTARY | DENMARK

La quatre du Groënland
FILM | DOCUMENTARY | FRANCE
Jean-Baptiste Charcot, director

1935/ 1936 *Med Leo Hansen paa Østgrønland*
FILM | DOCUMENTARY | DENMARK
Leo Hansen, director

1936 *Das große Eis*
FILM | DOCUMENTARY | GERMANY
Else Wegener, Paul Künheim, Svend Noldan, directors

Fra Thule til Kap Farvel
FILM | DOCUMENTARY | DENMARK

Petticoat Fever
FILM | NARRATIVE | USA
George Fitzmaurice, director
Metro-Goldwyn-Mayer

1937 *Patrol to the North West Passage*
FILM | DOCUMENTARY | CANADA
Richard Finnie, director

Thule – Polareskimoernes Land
Thule – Land of the Polar Eskimos
FILM | DOCUMENTARY | DENMARK

1938 *Med Gamma-ekspeditionen til Nordøstgrønland*
The Gamma Expedition to North East Greenland
FILM | DOCUMENTARY | DENMARK

Quatre du Groenland
FILM | DOCUMENTARY | FRANCE
Fred Matter, director

Spredte Træk fra Livet paa Grønland
Scenes from Everyday Life in Greenland
FILM | DOCUMENTARY | DENMARK

The Call of the Yukon
FILM | NARRATIVE | USA
John T. Coyle, B. Reeves Eason, directors
Republic Pictures

1939 *Arctic Springtime*
FILM | DOCUMENTARY | USA
Bernard Hubbard, director

Nanook of the North, 1922

Brydning af kul, marmor og kryolit i Grønland
Mining of Coal, Marble and Cryolite in Greenland
FILM | DOCUMENTARY | DENMARK
Jette Bang, director

Eskimo Trails
FILM | DOCUMENTARY | USA
Bernard Hubbard, director

Grønland Fiskeri I, Grønland Fiskeri II
Greenlandic Fishing I, Greenlandic Fishing II
FILM | DOCUMENTARY | DENMARK
Jette Bang, Paul Hansen, directors

Winter in Eskimo Land
FILM | DOCUMENTARY | USA
Bernard Hubbard, director

1940 *Girl from God's Country*
FILM | NARRATIVE | USA
Sidney Salkow, director
Republic Pictures

Inuit
FILM | DOCUMENTARY | DENMARK
Jette Bang, director

Rampart of Two Worlds
FILM | DOCUMENTARY | USA
Bernard Hubbard, director

1941 *Eskimo Children*
FILM | DOCUMENTARY | USA
Encyclopaedia Britannica Films

1942 *Billeder fra Grønland*
FILM | DOCUMENTARY | DENMARK
Julius Galster, Paul Hansen, directors
Globus Films

Filmography | 189

Palos Brudefærd, 1934

Grønland i Sommer og Sol
FILM | DOCUMENTARY | DENMARK
Paul Hansen, director
Globus Films

1943 *Eskimo Arts and Crafts*
FILM | DOCUMENTARY | CANADA
Laura Boulton, director
National Film Board of Canada

1944 *Arctic Hunters*
FILM | DOCUMENTARY | CANADA
Laura Boulton, director
National Film Board of Canada

Eskimo Summer
FILM | DOCUMENTARY | CANADA
Laura Boulton, director
National Film Board of Canada

1947 *Kai Karnøes optagelser fra Grønland*
Medical Doctor Kai Karnøe's Footage from Greenland
FILM | DOCUMENTARY | DENMARK

1948 *Chronique filmée de l'expédition française au Groënland*
FILM | DOCUMENTARY | FRANCE
Paul Gayet-Tancrèd (a.k.a. Samivel), director

Les hommes du phoques
FILM | DOCUMENTARY | FRANCE
Paul Gayet-Tancrède (a.k.a. Samivel), director

Printemps arctique
FILM | DOCUMENTARY | FRANCE
Paul Gayet-Tancrède (a.k.a. Samivel), director

Patrol to the North West Passage, 1937

1949 *Arctic Fury*
FILM | NARRATIVE | USA
Norman Dawn, director
Plymouth Pictures

Arctic Manhunt
FILM | NARRATIVE | USA
Ewing Scott, director
Universal Pictures

Eskimo Hunters of Northwest Alaska
FILM | DOCUMENTARY | USA
W. Kay Norton, director
Louis de Rochemont Associates

How to Build an Igloo
FILM | DOCUMENTARY | CANADA
Douglas Wilkinson, director
National Film Board of Canada

Terre des glaces
FILM | DOCUMENTARY | FRANCE
Jean-Jacques Languepin, director
Armor Films

1950 *Fiskeri på Grønland*
FILM | DOCUMENTARY | DENMARK
Paul Hansen, director
Teknisk Film Compagni

Grønland for de små
The Children in a Greenlandic Village
FILM | DOCUMENTARY | DENMARK
Paul Hansen, director

Grønland i sol
Greenland During Summertime
FILM | DOCUMENTARY | DENMARK
Hagen Hasselbalch, director
Minerva Film

Filmography | 191

Grønlandsindtryk
Impressions from Greenland
FILM | DOCUMENTARY | DENMARK

1952   *Arctic Saga*
FILM | DOCUMENTARY | CANADA
Douglas Wilkinson, director
National Film Board of Canada

Groenland – vingt mille lieues sur les glaces
FILM | DOCUMENTARY | FRANCE
Marcel Ichac, Jean-Jacques Languepin, directors
Marcel Ichac Films

Kongeparret på Grønland
FILM | DOCUMENTARY | DENMARK

Land of the Long Day
FILM | DOCUMENTARY | CANADA
Douglas Wilkinson, director
National Film Board of Canada

Med kongeparret i Grønland
FILM | DOCUMENTARY | DENMARK
Gunnar Wangel, director

Red Snow
FILM | NARRATIVE | USA
Boris Petroff, Harry S. Franklin, directors
All American Film Corporation

1953   *Angotee – Story of an Eskimo Boy*
FILM | DOCUMENTARY | CANADA
Douglas Wilkinson, director
National Film Board of Canada

Back to God's Country
FILM | NARRATIVE | USA
Joseph Pevney, director
Universal Pictures

Blyklippens gåde
FILM | DOCUMENTARY | DENMARK
Hagen Hasselbalch, director

The Alaskan Eskimo
FILM | DOCUMENTARY | USA
James Algar, director
Walt Disney

1954   *Et nyt Grønland*
Greenland, Denmark in the Arctic
FILM | DOCUMENTARY | DENMARK
Erik Ole Olsen, director
Arnø Studio

1955   *En sælfangst i Nordgrønland*
A Sealing in North Greenland
FILM | DOCUMENTARY | DENMARK
Astrid Henning-Jensen, director
Arnø Studio

Hvor bjergene sejler
Where Mountains Float
FILM | DOCUMENTARY | DENMARK
Bjarne Henning-Jensen, director
Arnø Studio

1956   *Our Northern Citizen*
FILM | DOCUMENTARY | CANADA
John Howe, director
National Film Board of Canada

Qivitoq
FILM | NARRATIVE | DENMARK
Erik Balling, director
Nordisk Film

1957   *Alaskan Sled Dog*
FILM | DOCUMENTARY | USA
Ben Sharpsteen, director
Walt Disney

1958   *The Living Stone*
FILM | DOCUMENTARY | CANADA
John Feeney, director
National Film Board of Canada

1959   *Down North*
FILM | DOCUMENTARY | CANADA
Hector Lemieux, director
National Film Board of Canada

Ice Palace
FILM | NARRATIVE | USA
Vincent Sherman, director
Warner Brothers

Pangnirtung
FILM | DOCUMENTARY | CANADA
John Feeney, director
National Film Board of Canada

1960 *The Savage Innocents*
FILM | DOCUMENTARY | ITALY
Nicholas Ray, director
Gray Film-Pathé

1962 *Ekspedisjon til Grønland*
FILM | DOCUMENTARY | NORWAY-DENMARK
Per Høst, director

Grønlands moskusokser
FILM | DOCUMENTARY | DENMARK
Christian Vibe, director

The Glacier Priest
FILM | DOCUMENTARY | USA
Bernard Hubbard, director

1963 *Eskimo Artist – Kenojuak*
FILM | DOCUMENTARY | CANADA
John Feeney, director
National Film Board of Canada

1964 *The Annanacks*
FILM | DOCUMENTARY | CANADA
René Bonnière, director
Crawley Films

1965 *Knud*
FILM | DOCUMENTARY | DENMARK
Jørgen Roos, director
Nunafilm

Stefansson – The Arctic Prophet
FILM | DOCUMENTARY | CANADA
National Film Board of Canada

1966 *Sisimiut*
FILM | DOCUMENTARY | DENMARK
Jørgen Roos, director
Minerva Film

Les hommes du phoque, 1948

Filmography | 193

How to Build an Igloo, 1949

Tuktu and His Eskimo Dogs
FILM | DOCUMENTARY | CANADA
Laurence Hyde, director
National Film Board of Canada

1967 *17 minutter Grønland*
17 Minutes Greenland
FILM | DOCUMENTARY | DENMARK
Jørgen Roos, director
Jørgen Roos Film, Minerva Film

En fangerfamilie i Thuledistriktet
FILM | DOCUMENTARY | DENMARK
Jørgen Roos, director
Jørgen Roos Film

Netsilik Eskimo (series)
FILM | DOCUMENTARY | USA
Quentin Brown, Robert Young, directors
Documentary Educational Resources

Tuktu and the Ten Thousand Fishes
FILM | DOCUMENTARY | CANADA
Laurence Hyde, director
National Film Board of Canada

Tuktu and the Trials of Strength
FILM | DOCUMENTARY | CANADA
Laurence Hyde, director
National Film Board of Canada

1968 *Aki'name*
On the Wall
FILM | DOCUMENTARY | CANADA
David Millar, director
National Film Board of Canada

Grønlandske dialektoptagelser og trommedans fra Thuledistriktet
FILM | DOCUMENTARY | DENMARK
Jørgen Roos, director
Jørgen Roos Film

Ultima Thule
FILM | DOCUMENTARY | DENMARK
Jørgen Roos, director
Jørgen Roos Film

1969 *En boplads i Østgrønland*
FILM | DOCUMENTARY | DENMARK
Kaj Mogens Jensen, Jette Bang, directors
Kaj Mogens A/S

Grønland I, Grønland II
FILM | DOCUMENTARY | DENMARK
Per Kirkeby, director

1970 *Kalâliuvit? (Er du grønlænder?)*
Are You Greenlander?
FILM | DOCUMENTARY | DENMARK
Jørgen Roos, director
Jørgen Roos Film

Snow Bear
TELEVISION | NARRATIVE | USA
Gunther von Fritsch, director
Walt Disney

1971 *Eskimos – A Changing Culture*
FILM | DOCUMENTARY | USA
Wayne Mitchell, director
Wayne Mitchell Film

River Is Boss
FILM | DOCUMENTARY | USA
Skyriver

Tununermiut
The People of Tununak
FILM | DOCUMENTARY | USA
Leonard Kamerling, Norman
Kamerling, directors
Alaska Native Heritage Film Project

Umialik
FILM | DOCUMENTARY | DENMARK
Jens Rosing, director
Kaj Mogens A/S

1972 *Da myndighederne sagde stop*
FILM | DOCUMENTARY | DENMARK
Per Kirkeby, Aqqaluk Lynge, directors
Flip Film Production

Emilie fra Sarqaq
Emilie from Sarqaq
FILM | DOCUMENTARY | DENMARK
Sune Lund-Sørensen, director

Havet ved Grønland
The Sea Around Greenland
FILM | DOCUMENTARY | DENMARK
Sune Lund-Sørensen, director
Laterna Film

The Emerging Eskimo
FILM | DOCUMENTARY | USA
Brayton-Kendall Productions, Centron
Educational Films

The Netsilik Eskimo Today
FILM | DOCUMENTARY | CANADA, USA
Gilles Blais, director
National Film Board of Canada, Education
Development Center (Cambridge)

To mænd i ødemarken
FILM | DOCUMENTARY | DENMARK
Jørgen Roos, director
Minerva Film

Ulare písarganartumik okalugtuarpok
Ulrik Is Telling a Legend
FILM | DOCUMENTARY | DENMARK
Jørgen Roos, director
Minerva Film

1973 *A Wedge of Rock*
FILM | DOCUMENTARY | DENMARK
Nic Lichtenberg, director
Arnø Studio

Animation from Cape Dorset
FILM | NARRATIVE | CANADA
National Film Board of Canada

For fremtiden
FILM | DOCUMENTARY | DENMARK
Jørgen Roos, director
Minerva Film

Hverdag I Grønland
FILM | DOCUMENTARY | DENMARK
Sven Thomsen, director

Labrador North
FILM | DOCUMENTARY | CANADA
Roger Hart, director
National Film Board of Canada

Naalakkersuisut Oqarput Tassagooq
And the Authorities Said Stop
FILM | DOCUMENTARY | DENMARK
Aqqaluk Lynge, Per Kirkeby, directors
Minerva Film

Owl and the Raven –
An Eskimo Legend
FILM | NARRATIVE | CANADA
Co Hoedeman, director
National Film Board of Canada

Some Natives of Churchill
FILM | DOCUMENTARY | CANADA
Cynthia Scott, director
National Film Board of Canada

The Greenlanders
FILM | DOCUMENTARY | CANADA
Hubert Schuurman, director
National Film Board of Canada

1974 *At the Time of Whaling*
FILM | DOCUMENTARY | USA
Sarah Elder, Leonard Kamerling, directors
Alaska Native Heritage Film Project

In Search of the Bowhead Whale
FILM | DOCUMENTARY | CANADA
Bill Mason, director
National Film Board of Canada

North of the Sun
FILM | DOCUMENTARY | USA
Gordon Eastman, director
Eastman's Outdoor World, Gordon
Eastman Productions

The Owl Who Married a Goose
FILM | NARRATIVE | CANADA
Caroline Leaf, director
National Film Board of Canada

The White Dawn
FILM | NARRATIVE | USA, CANADA
Philip Kaufman, director
American Film Properties, Filmways
Pictures, Paramount Pictures

Two Against the Arctic
TELEVISION | NARRATIVE | USA
William Beaudine Jr., director
Walt Disney

1975 *Arbejderkvinder i Grønland*
Women Workers in Greenland
FILM | DOCUMENTARY | DENMARK
Lene Aidt, Merete Borker, directors
Ebbe Preisler Film

Dersu Uzala
FILM | NARRATIVE | RUSSIA, JAPAN
Akira Kurosawa, director
Daiei Film, Mosfilm

Les Derniers Rois de Thulé
FILM | DOCUMENTARY | FRANCE
Jean Malaurie, director

Lumaaq – An Eskimo Legend
FILM | NARRATIVE | CANADA
Co Hoedeman, director
National Film Board of Canada

Natsik Hunting
FILM | DOCUMENTARY | CANADA
Mosha Michael, director
National Film Board of Canada

On the Spring Ice
FILM | DOCUMENTARY | USA
Sarah Elder, Leonard Kamerling, directors
Alaska Native Heritage Film Project

The Man and the Giant –
An Eskimo Legend
FILM | NARRATIVE | CANADA
Co Hoedeman, director
National Film Board of Canada

1976 *Labrador Resources Advisory Council*
FILM | DOCUMENTARY | CANADA
Memorial University of Newfoundland Extension Service

Mumitsiniarpugut
FILM | DOCUMENTARY | NORWAY
Jan Knutzen, Malte Wadman, directors

Umanak 75
FILM | DOCUMENTARY | DENMARK
Jørn Kjær Nielsen, director
Zepia Film

1977 *Asivaqtiin*
The Hunters
FILM | DOCUMENTARY | CANADA
Mosha Michael, director
National Film Board of Canada

From the First People
FILM | DOCUMENTARY | USA
Sarah Elder, Leonard Kamerling, directors
Alaska Native Heritage Film Project

Labrador Land Use Conference
FILM | DOCUMENTARY | CANADA
Memorial University of Newfoundland Extension Service

Nanook Taxi
FILM | NARRATIVE | USA
Edward Folger, director
Tulugak

Qilaluganiatut
Whale Hunting
FILM | DOCUMENTARY | CANADA
Mosha Michael, director
National Film Board of Canada

1978 *Nuuk ukiut 250-ignorneráne*
FILM | DOCUMENTARY | KALAALLIT NUNAAT
Kalaallit Nunaata Radioa

Tolerance
FILM | DOCUMENTARY | DENMARK
Anders Odsbjerg, director
Laterna Film (Arnø Studio)

Qivitoq, 1956

Filmography | 197

The Living Stone, 1958

1979 *Grønlandske kvindearbejder*
FILM | DOCUMENTARY | DENMARK
Franz Ernst, director

Narsaq – ung by i Grønland
FILM | DOCUMENTARY | KALAALLIT NUNAAT
Claus Hermansen, director

Of Seals and Men
FILM | DOCUMENTARY | DENMARK
Mai Zetterling, director

1980 *Aussivik 77*
FILM | DOCUMENTARY | DENMARK
Mike Siegstad, director
Flip Film Production

Hvis der skal være havgående fiskeri
FILM | DOCUMENTARY | DENMARK
Mike Siegstad, director

Rikke på Grønland – 1. Vinter og sælfangst, 2. Forår og trommedans, 3. Sommer og udflugter
FILM | DOCUMENTARY | DENMARK
Annelise Alexandrovitsch, Lennart Steen Alexandrovitsch, directors
Lennart Steen Film

1980– *Qaggiq*
2005 TELEVISION SERIES | CANADA
Inuit Broadcasting Corporation

1981 *Byen under kællingehætten*
FILM | DOCUMENTARY | DENMARK

Grønland
FILM | DOCUMENTARY | DENMARK
Jørgen Roos, director

198 | Inuit TakugatsaliuKatiget / On Inuit Cinema

Northern Games
FILM | DOCUMENTARY | CANADA
Ken Buck, director
National Film Board of Canada

Slædepatruljen Sirius
The Sirius Patrol
FILM | DOCUMENTARY | DENMARK
Jørgen Roos, director
Jørgen Roos Film

1982 *Knud Rasmussens mindeekspedition til Kap Seddon*
FILM | DOCUMENTARY | DENMARK
Jørgen Roos, director
Jørgen Roos Film

The Children of Eek and Their Art
FILM | DOCUMENTARY | USA
Commercial Film Productions

1983 *Never Cry Wolf*
FILM | NARRATIVE | USA
Carroll Ballard, director
Walt Disney, Amarok Productions

Our Land, Our Truth
FILM | DOCUMENTARY | CANADA
Maurice Bulbulian, director
National Film Board of Canada

Qallunaani
FILM | DOCUMENTARY | CANADA
Stavros Stavrides, Barbara Stocking, directors
One-Six Productions

Unitas Fratrum – The Moravians in Labrador
FILM | DOCUMENTARY | CANADA
Hubert Schuurman, director
National Film Board of Canada

1983– *Labradorimiut*
2011 TELEVISION SERIES | DOCUMENTARY | CANADA
OKâlaKatiget Society

1984 *Eyes of the Spirit*
FILM | DOCUMENTARY | USA
Alexie Isaac, director

Tukuma
FILM | NARRATIVE | DENMARK
Palle Kjærulff-Schmidt, director
Crone Film

1985 *Inughuit – folket vid jordens navel*
The Inuit – The People at the Navel of the Earth
FILM | DOCUMENTARY | SWEDEN
Staffan Julén, Ylva Julén, directors

Justice blanche
FILM | DOCUMENTARY | CANADA
Françoise Wera, Morgane Laliberté, directors
InformAction

Nabo til Nordpolen
FILM | DOCUMENTARY | DENMARK
Teit Jørgensen, Per Ingolf Mannstaedt, Mike Siegstad, directors
Flip Film Production, Tusarliivik, Grønlands Hjemmestyre, Statens Filmcentral, Udenrigsministeriet

Shungnak – A Village Profile
FILM | DOCUMENTARY | USA
Daniel Housberg, director

The Last Days of Okak
FILM | DOCUMENTARY | CANADA
Anne Budgell, Nigel Markham, directors
National Film Board of Canada

Uuttoq (Uuttoq – Kaali på sælfangst)
FILM | DOCUMENTARY | DENMARK, KALAALLIT NUNAAT
Tørk Haxthausen, director
Flip Film Production, Statens Filmcentral, Tusarliivik

Verdens største nationalpark
FILM | DOCUMENTARY | DENMARK, KALAALLIT NUNAAT
Tue Ritzau, director

1986 *De grønlandske mumier*
FILM | DOCUMENTARY | DENMARK
Jørgen Roos, director

Edge of Ice
FILM | DOCUMENTARY | CANADA
William Hansen, director
National Film Board of Canada

Inukshuk
FILM | DOCUMENTARY | CANADA

1986– 1987 *Takujuminaqtut / Takuyuminaqtut*
TELEVISION SERIES | DOCUMENTARY | CANADA
Inuvialuit Communications Society

1987 *Et hul i jorden*
A Hole in the Ground
FILM | DOCUMENTARY | DENMARK
Peter Ronild, director
Jørgen Roos Film

Following the Star
FILM | DOCUMENTARY | USA
Alexie Isaac, director

1987– 2010 *Qaujisaut*
TELEVISION SERIES | DOCUMENTARY | CANADA
Inuit Broadcasting Corporation

1988 *Ekspeditionen*
FILM | DOCUMENTARY | DENMARK
Per Kirkeby, director
Kraka Film

Esbjergfiskerne drog til Grønland i 1948
The Esbjerg Fishermen Went to Greenland in 1948
FILM | DOCUMENTARY | DENMARK
Katrine Borre, director
Det Danske Videoværksted

In Iirgu's Time
FILM | DOCUMENTARY | USA
Sarah Elder, Leonard Kamerling, directors
Alaska Native Heritage Film Project

Joe Sun
FILM | DOCUMENTARY | USA
Katrina Waters, Director
Alaska Native Heritage Film Project

Lypa
FILM | DOCUMENTARY | CANADA
Shelagh Mackenzie, Sharon Van Raalte, directors
National Film Board of Canada

Qaggiq
Gathering Place
FILM | NARRATIVE | CANADA
Zacharias Kunuk, Norman Cohn, Pauloosie Qulitalik, directors
Igloolik Isuma

The Reindeer Thief
FILM | DOCUMENTARY | USA
Sarah Elder, Leonard Kamerling, directors
Alaska Native Heritage Film Project

Uksuum Cauyai – Drums of Winter
FILM | DOCUMENTARY | USA
Sarah Elder, Leonard Kamerling, directors
Alaska Native Heritage Film Project

1989 *Kamik*
FILM | DOCUMENTARY | CANADA
Elise Swerhone, director
National Film Board of Canada

Nissebanden i Grønland
TELEVISION SERIES | NARRATIVE | DENMARK
Per Pallesen, director
DR [TV-B&U-afdelingen]

1990 *Between Two Worlds*
FILM | DOCUMENTARY | CANADA
Barry Greenwald, director
National Film Board of Canada, Investigative Productions

Kolonihaven – om nogen grønlændere i Danmark
About Greenlanders in Denmark
FILM | DOCUMENTARY | DENMARK
Lise Roos, director

Nanook Revisited
FILM | DOCUMENTARY | USA
Claude Massot, director
Films Media Group

1991 *Nunaqpa*
Going Inland
FILM | DOCUMENTARY | CANADA
Zacharias Kunuk, director
Igloolik Isuma

Salmonberries
FILM | NARRATIVE | GERMANY
Percy Adlon, director
Pelemele Film

Starting Fire with Gunpowder
FILM | DOCUMENTARY | CANADA
William Hansen, David Poisey, directors
Tamarack Productions, National Film Board of Canada

1992 *Attagutaaluk*
Starvation
FILM | DOCUMENTARY | CANADA
Arnait Video Productions

Coppermine
FILM | DOCUMENTARY | CANADA
Ray Harper, director
National Film Board of Canada

Kingulliit
The Next Generation
FILM | DOCUMENTARY | CANADA
Zacharias Kunuk, Paul Quassa, directors
Igloolik Isuma

Lauge Koch – grønlandsforskeren
FILM | DOCUMENTARY | DENMARK
Jørgen Roos, director
Jørgen Roos Film

The Annanacks, 1964

Sedna – The Making of a Myth
FILM | DOCUMENTARY | CANADA
John Paskievich, director
National Film Board of Canada, Zemma Pictures

L'ours renifleur
The Sniffing Bear
FILM | NARRATIVE | CANADA
Co Hoedeman, director
National Film Board of Canada

1992-2001 *Qimaivvik*
TELEVISION SERIES | DOCUMENTARY | CANADA
Inuit Broadcasting Corporation

1993 *Keeping Our Stories Alive – The Sculpture of Canada's Inuit*
FILM | DOCUMENTARY | CANADA
Denise Withers, director
Indian and Northern Affairs Canada

Labrador Inuit – Part One: The Land, The Sea, and The People, Part Two: Negotiating the Claim
FILM | DOCUMENTARY | CANADA
Labrador Inuit Association, OKâlaKatiget Society

Map of the Human Heart
FILM | NARRATIVE | AUSTRALIA, CANADA, FRANCE, UK
Vincent Ward, director
Working Title Films, PolyGram Filmed Entertainment, Australian Film Finance Corporation

Qulliq
Oil Lamp
FILM | DOCUMENTARY | CANADA
Arnait Video Productions

Netsilik Eskimo (series), *Fishing at the Stone Weir, Part 1*, 1967

Saputi
Fish Traps
FILM | DOCUMENTARY | CANADA
Zacharias Kunuk, Pauloosie Qulitalik, Norman Cohn, directors
Igloolik Isuma

Shadow of the Wolf
FILM | NARRATIVE | CANADA
Jacques Dorfmann, Pierre Magny, directors
Canal+, Eiffel Productions

1994 *Arviq!*
Bowhead!
FILM | DOCUMENTARY | CANADA
Paul Apak Angilirq, Zacharias Kunuk, directors
Igloolik Isuma

Kabloonak
FILM | NARRATIVE | CANADA
Claude Massot, director
Bloom Films

Piujuk and Angutautuq
FILM | DOCUMENTARY | CANADA
Arnait Video Productions

Trial at Fortitude Bay
FILM | NARRATIVE | CANADA
Vic Sarin, director

Vor enestående tid
FILM | DOCUMENTARY
Ivars Silis, director

1995 *Arctic Hysteria*
FILM | EXPERIMENTAL | KALAALLIT NUNAAT
Pia Arke, director

Owl and the Raven – An Eskimo Legend, 1973

Filmography | 203

Natsik Hunting, 1975

Broken Promises – The High Arctic Relocation
FILM | DOCUMENTARY | CANADA
Patricia Tassinari, director
National Film Board of Canada

Cry of the Ancestors – The Art of Manasie Akpaliapik
FILM | DOCUMENTARY | CANADA
Cathy Gulking, director
Breakthrough Films and Television

Frostfire
FILM | NARRATIVE | CANADA
David Greene, director
Crescent Entertainment, Howe Sound Films, Nagarauk Films

In the Reign of Twilight
FILM | DOCUMENTARY | USA
Kevin McMahon, director
Primitive Features

Northern Justice
FILM | DOCUMENTARY | CANADA
Simcha Jacobovici, Elliott Halpern, directors

Nunavut – Our Land
TELEVISION SERIES | DOCUMENTARY | CANADA
Zacharias Kunuk, Pauloosie Qulitalik, directors
Igloolik Isuma

Spirit of the Arctic
FILM | DOCUMENTARY | CANADA
Alex Hamilton-Brown, director

1995–2007 *Nunatinni*
At Our Place
TELEVISION SERIES | CURRENT EVENTS | CANADA
Nunavut Independent Television Network

1996 *Aqtuqsi*
The Nightmare
FILM | NARRATIVE | CANADA
Mary Kunuk, director
Arnait Video Productions

Donald and Winifred Marsh's Missionary Encounter with the Padlimiut
FILM | DOCUMENTARY | CANADA
Keith Packwood, director
National Film Board of Canada

Grønland på vej
FILM | DOCUMENTARY | DENMARK
Ivars Silis, director

Travelers
FILM | DOCUMENTARY | CANADA
Marie-Hélène Cousineau, director
Arnait Video Productions

Unikausiq
Stories
FILM | NARRATIVE | CANADA
Mary Kunuk, director
Arnait Video Productions

1997 *Eye of the Storm*
FILM | DOCUMENTARY | CANADA
Nigel Markham, director
National Film Board of Canada, Lazybank Productions

Inuttut Oqaatsikka – mit sprog som menneske
FILM | DOCUMENTARY | DENMARK
Karin Parbst, director

Jørgen Roos og Grønland
FILM | DOCUMENTARY | DENMARK
Jørgen Roos, director

Smilla's Sense of Snow
FILM | NARRATIVE | DENMARK, GERMANY, SWEDEN
Bille August, director
Bavaria Film, Constantin Film, Det Danske Filminstitut, Greenland Film Production, Nordisk Film

1998 *Amarok's Song – The Journey to Nunavut*
FILM | DOCUMENTARY | CANADA
Martin Kreelak, Ole Gjerstad, directors
National Film Board of Canada

Grønland på cykel!
Greenland By Bike
FILM | DOCUMENTARY | DENMARK
Stig Hartkopf, director
Zentropa Productions

Qaamarngup uummataa
Heart of Light
FILM | NARRATIVE | KALAALLIT NUNAAT, DENMARK
Jacob Grønlykke, director
ASA Film Production

c. 1998 *Visions of Makkovik*
FILM | DOCUMENTARY | CANADA
James Robert Andersen, director

1999 *Gensyn med Østgrønland ... Kirsten Bang*
East Greenland Revisited ... Kirsten Bang
FILM | DOCUMENTARY | DENMARK
Karen Littauer, director
Nuka Film

John Houston Trilogy, Part 1: Songs in Stone – An Arctic Journey Home
FILM | DOCUMENTARY | CANADA
John Houston, director
Houston Productions

Nipi
Voice
FILM | DOCUMENTARY | CANADA
Zacharias Kunuk, director
Igloolik Isuma

Saputjinik
Healing Each Other
FILM | DOCUMENTARY | CANADA
Fran Williams, director
Memorial University of Newfoundland

Sinilluarit
Goodnight
FILM | NARRATIVE | KALAALLIT NUNAAT
Inuk Silis Høegh, director
Nuna Manna Pictures

Tunit – det forsvundne folk
FILM | DOCUMENTARY | DENMARK, KALAALLIT NUNAAT

Welcome to Nunavut
FILM | DOCUMENTARY | CANADA
Joe Moulins, George Hargrave, directors
National Film Board of Canada, Nutaaq Media

1999– *Takuginai*
TELEVISION SERIES | CHILDREN'S PROGRAM | CANADA
Inuit Broadcasting Corporation

Labradorimiut, "Nunaksiamut," 1983

2000 *Bug*
FILM | EXPERIMENTAL | CANADA
Lindsay McIntyre, director

Fragments of Lost History
FILM | DOCUMENTARY | CANADA
National Film Board of Canada

Ikíngut
FILM | NARRATIVE | ICELAND, DENMARK, NORWAY
Gísli Snær Erlingsson, director
Icelandic Film Corporation, Filmhuset Produksjoner AS, Zentropa Productions

Kikkik
FILM | DOCUMENTARY | CANADA
Ole Gjerstad, Elisapee Karetak, directors
Words & Pictures Video, WTN Women's Television Network, Filmoption International

Kitikmeot (series): *The Drum Dancer; Journey of the Stone; Uvajuq, The Origin of Death*
FILM | DOCUMENTARY | CANADA
Danielle Beaudry, director
Les Productions Vic Pelletier

Nanoq
FILM | NARRATIVE | DENMARK
Kunuk Platoú, director
Den Danske Filmskole

Nanugiurutiga
My First Polar Bear
FILM | DOCUMENTARY | CANADA
Zacharias Kunuk, director
Igloolik Isuma

Uksuum Cauyai – Drums of Winter, 1988

Filmography | 207

Ningiura
My Grandmother
FILM | DOCUMENTARY | CANADA
Mary Kunuk, Marie-Helene Cousineau,
directors
Arnait Video Productions

På Fremmed Is
FILM | DOCUMENTARY | KALAALLIT NUNAAT
Inuk Silis Høegh, director
Ánorâk Film

2000 *Smoke*
FILM | EXPERIMENTAL | CANADA
Lindsay McIntyre, director

2001 *A Traditional Seal Hunt in Nunatsiavut*
FILM | DOCUMENTARY | CANADA
Sarah Abel, director
OKâlaKatiget Society

Ajainaa!
Almost!
FILM | DOCUMENTARY | CANADA
Zacharias Kunuk, director
Igloolik Isuma

Anaana
Mother
FILM | DOCUMENTARY | CANADA
Mary Kunuk, Marie-Hélène Cousineau,
directors
Arnait Video Productions

Artcirq
FILM | DOCUMENTARY | CANADA
Natar Ungalaaq, Guillaume Saladin,
directors
Igloolik Isuma

Atanarjuat – The Fast Runner
FILM | NARRATIVE | CANADA
Zacharias Kunuk, director
Igloolik Isuma, National Film Board of
Canada

Eskimo Weekend
FILM | NARRATIVE | KALAALLIT NUNAAT
Inuk Silis Høegh, director
Ánorâk Film

Fetish
FILM | EXPERIMENTAL | CANADA
Lindsay McIntyre, director

Great North
FILM | DOCUMENTARY | CANADA
Martin J. Dignard, William Reeve,
directors
TVA International, Swedish Museum of
Natural History, Imagica

Ommatimmiutagennaniattavut – IkKaumset Hebaronimit Notitausimanningit
Forever in Our Hearts – Memories of the Hebron Relocation
FILM | DOCUMENTARY | CANADA
Nigel Markham, director
OKâlaKatiget Society

The End
FILM | EXPERIMENTAL | CANADA
Lindsay McIntyre, director

2002 *Andala og Sofiannguaq*
Our Farm – Under the Northern Lights
FILM | DOCUMENTARY | DENMARK
Ivars Silis, director
Sonne

Drengen der ville gøre det umulige
The Boy Who Wanted to Be a Bear
FILM | NARRATIVE | DENMARK, FRANCE
Jannik Hastrup, director
Dansk Tegnefilm, France 3 Cinéma

Forbrydelse og straf i Grønland
Arctic Crime and Punishment
FILM | DOCUMENTARY | DENMARK
Sasha Snow, director
Diverse Production

Qulliq, 1993

I samme båd
FILM | DOCUMENTARY | KALAALLIT NUNAAT
Inuk Silis Høegh, director
Ánorâk Film

Inuk Woman City Blues
FILM | DOCUMENTARY | DENMARK
Laila Hansen, director
Nils Vest Film

Jeg husker ... Fortællinger fra Grønland
FILM | DOCUMENTARY | DENMARK
Karen Littauer, director
Magic Hour Films, Nuka Film

John Houston Trilogy, Part 2: Nuliajuk – Mother of the Sea Beasts
FILM | DOCUMENTARY | CANADA
John Houston, director
Houston Productions

Taking Flight
FILM | EXPERIMENTAL | CANADA
Lindsay McIntyre, director

2003 *Angakkuiit*
Shaman Stories
FILM | DOCUMENTARY | CANADA
Pauloosie Qulitalik, Zacharias Kunuk, directors
Igloolik Isuma

Angimajuka Tinnagu – Notitausimanningi Inuit Labrador Tagganimiut
Without Consent – The Resettlement of Inuit of Northern Labrador
FILM | DOCUMENTARY | CANADA
Nigel Markham, director
OKâlaKatiget Society

Brother Bear
FILM | NARRATIVE | CANADA
Aaron Blaise, Robert Walker, directors
Walt Disney

Climate on the Edge
FILM | DOCUMENTARY | CANADA
Alain Belhumeur, Jean Lemire, directors
National Film Board of Canada

Dage med Kathrine
FILM | DOCUMENTARY | DENMARK
Ulla Boye, director
Koncern TV- og Filmproduktion

E1-472 Kikkik
FILM | DOCUMENTARY | CANADA
Martin Kreelak, director
Inuit Broadcasting Corporation

How to Make a Phantastik Film
FILM | EXPERIMENTAL | CANADA
Lindsay McIntyre, director

If the Weather Permits
FILM | DOCUMENTARY | CANADA
Elisapie Isaac, director
National Film Board of Canada

Islet
FILM | NARRATIVE | CANADA
Nicolas Brault, director
National Film Board of Canada

Lords of the Arctic
FILM | DOCUMENTARY | CANADA
Caroline Underwood, Jean Lemire, directors
National Film Board of Canada

Nunavut – Our Land, "Quviasukvik," 1995

People of the Ice
FILM | DOCUMENTARY | CANADA
Carlos Ferrand, Jean Lemire, directors
National Film Board of Canada

The Great Adventure
FILM | DOCUMENTARY | CANADA
Jean Lemire, Thierry Piantanida, directors
National Film Board of Canada

The Snow Walker
FILM | NARRATIVE | CANADA
Charles Martin Smith, director
Snow Walker/Walk Well Productions

2004 **Inuuvunga – I Am Inuk, I Am Alive**
FILM | DOCUMENTARY | CANADA
Bobby Echalook, Sarah Idlout, Laura
Iqaluk, Linus Kasudluak, Dora
Ohaituk, Rita-Lucy Ohaituk, Willia
Ningeok, Caroline Ningiuk, Mila Aung-
Thwin, Daniel Cross, Brett Gaylor, directors
National Film Board of Canada

**John Houston Trilogy, Part 3:
Diet of Souls**
FILM | DOCUMENTARY | CANADA
John Houston, director
Houston Productions

Kunuk Family Reunion
FILM | DOCUMENTARY | CANADA
Zacharias Kunuk, director
Igloolik Isuma

La longue trace
FILM | DOCUMENTARY | FRANCE
Mike Magidson, director

Sooq Akersuuttugut
Why We Fight
FILM | EXPERIMENTAL | KALAALLIT NUNAAT
Inuk Silis Høegh, director
Ánorâk Film

2005 **A B Movie**
FILM | EXPERIMENTAL | CANADA
Lindsay McIntyre, director

**Aboriginal Architecture
Living Architecture**
FILM | DOCUMENTARY | CANADA
Paul M. Rickard, director
Mushkeg Productions, National Film Board
of Canada

Compulsion (Part I/III)
FILM | EXPERIMENTAL | CANADA
Lindsay McIntyre, director

I Can Make Art ... Like Andrew Qappik
FILM | DOCUMENTARY | CANADA
Jane Churchill, director
National Film Board of Canada

**I, Nuligak – An Inuvialuit History
of First Contact**
FILM | DOCUMENTARY | CANADA
Tom Radford, Peter Raymont,
Patrick Reed, directors
National Film Board of Canada

Minik
FILM | DOCUMENTARY | GERMANY
Axel Engstfeld, director

Not Waving But Drowning
FILM | EXPERIMENTAL | CANADA
Lindsay McIntyre, director

Qallunajatut
Urban Inuk
FILM | DOCUMENTARY | CANADA
Jobie Weetaluktuk, director
Kunuk Cohn Productions, Igloolik Isuma

Quando i bambini giocano in cielo
When Children Play in the Sky
FILM | NARRATIVE | ITALY, DENMARK, ICELAND, UK
Lorenzo Hendel, director
Zentropa Entertainments, Orione
Cinematografica

Silent Messengers
FILM | DOCUMENTARY | CANADA
William D. MacGillivray, director
National Film Board of Canada, Picture Plant

Unakuluk
Dear Little One
FILM | DOCUMENTARY | CANADA
Marie-Hélène Cousineau, Mary Kunuk,
directors
Arnait Video Productions

2006 *Annie Pootoogook*
FILM | DOCUMENTARY | CANADA
Marcia Connolly, director
Site Media

Kiviaq versus Canada
FILM | DOCUMENTARY | CANADA
Zacharias Kunuk, director
Igloolik Isuma, Kunuk Cohn Productions

*Menneskenes land – min film
om Grønland*
The Land of Human Beings
FILM | DOCUMENTARY | DENMARK
Anne Regitze Wivel, director
Barok Film

*Qallunaat! Why White People
Are Funny*
FILM | DOCUMENTARY | CANADA
Mark Sandiford, director
National Film Board of Canada

The Journals of Knud Rasmussen
FILM | NARRATIVE | CANADA
Zacharias Kunuk, Norman Cohn, directors
Igloolik Isuma

2006– *Niqitsiat*
2018 TELEVISION SERIES | DOCUMENTARY | CANADA
Inuit Broadcasting Corporation

2006– *Qanuq Isumavit?*
TELEVISION SERIES | CURRENT EVENTS | CANADA
Inuit Broadcasting Corporation

2007 *30 Days of Night*
FILM | NARRATIVE | USA
David Slade, director
Columbia Pictures, Dark Horse
Entertainment,
Ghost House Pictures

Issaittuq
Waterproof
FILM | NARRATIVE | CANADA
Bruce Haulli, director
Igloolik Isuma, Artcirq

Tarrarsornerit / Spejlinger
FILM | DOCUMENTARY | KALAALLIT NUNAAT
Inuk Silis Høegh, director
Ánorâk Film

The Prize of the Pole
FILM | DOCUMENTARY | DENMARK
Staffan Julén, director

Umiaq
FILM | DOCUMENTARY | CANADA
Madeline Ivalu, director
Arnait Video Productions

2007– *Testimony – Residential Schools*
2018 FILM | DOCUMENTARY | CANADA
Zacharias Kunuk, Peter Irniq, directors
Igloolik Isuma

2008 *Before Tomorrow*
FILM | NARRATIVE | CANADA
Marie-Hélène Cousineau, Madeline Ivalu,
directors
Igloolik Isuma, Kunuk Cohn Productions,
Arnait Video Productions

Ce qu'il faut pour vivre
The Necessities of Life
FILM | NARRATIVE | CANADA
Benoît Pilon, director
Association Coopérative des Productions
Audio-Visuelles

*James Andersen – Over 50 Years
of Taking Pictures*
FILM | DOCUMENTARY | CANADA
Rhonda Buckley, director
Torngâsok Cultural Centre

Martha of the North
FILM | DOCUMENTARY | CANADA
Marquise Lepage, director
National Film Board of Canada

Passage
FILM | DOCUMENTARY | CANADA
John Walker, director
John Walker Productions, PTV Productions, National Film Board of Canada

though she never spoke, this is where her voice would have been
FILM | EXPERIMENTAL | CANADA
Lindsay McIntyre, director

Tikeq, Qiterleq, Mikileraq, Eqeqqoq
Fore Finger, Middle Finger, Ring Finger, Little Finger
FILM | NARRATIVE | KALAALLIT NUNAAT
Ujarneq Fleischer, director

Umiaq Skin Boat
FILM | DOCUMENTARY | CANADA
Jobie Weetaluktuk, director
Catbird Productions

2009 *Exile Nutaunikut*
FILM | DOCUMENTARY | CANADA
Zacharias Kunuk, director
Igloolik Isuma

Hinnarik Sinnattunilu
FILM | NARRATIVE | KALAALLIT NUNAAT
Angayo Lennert-Sandgreen, director
Tumit Productions

Inuit Odyssey
TELEVISION | DOCUMENTARY | CANADA
Tom Radford, Niobe Thompson, directors
Clearwater Media

Inuit Piqutingit
What Belongs to Inuit
FILM | DOCUMENTARY | CANADA
Zacharias Kunuk, Bernadette Dean, directors
Igloolik Isuma

Kakkalaakkuvik
Where the Children Dwell
FILM | DOCUMENTARY | CANADA
Jobie Weetaluktuk, director
Catbird Productions

Nuummioq
FILM | NARRATIVE | KALAALLIT NUNAAT
Otto Rosing, Torben Bech, directors
3900 Pictures

Atanarjuat – The Fast Runner, 2001

Before Tomorrow, 2008

This Land
FILM | DOCUMENTARY | CANADA
Dianne Whelan, director
National Film Board of Canada

Traditional Clothing Igloolik Style
FILM | DOCUMENTARY | CANADA
Susan Avingaq, director
Arnait Video Productions

Tro, Håb og Grønland
Faith, Hope and Greenland
FILM | DOCUMENTARY | GERMANY, KALAALLIT NUNAAT
Ivalo Frank, director

Uncle Jim's Northern Labrador Traditions
FILM | DOCUMENTARY | CANADA
James Andersen, Tony Dawson, directors

Vistas – InukShop
FILM | EXPERIMENTAL | CANADA
Jobie Weetaluktuk, director
National Film Board of Canada

2010 **A Film Without Kayaks**
FILM | DOCUMENTARY
Andreas Rydbacken, director
Royback Production

Echoes
FILM | DOCUMENTARY
Ivalo Frank, director

Eksperimentet
The Experiment
FILM | NARRATIVE | DENMARK
Louise Friedberg, director
Nimbus Film

focus
FILM | EXPERIMENTAL | CANADA
Lindsay McIntyre, director

Ghost Noise
FILM | DOCUMENTARY | CANADA
Marcia Connolly, director

I Am But a Little Woman
FILM | NARRATIVE | CANADA
Gyu Oh, director
National Film Board of Canada, Inuit
Broadcasting Corporation

Inuit High Kick
FILM | DOCUMENTARY | CANADA
Alethea Arnaquq-Baril, director

Inuit Knowledge and Climate Change
FILM | DOCUMENTARY | CANADA
Ian Mauro, Zacharias Kunuk, directors
Igloolik Isuma, Kunuk Cohn Productions

*Kinngait – Riding Light
into the World*
FILM | DOCUMENTARY | CANADA
Annette Mangaard, director
Site Media

Lumaajuuq
FILM | NARRATIVE | CANADA
Alethea Arnaquq-Baril, director
National Film Board of Canada, Inuit
Broadcasting Corporation

Qalupalik
FILM | NARRATIVE | CANADA
Ame Papatsie, director
National Film Board of Canada, Inuit
Broadcasting Corporation

Qimmit – A Clash of Two Truths
FILM | DOCUMENTARY | CANADA
Ole Gjerstad, Joelie Sanguya, directors
National Film Board of Canada, Piksuk
Media

Queen of the Quest
FILM | DOCUMENTARY | CANADA
Carol Kunnuk, director
Arnait Video Productions

*Show Me on the Map – Part 1:
A Changing World, Part 2:
People Can Stand Up*
FILM | DOCUMENTARY | CANADA
Marie-Hélène Cousineau, Carol Kunnuk,
directors
Arnait Video Productions

Teenagerdrømme i Grønland
FILM | DOCUMENTARY | DENMARK
Lotte Andersen, director

The Bear Facts
FILM | NARRATIVE | CANADA
Jonathan Wright, director
National Film Board of Canada

The White Archer
FILM | DOCUMENTARY | CANADA
John Houston, director
Houston Productions

*Tunniit – Retracing the Lines
of Inuit Tattoos*
FILM | DOCUMENTARY | CANADA
Alethea Arnaquq-Baril, director

2011   *Charlie Pisuk*
FILM | DOCUMENTARY | CANADA
Marie-Hélène Cousineau, director
Arnait Video Productions

On the Ice
FILM | NARRATIVE | USA
Andrew Okpeaha MacLean, director
On the Ice Productions, Silverwood Films,
Treehead Films

People of a Feather
FILM | DOCUMENTARY | CANADA
Joel Heath, director

Qaqqat Alanngui
FILM | NARRATIVE | KALAALLIT NUNAAT
Malik Kleist, director
Tumit Productions

*Stories from Our Land 1.5 – If You
Want to Get Married ... You Have to
Learn How to Build an Igloo!*
FILM | DOCUMENTARY | CANADA
Allen Auksaq, director
National Film Board of Canada

The Tundra Book
FILM | DOCUMENTARY | RUSSIA
Aleksei Vakhrushev, director
High Latitudes

The Uluit – Champion of the North
TELEVISION SERIES | DOCUMENTARY |
CANADA
Ari A. Cohen, director
Arnait Video Productions

Throat Song
FILM | NARRATIVE | CANADA
Miranda de Pencier, director
Puhitaq, Northwood Productions

2011–
2019

Qanurli?
TELEVISION SERIES | NARRATIVE | CANADA
Qanukiaq Studios

Tamânevugut
TELEVISION SERIES | DOCUMENTARY | CANADA
OKâlaKatiget Society

2012   *A Step Towards the Arctic –
Reflections and Visions of the North*
FILM | DOCUMENTARY | CANADA
Anne-Marie Tougas, director
National Film Board of Canada

Bloodline
FILM | EXPERIMENTAL | CANADA
Lindsay McIntyre, director

Charlottes rejse til Grønland
FILM | DOCUMENTARY | DENMARK
Birgitte Kristensen, director
Aarhus Filmværksted

Her Silent Life
FILM | EXPERIMENTAL | CANADA
Lindsay McIntyre, director

*In the Shadow of the Kayaks –
The Political History of Greenland
1939–79*
FILM | DOCUMENTARY | KALAALLIT NUNAAT
Tupaarnaq Rosing Olsen, director

Inuk
FILM | NARRATIVE | KALAALLIT NUNAAT, FRANCE
Mike Magidson, director
Uummannaq Polar Institute

*Katinniq
Vanishing Point*
FILM | DOCUMENTARY | CANADA
Stephen A. Smith, Julia Szucs, directors
National Film Board of Canada

*Till We Meet Again – Moravian Music
in Labrador*
FILM | DOCUMENTARY | CANADA
Nigel Markham, director
Lazybank Productions

Timuti
FILM | DOCUMENTARY | CANADA
Jobie Weetaluktuk, director
National Film Board of Canada

Village at the End of the World
FILM | DOCUMENTARY | UK, DENMARK
David Katznelson, Sarah Gavron,
directors
Met Film Production, Made in
Copenhagen, Film4

Where She Stood in the First Place
FILM | EXPERIMENTAL | CANADA
Lindsay McIntyre, director

2013   *Aningaaq*
FILM | NARRATIVE | USA
Jonás Cuarón, director
Warner Brothers

bernard gaspé
FILM | EXPERIMENTAL | CANADA
Lindsay McIntyre, director

darg – construction
FILM | EXPERIMENTAL | CANADA
Lindsay McIntyre, director

Maïna
FILM | NARRATIVE | CANADA
Michel Poulette, director
Les Productions Nuit Blanche, Médiamax,
Productions Thalie

Nothing on Earth
FILM | DOCUMENTARY | AUSTRALIA
Michael Angus, director
Jerrycan Films

Oqarit Inuullutillu
The Ravens Storm
FILM | DOCUMENTARY | KALAALLIT NUNAAT
Pipaluk Jørgensen, director
Karitas Production

Sivummut – Going Forward
TELEVISION SERIES | DOCUMENTARY | CANADA
Arnait Video Productions

Stories from Our Land Vol. 2 –
Finding Home
FILM | DOCUMENTARY | CANADA
Nyla Innuksuk, director
National Film Board of Canada

Stories from Our Land Vol. 2 –
Strength, Flexibility, and Endurance
FILM | DOCUMENTARY | CANADA
Allen Auksaq, director
National Film Board of Canada

Stories from Our Land Vol. 2 –
Taking Shape
FILM | DOCUMENTARY | CANADA
Sarah McNair-Landry, director
National Film Board of Canada

Stories from Our Land Vol. 2 –
The Vending Machine
FILM | DOCUMENTARY | CANADA
Jessica Kotierk, director
National Film Board of Canada

The Legend of Sarila
FILM | NARRATIVE | CANADA
Nancy Florence Savard, director
10th Ave Productions, CarpeDiem Film & TV

The Wings of Johnny May
FILM | DOCUMENTARY | CANADA, FRANCE
Marc Fafard, director
National Film Board of Canada, K'ien Productions, Productions Thalie

Two Inuit Lives
FILM | DOCUMENTARY | FRANCE
Yves Maillard, director
K'ien Productions, ARTE France

SUMÉ – Mumisitsinerup Nipaa, 2014

Ukiuktaqtumi, 2016

Uvanga
FILM | NARRATIVE | CANADA
Marie-Hélène Cousineau, Madeline Ivalu, directors
Arnait Video Productions, Kunuk Cohn Productions

2014 *Attatama Nunanga*
My Father's Land
FILM | DOCUMENTARY | CANADA
Zacharias Kunuk, Norman Cohn, directors
Igloolik Isuma, Kingulliit Productions

Aviliaq – Entwined
FILM | NARRATIVE | CANADA
Alethea Arnaquq-Baril, director

Fish Plane, Heart Clock
FILM | EXPERIMENTAL | CANADA
Arvo Leo, director

Kajutaijuq – The Spirit That Comes
FILM | NARRATIVE | CANADA
Scott Brachmayer, director
North Creative

Kiawak Ashoona
FILM | DOCUMENTARY | CANADA
Koomuatuk Curley, director

Sol
FILM | DOCUMENTARY | CANADA
Marie-Hélène Cousineau, Susan Avingaq, directors
Arnait Video Productions

SUMÉ – Mumisitsinerup Nipaa
SUMÉ – The Sound of a Revolution
FILM | DOCUMENTARY | KALAALLIT NUNAAT
Inuk Silis Høegh, director
Ánorâk Film

The Big Lemming
FILM | NARRATIVE | CANADA
Mosha Folger, director

ThuleTuvalu
FILM | DOCUMENTARY | SWITZERLAND, TUVALU, KALAALLIT NUNAAT
Matthias von Gunten, director
HesseGreutert Film, Odysseefilm, Schweizer Radio und Fernsehen

Unnuap Taarnerpaaffiani
When the Darkness Comes
FILM | NARRATIVE | KALAALLIT NUNAAT
Malik Kleist, director
Tumit Productions

Where We Stand
FILM | EXPERIMENTAL | CANADA
Lindsay McIntyre, director

2015 *Chloe and Theo*
FILM | NARRATIVE | USA
Ezna Sands, director
Arctica Films

Elisapee Ishulutaq's Yesterday and Today
FILM | DOCUMENTARY | CANADA
Ivan Hughes, director
Winnipeg Art Gallery

Eskimo Diva
FILM | DOCUMENTARY | DENMARK
Lene Stæhr, director
Space Rocket Nation

Half & Half
FILM | DOCUMENTARY | DENMARK, KALAALLIT NUNAAT
Aka Hansen, director
Inuit Broadcasting Corporation

Ilinniq
TELEVISION SERIES | DOCUMENTARY | CANADA
Inuit Broadcasting Corporation

In the Backyarden
FILM | EXPERIMENTAL | CANADA
Lindsay McIntyre, director

Napagunnaqullusi – So That You Can Stand
FILM | DOCUMENTARY | CANADA
Ole Gjerstad, director
Pascal Blais Studios

Nowhere Land
FILM | DOCUMENTARY | CANADA
Rosie Bonnie Ammaaq, director
National Film Board of Canada

Of Ravens and Children
FILM | DOCUMENTARY | CANADA
Marie-Hélène Cousineau, director
Arnait Video Productions

of the North
FILM | EXPERIMENTAL | CANADA
Dominic Gagnon, director

Okpik's Dream
FILM | DOCUMENTARY | CANADA
Laura Rietveld, director
Catbird Films

Trash Heaven
FILM | EXPERIMENTAL | CANADA
Lindsay McIntyre, director

2016 *Angry Inuk*
FILM | DOCUMENTARY | CANADA
Alethea Arnaquq-Baril, director
Unikkaat Studios Inc, Eyesteel Film, National Film Board of Canada

Breaths
FILM | DOCUMENTARY | CANADA
Nyla Innuksuk, director
National Film Board of Canada

Call of the Ice
FILM | DOCUMENTARY | FRANCE, KALAALLIT NUNAAT
Mike Magidson, Xavier Liberman, directors
MFP Films, UPI Films, Planète+

Il carro, il carro arrugginito, e il mucchio di spazzatura
FILM | EXPERIMENTAL | CANADA
Lindsay McIntyre, director

Ilik
FILM | DOCUMENTARY | KALAALLIT NUNAAT
Ánorâk Film

Ilimanaq – oqaluttuarisaaneq siuarsaasoralugu
TELEVISION SERIES | DOCUMENTARY | KALAALLIT NUNAAT
Inuk Silis Høegh, director
Ánorâk Film

Iqaluit
FILM | NARRATIVE | CANADA
Benoît Pilon, director
Association Coopérative des Productions Audio-Visuelles

Filmography | 219

Journey to Greenland
FILM | NARRATIVE | FRANCE
Sébastien Betbeder, director
UFO, Envie de tempête Productions,
Bobi Lux

*Kablunât – Legend of the Origin
of the White People*
FILM | NARRATIVE | CANADA
Glenn Gear, director

Killormut
Upside Down
FILM | NARRATIVE | KALAALLIT NUNAAT
Ulannaq Ingemann, director

Living With Giants
FILM | DOCUMENTARY | CANADA
Aude Leroux-Lévesques, Sébastien Rist,
directors
MC2 Communication Média

Maliglutit
Searchers
FILM | NARRATIVE | CANADA
Zacharias Kunuk, Natar Ungalaaq,
directors
Kinguliit Productions

Polar Sun
FILM | NARRATIVE | USA
Katie Doane Avery, director

They Called Her Sam
FILM | DOCUMENTARY | CANADA
Mosha Folger, director

Trapped in a Human Zoo
FILM | DOCUMENTARY | CANADA
Guilhem Rondot, director
National Film Board of Canada

Tuktuq
FILM | NARRATIVE | CANADA
Robin Aubert, director
Lynx Films, PRIM Centre D'arts
Médiatiques, Post-Moderne

Two Lovers and a Bear
FILM | NARRATIVE | CANADA
Kim Nguyen, director

Two Soft Things, Two Hard Things
FILM | DOCUMENTARY | CANADA
Mark Kenneth Woods, Michael Yerxa,
directors
MKW Productions

Ujarangniqtiuvalauqtut
Beneath the Surface
FILM | DOCUMENTARY | CANADA
Frank Tester, director

Ukiuktaqtumi
FILM | DOCUMENTARY | CANADA
Stephen Agluvak Puskas, director

Uninnak – Sungiussiartuaarit
FILM | DOCUMENTARY | KALAALLIT NUNAAT
Emile Hertling Péronard, director
Ánorâk Film

Upinnaqusittik
Lucky
FILM | EXPERIMENTAL | CANADA
asinnajaq, director

2017 *Handmade Film*
FILM | EXPERIMENTAL | CANADA
Lindsay McIntyre, director

Old Films of the New Tale
FILM | EXPERIMENTAL | KALAALLIT NUNAAT
Inuuteq Storch, director

Polar
TELEVISION SERIES | NARRATIVE | KALAALLIT
NUNAAT

Shaman
FILM | NARRATIVE | CANADA
Echo Henoche, director
National Film Board of Canada

The Last Walk
FILM | NARRATIVE | CANADA, KALAALLIT
NUNAAT, USA
Arctic Film Circle

There Is a House Here
FILM | DOCUMENTARY | CANADA
Alan Zweig, director
Primitive Entertainment

Three Thousand
FILM | EXPERIMENTAL | CANADA
asinnajaq, director
National Film Board of Canada

2018 *Akornatsinniitut – Tarratta Nunaanni*
Among Us – In the Land of Our Shadows
FILM | NARRATIVE | KALAALLIT NUNAAT
Marc Fussing Rosbach, director

Anori
FILM | NARRATIVE | KALAALLIT NUNAAT
Pipaluk Jørgensen, director
Karitas Production

Iglu – Angirraq
House – Home
FILM | DOCUMENTARY | CANADA
Mosha Folger, director
Folger Tulugaq Productions

Katatjatuuk Kangirsumi
Throat Singing in Kangirsuk
FILM | DOCUMENTARY | CANADA
Eva Kaukai, Manon Chamberland, directors
Wapikoni Mobile

Kivitoo – What They Thought of Us
FILM | DOCUMENTARY | CANADA
Zacharias Kunuk, director
Igloolik Isuma

Light Moving in Time
FILM | EXPERIMENTAL | CANADA
Lindsay McIntyre, director

Lykkelænder
The Raven and the Seagull
FILM | DOCUMENTARY | DENMARK
Lasse Lau, director
Kran Film Collective, Tambo Film

Nutsigassat
Translations
FILM | EXPERIMENTAL | KALAALLIT NUNAAT,
CANADA, DENMARK
Tinne Zinner, director

The Book of the Sea
FILM | DOCUMENTARY | RUSSIA
Aleksei Vakhrushev, director
High Latitudes

Three Thousand, 2017

Filmography | 221

The Fifth Region
FILM | DOCUMENTARY | CANADA
Aeyliya Husain, Gabriel Nuraki Koperqualuk, directors

The Grizzlies
FILM | NARRATIVE | CANADA
Miranda de Pencier, director
Mongrel Media

Tia and Piujuq
FILM | NARRATIVE | CANADA
Lucy Tulugarjuk, director
Arnait Video Productions

Une année polaire
A Polar Year
FILM | DOCUMENTARY | FRANCE
Samuel Collardey, director
Geko Films, France 3 Cinéma

2019 *Gently, Jennifer*
FILM | NARRATIVE | USA
Katie Doane Avery, director

Nanurluk
Giant Bear
FILM | NARRATIVE | CANADA
Neil Christopher, Daniel Gies, directors
E→D Films, Taqqut Productions

One Day in the Life of Noah Piugattuk
FILM | NARRATIVE | CANADA
Zacharias Kunuk, director
Igloolik Isuma

Restless River
FILM | NARRATIVE | CANADA
Marie-Hélène Cousineau, Madeline Ivalu, directors
Arnait Video Productions

Winter's Yearning
FILM | DOCUMENTARY | NORWAY, DENMARK, KALAALLIT NUNAAT
Sidse Torstholm Larsen, Sturla Pilskog, directors
Blåst Film, Bullitt Film, Ánorâk Film

Winter's Yearning, 2019

222 | Inuit TakugatsaliuKatiget / On Inuit Cinema

2020 *Kajanaqtuq*
FILM | EXPERIMENTAL | CANADA
Ella Morton, director

The Fight for Greenland
FILM | DOCUMENTARY | KALAALLIT NUNAAT, DENMARK, NORWAY
Kenneth Sorento, director
Copenhagen Film Company Short & Doc

2021 *Alanngut Killinganni*
FILM | NARRATIVE | KALAALLIT NUNAAT
Malik Kleist, director
PaniNoir Films

Angakusajaujuq – The Shaman's Apprentice
FILM | NARRATIVE | CANADA
Zacharias Kunuk, director
Taqqut Productions, Kingulliit Productions

Evan's Drum
FILM | DOCUMENTARY | CANADA
Ossie Michelin, director
National Film Board of Canada

Nalujuk Night
FILM | DOCUMENTARY | CANADA
Jennie Williams, director
National Film Board of Canada

Tuulik
FILM | NARRATIVE | KALAALLIT NUNAAT
Berda Larsen, director
Ánorâk Film

2022 *Arctic Song*
FILM | NARRATIVE | CANADA
Germaine Arnattaujuq (Arnaktauyok), Neil Christopher, Louise Flaherty, directors
National Film Board of Canada, Taqqut Productions

Slash/Back
FILM | NARRATIVE | CANADA
Nyla Innuksuk, director
Good Question Media, Mixtape VR, Red Marrow Media, Scythia Films, Stellar Citizens

Nalujuk Night, 2021

Filmography | 223

Image Credits

Esquimaux Game of Snap-the-Whip, fame enlargement, 1901. Library of Congress control number 00694349 | p. 184

Grønland 1914 I-III, 1914 | p. 185

Heritage of Adventure, frame enlargement, 1920. Hudson's Bay Company Archives, Archives of Manitoba, F122 | p. 186

Nanook of the North, frame enlargement, 1922 | p. 189

Palos Brudefærd, frame enlargement, 1934 | p. 190

Patrol to the North West Passage, frame enlargement, 1937. Reproduced by permission from Library and Archives Canada, ISN 5670. © Estate of Richard S. Finnie | p. 191

Les hommes du phoque, frame enlargement. Samivel, 1948. © Cinematheque de Bretagne / Expéditions Polaires Françaises | p. 193

How to Build an Igloo, frame enlargement, 1949. © National Film Board of Canada | p. 194

Qivitoq, frame enlargement, 1956. © Nordisk Film Production A/S | p. 197

The Living Stone, frame enlargement, 1958. © National Film Board of Canada | p. 198

The Annanacks, frame enlargement, 1964. © Crawley Films | p. 201

Netsilik Eskimo: Fishing at the Stone Weir, Part 1, frame enlargement, 1967. Quentin Brown, director. Image courtesy of Documentary Educational Resources | p. 202

Owl and the Raven – An Eskimo Legend, frame enlargement, 1973. © National Film Board of Canada | p. 203

Natsik Hunting, frame enlargement, 1975. © National Film Board of Canada | p. 204

Labradorimiut, "Nunaksiamut," frame enlargement, 1983. © OKâlaKatiget Society | p. 206

Uksuum Cauyai – Drums of Winter, frame enlargement, 1988. Sarah Elder, Leonard Kamerling, directors. Image courtesy of Documentary Educational Resources | p. 207

Qulliq, frame enlargement, 1993. © Arnait Video Productions | p. 209

Nunavut – Our Land, "Quviasukvik," frame enlargement, 1995. © Isuma | p. 210

Atanarjuat – The Fast Runner, frame enlargement, 2001. © Isuma | p. 213

Before Tomorrow, frame enlargement, 2008. © Isuma | p. 214

SUMÉ – Mumisitsinerup Nipaa, frame enlargement, 2014. © Ánorâk Film | p. 217

Ukiuktaqtumi, frame enlargement, 2016. Reproduced by permission of Stephen Agluvak Puskas, Alethea Arnaquq-Baril, and Pudloo Arnaquq| p. 218

Three Thousand, frame enlargement, 2017. © National Film Board of Canada | p. 221

Winter's Yearning, frame enlargement, 2019. © Blåst Film and Ánorâk Film | p. 222

Nalujuk Night, frame enlargement, 2021. © National Film Board of Canada | p. 223

Bibliography

"About," Greenland Eyes Film Festival. http://greenlandeyes.com/about/.

"About Us." Inuit Art Foundation. https://www.inuitartfoundation.org/about.

Alexander, Cynthia J., Agar Adamson, Graham R. Daborn, John Huston, and Victor Tootoo. "Inuit Cyberspace: The Struggle for Access for Inuit Qaujimajatuqangit." *Journal of Canadian Studies* 43, no. 2 (2009): 220–49. https://doi.org/10.3138/jcs.43.2.220.

"Approval of Inuktut Resolution," Inuit Tapiriit Kanatami. Last updated April 7, 2016, https://www.itk.ca/wp-content/uploads/2019/08/B16-04-03-Approval-of-Inuktut-Resolution.pdf.

"Arctic Indigenous Film Fund Announced." Canadian Media Fund. Last modified March 8, 2018, https://cmf-fmc.ca/news/arctic-indigenous-film-fund-announced/.

Arnait Video Productions. *Ikuma, carnet de tournage.* Montréal: Mémoire d'encrier, 2008.

"Arnait Video Productions: Voicing A Unique Canadian View." Arnait Video Productions. http://www.arnaitvideo.ca/about-us.html.

Arnaquq-Baril, Alethea Aggiuq. "Filmmaking and Media." *Canadian Geographic Indigenous Peoples Atlas of Canada.* Last modified June 14, 2018, https://indigenouspeoplesatlasofcanada.ca/article/inuit-film-and-broadcasting/.

Athens, Allison K. "Saviors, 'Sealfies,' and Seals: Strategies for Self-Representation in Contemporary Inuit Films." *Ecozon@* 5, no. 2 (2014): 41–56.

Atkin, Ian, ed. *Encyclopedia of the Documentary Film.* New York: Routledge, 2006.

"Basic Information About the Arctic." University of Lapland Arctic Centre. https://www.arcticcentre.org/EN/arcticregion.

Berger, Sally. "Time Travellers." *Inuit Art Quarterly* 11, no. 2 (1996): 4–11.

Bertrand, Karine. "Le Collectif Arnait Video Productions et le cinéma engagé des femmes inuits: Guérison communautaire et mémoire Culturelle." *Canadian Review of Comparative Literature/Revue Canadienne de Littérature Comparée* 44, no. 1 (2018): 36–53. https://doi.org/10.1353/crc.2017.0002.

———. "Cinéma inuit et post-colonialisme: la revendication de la parole des femmes dans le film Le jour avant le lendemain (2008) de Marie-Hélène Cousineau et Madeleine Ivalu." *Studies French Cinema* 13, no. 3 (2014): 197–213. https://doi.org/10.1386/sfc.13.3.197_1.

Burelle, Julie. "Inuit Visual and Sensate Sovereignty in Alethea Arnaquq-Baril's *Angry Inuk*." *Canadian Journal of Film Studies* 29, no. 1 (2020): 145–62.

Caron, Andre H. "First-Time Exposure to Television: Effects on Inuit Children's Cultural Images." *Communication Research* 6, no. 2 (1979): 135–54. https://doi.org/10.1177/009365027900600202.

Carry, Catherine L., Kath Clarida, Denise Rideout, Dianne Kinnon, and Rhonda M. Johnson. "Perspective: *Qanuqtuurniq – Finding the Balance;* An IPY Television Series Using Community Engagement." *Polar Research* 30, no. 1 (2011): 1–10. https://doi.org/10.3402/polar.v30i0.11514.

Chisholm, Dianne. "The Enduring Afterlife of *Before Tomorrow*: Inuit Survivance and the Spectral Cinema of Arnait Video Productions." *Études Inuit Studies* 40, no. 1 (2016): 211–27.: https://doi.org/10.7202/1040152ar.

"A Circumpolar Inuit Declaration on Sovereignty in the Arctic." Inuit Circumpolar Council. April 2009. https://iccalaska.org/wp-icc/wp-content/uploads/2016/01/Signed-Inuit-Sovereignty-Declaration-11x17.pdf.

Coelho, Kareena. "New Uses of 'Old' Media: Exploring Technologies-in-Use in Nunavut." *Canadian Journal of Communication* 43, no. 4 (2018): 507–24. https://doi.org/10.22230/cjc.2018v43n4a3222.

Cohn, Norman, and Zacharias Kunuk. "Our Baffinland: Digital Indigenous Democracy." *Northern Public Affairs* Spring (2012): 50–52.

Coldevin, Gary O., and Thomas C. Wilson, "Effects of a Decade of Satellite Television in the Canadian Arctic: Euro-Canadian and Inuit Adolescents Compared." *Journal of Cross-Cultural Psychology* 16, no. 3 (1985): 329–54. https://doi.org/10.1177/0022002185016003005.

Coldevin, Gary O., and Thomas C. Wilson. "Education, Télévision par Satellite et Impuissance Apprise chez des Adolescents Inuit du Canada." *Études Inuit Studies* 6, no. 1 (1982): 29–37.

Cook, Sarah. "Filming the 'Northern Front': The Motion Pictures of the Canadian Arctic Expedition." *Northern Review* 44 (2017): 427–55. https://doi.org/10.22584/nr44.2017.019.

Cornellier, Bruno. "Extracting Inuit: The *of the North* Controversy and the White Possessive." *American Indian Culture and Research Journal* 40, no. 4 (2016): 23–48.

Cranston, Paul. "Inuit Television Broadcasting: Cultural Identity and Expression in a New Medium." Master's thesis, McGill University, 1985.

Dorais, Louis-Jacques. *The Language of the Inuit: Syntax, Semantics, and Society in the Arctic*. Montreal: McGill-Queen's University Press, 2010.

Elder, Sarah. "Collaborative Filmmaking: An Open Space for Making Meaning, A Moral Ground for Ethnographic Film." *Visual Anthropology Review* 11, no. 2 (1995): 94–101. https://doi.org/10.1525/var.1995.11.2.94.

Evans, Michael Robert. *Isuma: Inuit Video Art*. Montreal: McGill-Queens University Press, 2008.

———. "Frozen Light and Fluid Time: The Folklore, Politics, and Performance of Inuit Video." PhD diss., Indiana University, 1999.

Feest, Christian F., ed., *Indians in Europe: An Interdisciplinary Collection of Essays*. Lincoln: Nebraska University Press, 1989.

Fienup-Riordan. *Freeze Frame: Alaska Eskimos in the Movies*. Seattle: University of Washington Press, 1995.

"Film, Television and Digital Media Development Contribution Policy." Government of Nunavut, Department of Economic Development and Transportation, April 1, 2017.

Fleming, Kathleen. "Igloolik Video: An Organic Response from a Culturally Sound Community." *Inuit Art Quarterly* 11, no. 1 (1996): 26–34.

———. "Marie-Hélène Cousineau: Videomaker." *Inuit Art Quarterly* 11, no. 2 (1996): 12–20.

———. "Mary Kunuk: From Printmaking to Computer-Animated Video." *Inuit Art Quarterly* 11, no. 1 (1996): 36–41.

Fox, Matthew. "Women Helping Each Other." *Inuit Art Quarterly* 13, no. 1 (1998): 6–17.

Freuchen, Peter. *Der Eskimo: ein Roman von der Hudson-Bai*. Berlin: Safari-Verlag, 1928.

———. *Die Flucht ins weiße: Land Ein Eskimo-Roman*. Berlin: Safari-Verlag, 1929.

Gagnon, Olivia Michiko. "Singing With Nanook of the North: On Tanya Tagaq, Feeling Entangled, and Colonial Archives of Indigeneity." *ASAP Journal* 5, no. 1 (2020): 45–78. https://doi.org/10.1353/asa.2020.0002.

Gauthier, Jennifer L. "Speaking Back with Similar Voices: The Dialogic Cinema of Zacharias Kunuk and Pierre Perrault." *Quarterly Review of Film and Video* 27, no. 2 (2010): 108–20. https://doi.org/10.1080/10509200802241456.

Geller, Peter. *Northern Exposures: Photographing and Filming the Canadian North, 1920–45*. Vancouver: UBC Press, 2005.

Ginsburg, Faye. "*Atanarjuat* Off-Screen: From 'Media Reservations' to the World Stage." *American Anthropologist* 105, no. 4 (2003): 827–31.

Graburn, Nelson H.H. "Television and the Canadian Inuit." *Études Inuit Studies* 6, no. 1 (1982): 7–17.

Grace, Sherrill. "Exploration as Construction: Robert Flaherty and *Nanook of the North.*" *Essays on Canadian Writing* 59 (Fall 1996): 123–46.

Griffiths, Allison. *Wondrous Difference: Cinema, Anthropology and Turn-of-the-Century Visual Culture.* New York: Columbia University Press, 2002.

Gunderson, Sonia. "Arnait Video Productions: Women Telling Their Own Stories." *Inuit Art Quarterly* 24, no. 2 (2009): 10–13.

———. "Zacharias Kunuk: Giving Inuit a Voice." *Inuit Art Quarterly* 21, no. 1 (2006): 12–20.

Harley Eber, Dorothy. "A Winter of Memories: Recollections." *Inuit Art Quarterly* 15, no. 3 (2000): 20–27.

Harper, Kenn. "Silent Movie Actor Perishes in Labrador Spanish Flu Epidemic." *Nunatsiaq News.* Last modified May 15, 2020. https://nunatsiaq.com/stories/article/taissumani-may-15/.

———. "Nancy Columbia: Inuit Star of Stage, Screen and Camera." *Above & Beyond – Canada's Arctic Journal.* Last modified July 3, 2014. http://arcticjournal.ca/featured/nancy-columbia-   inuit-star-of-stage-screen-and-camera/.

Harper, Kenn, and Russell Potter. "Early Arctic Films of Nancy Columbia and Esther Eneutseak," *Nimrod: The Journal of the Ernest Shackleton Autumn School* Vol. 4 (2010): 48–105.

Hart, Kylo-Patrick R., ed. *Arctic Cinemas: Essays on Polar Spaces and the Popular Imagination.* Jefferson, NC: McFarland, 2021.

Hearne, Joanna. "'Who We Are Now': Iñupiaq Youth On the Ice." *MediaTropes* 7, no. 1 (2017): 185–202.

Hjort, Mette, and Duncan J. Petrie. *The Cinema of Small Nations.* Edinburgh: Edinburgh University Press, 2007.

"Home to the Vibrant Film Community in Greenland," FILM-GL. https://film.gl.

Huhndorf, Shari. "*Atanarjuat, The Fast Runner*: Culture, History, and Politics in Inuit Media." *American Anthropologist* 105, no. 4 (2003): 822–26. https://doi.org/10.1525/aa.2003.105.4.822.

Igloliorte, Heather. "Tilllutarniit: History, Land, and Resilience in Inuit Film and Video." *PUBLIC* 27, no. 54 (2016): 104–9. https://doi.org/10.1386/public.27.54.104_7. *Inuit Art Quarterly: Film* 32, no. 2 (2019).

Inuit Tapiriit Kanatami. "ITK Releases Inuit Nunangat Chapter of Arctic and Northern Policy Framework." Last modified September 10, 2019, https://www.itk.ca/itk-releases-inuit-nunangat-chapter-of-arctic-and-northern-policy-framework/.

———. "ITK Board of Directors Adopts Inuktut Qaliujaaqpait as Unified Orthography for Inuktut." Last updated September 26, 2019, https://www.itk.ca/itk-board-of-directors-adopts-inuktut-qaliujaaqpait-as-unified-orthography-for-inuktut/.

———. "Approval of Inuktut Resolution," Last modified April 7, 2016, https://www.itk.ca/wp-content/uploads/2019/08/B16-04-03-Approval-of-Inuktut-Resolution.pdf.

The Inuit Way: A Guide to Inuit Culture. 2nd ed. Ottawa, ON: Pauktuutit Inuit Women of Canada, 2006.

"ITK Releases Inuit Nunangat Chapter of Arctic and Northern Policy Framework." Inuit Tapiriit Kanatami, last modified September 10, 2019. https://www.itk.ca/itk-releases-inuit-nunangat-chapter-of-arctic-and-northern-policy-framework/.

Iversen, Gunnar. "Roos, Jørgen." *Encyclopedia of the Documentary Film*, edited by Ian Atkin, 1144–45. New York: Routledge, 2006.

Jasen, Sylvie. "The Archive and Reenactment: Performing Knowledge in the Making of *The Journals of Knud Rasmussen*." *The Velvet Light Trap* 71, no. 1, (2013): 3–14. https://doi.org/10.7560/VLT7102.

Johnson, Rhonda, Robin Morales, Doreen Leavitt, Catherine Carry, Dianne Kinnon, Denise Rideout, and Kath Clarida. "Pan-Arctic TV Series on Inuit Wellness: A Northern Model of Communication for Social Change?" *International Journal of Circumpolar Health* 70, no. 3 (2011): 236–44. https://doi.org/10.3402/ijch.v70i3.17827.

Kaganovsky, Lilya, Scott MacKenzie, and Anna Westerståhl Stenport, eds. *Arctic Cinemas and the Documentary Ethos*. Bloomington: Indiana University Press, 2019.

Kamboureli, Smaro. "Opera in the Arctic: Knud Rasmussen, Inside and Outside Modernity." *IdeAs* 11 (Spring/Summer 2018): 1–20. https://doi.org/10.4000/ideas.2553.

Kennedy, Timothy. *Where the Rivers Meet the Sky: A Collaborative Approach to Participatory Development*. Penang, Malaysia: Southbound, 2008.

Kilbourn, Russell J.A. "The '*Fast Runner*' Trilogy – Inuit Cultural Memory, and Knowledge." *Zeitschrift für Anglistik und Amerikanistik* 68, no. 2 (2020): 191–208. https://doi.org/10.1515/zaa-2020-0019.

———. "If This Is Your Land, Where Is Your Camera?: *Atanarjuat*, *The Journals of Knud Rasmussen* and Post-Cinematic Adaptation." *Journal of Adaptation in Film and Performance* 7, no. 2 (2014): 195–207. https://doi.org/10.1386/jafp.7.2.195_1.

———. "'When I Swallow His Heart and Lungs, Jesus Is Pleased': The Transmediation of Sacrifice in *The Journals of Knud Rasmussen*." *Angelaki* 19, no. 4 (2014): 95–110. https://doi.org/10.1080/0969725X.2014.984445.

Knopf, Kerstin. "*Atanarjuat*: Fast Running and Electronic Storytelling in the Arctic." In *Transcultural English Studies: Theories, Fictions, Realities*, edited by Frank Schulze-Engler and Sissy Helff, 201–20. Amsterdam: Rodopi, 2008.

Kunnuk, Simeonie. "Natar Ungalaq Talks About His Art and His Goals." *Inuit Art Quarterly* 8, no. 3 (1993): 16–23.

Kunuk, Zacharias, and Bernard Saladin d'Anglure. *Au pays des Inuit un film, un peuple, une légende: conçu à partir du film Atanarjuat, la légende de l'homme rapide*. Montpellier: Indigène, 2002.

Larsson, Mariah, and Anna Westerståhl Stenport. "Documentary Filmmaking as Colonialist Propaganda and Cinefeminist Intervention: Mai Zettterling's *Of Seals and Men* (1979)." *Film History: An International Journal* 27, no. 4 (2015): 106–29. https://doi.org/10.2979/filmhistory.27.4.106.

Laugrand, Frédéric, and Galo Luna-Penna. "IsumaTV, la Babel du Grand Nord: Religions, images autochtones et médias électroniques." *Recherches amérindiennes au Québec* 43, no. 2–3 (2013): 31–47. https://doi.org/10.7202/1026105ar.

MacKenzie, Scott, and Anna Westerståhl Stenport. "An Alternative History of the Arctic: The Origins of Ethnographic Filmmaking, the Fifth Thule Expedition, and Indigenous Cinema." *Visual Anthropology Review* 36, no. 1 (2020): 137–62. https://doi.org/10.1111/var.12195.

———. "Arnait Video Productions: Inuit Women's Collective Filmmaking, Coalitional Politics, and a Globalized Arctic." *Camera Obscura* 31, no. 3 (2016): 153–63. https://doi.org/10.1215/02705346-3662066.

———. *Films on Ice: Cinemas of the Arctic*. Edinburgh: Edinburgh University Press, 2015.

MacRae, Ian J., and Samantha MacKinnon. "The Sense of a Better Ending: Legal Pluralism and Performative Jurisprudence in *Atanarjuat – The Fast Runner*." *Journal of Canadian Studies/Revue d'études canadiennes* 51, no. 3 (2017): 547–70. https://doi.org/10.3138/jcs.2016-0005.r1.

"Maps of Inuit Nunangat (Inuit Regions of Canada)." Last updated June 10, 2009, https://www.itk.ca/maps-of-inuit-nunangat/.

Marchessault, Janine, and Will Straw, eds. *The Oxford Handbook of Canadian Cinema*. Oxford: Oxford University Press, 2019.

Marcus, Alan. "*Nanook of the North* as Primal Drama." *Visual Anthropology* 19, no. 3–4 (2006): 201–22. https://doi.org/10.1080/08949460600656543.

Marks, Laura U. *The Skin of the Film: Intercultural Cinema, Embodiment, and the Senses*. Durham, NC: Duke University Press, 2000.

———. "Reconfigured Nationhood: A Partisan History of the Inuit Broadcasting Corporation." *Afterimage* 21, no. 8 (1994): 4–8.

———. "Inuit Auteurs and Arctic Airwaves: Questions of Southern Reception." *Fuse* 22, no. 1 (1998): 13–17.

McCall, Sophie. "I Can Only Sing This Song to Someone Who Understands It: Community Filmmaking and the Politics of Partial Translation in *Atanarjuat – The Fast Runner*." *Essays on Canadian Writing* 83 (2004): 19–46.

Miller, Cynthia. "Ethnographic Documentary Filmmakers Sarah Elder and Leonard Kamerling: An Interview." *Post Script: Essays in Film and the Humanities* 27, no. 1 (2007): 90–109.

Mitchell, Marybelle. "Inuit Art Is Inuit Art (Part 2)" *Inuit Art Quarterly* 12, no. 2 (1997): 4–15.

Morton, Erin, and Taryn Sirove. "Structuring Knowledges: Caching Inuit Architecture Through Igloolik Isuma Productions." *Post Script: Essays in Film and the Humanities* 29, no. 3 (2010): 58–136.

"Mosha Michael." National Film Board of Canada. https://www.nfb.ca/directors/mosha-michael/.

"New Artists, New Media, New Techniques." *Inuit Art Quarterly* 26, no. 1 (2011): 19–23.

Morgan, Lael. *Eskimo Star: From the Tundra to Tinseltown; The Ray Mala Story*. Kenmore, WA: Epicenter Press, 2011.

Nørrested, Carl. *Grønlandsfilm: Blandt eskimoer, eventyrer kolonisatorer og etnografer | Greenland on Film: Amongst Eskimos, Adventurers, Colonisers and Ethnographers*. Copenhagen: North, 2011.

Olson, Michael, and Henry Kudluk. "*Atanarjuat –The Fast Runner:* Impressions of the Film from Inuit Artists." *Inuit Art Quarterly* 17, no. 3 (2002): 36–39.

Owlijoot, Pelagie. *Guidelines for Working with Inuit Elders: Maligaksait Piliriqatiqangnirmik Inuit Innanginnik*. Iqaluit: Nunavut Arctic College, 2008.

Perrot, Michel. "La radio et la télévision dans les sociétés inuit: Groenland, Canada, Alaska et Tchoukotka." *Études Inuit Studies* 16, no. 1–2 (1992): 257–89.

Petrasek MacDonald, Joanna, James Ford, Ashlee Cunsolo Willox, Claudia Mitchell, Konek Productions, My Word Storytelling and Digital Media Lab, and Rigolet Inuit Community Government. "Youth-Led Participatory Video as a Strategy to Enhance Inuit Youth Adaptive Capacities for Dealing with Climate Change." *Arctic* 68, no. 4 (2015): 486–99.

Raheja, Michelle H. "Reading Nanook's Smile: Visual Sovereignty, Indigenous Revisions of Ethnography, and *Atanarjuat (The Fast Runner)*." *American Quarterly* 59, no. 4, (2007): 1159–85.

Rothfels, Nigel. *Savages and Beasts: The Birth of the Modern Zoo*. Baltimore: Johns Hopkins University Press, 2002.

Rosing, Peter Frederick, and Marianne Stenbaek. *Radiormiut: Kalaallit Nunaata Radioa, Grønlands Radio, Radio Greenland, 1958–1998*. Nuuk, Greenland: Atuakkiorfik, 1999.

Roth, Lorna. *Something New in the Air: The Story of First Peoples Broadcasting in Canada*. Montreal: McGill-Queen's University Press, 2005.

Sanader, Daniella. "Soft Shapes and Hard Mattresses: Sex and Desire in Contemporary Inuit Graphic Art and Film." *Inuit Art Quarterly* 31, no. 2 (2018): 40–47.

Santo, Avi. "Act Locally, Sell Globally: Inuit Media and the Global Cultural Economy." *Continuum: Journal of Media & Cultural Studies* 22, no. 3 (2008): 327–40.

———. "Nunavut: Inuit Television and Cultural Citizenship." *International Journal of Cultural Studies* 7, no. 4 (2004): 379–97.

"Sharing Power." *Inuit Art Quarterly* 26, no. 1 (2011): 27–31.

Siebert, Monika. "*Atanarjuat* and the Ideological Work of Contemporary Indigenous Filmmaking." *Public Culture* 18, no. 3 (2006): 531–50.

Silis Høegh, Inuk, Asmund Havsteen-Mikkelsen, and Nordatlantens Brygge. *Melting Barricades*. Copenhagen: Nordatlantens Brygge, 2004.

Simma, Åsa (Sámi), and Darlene Johnson (Dunghutti). "Declaration of Indigenous Cinema." Māoriland. https://maorilandfilm.co.nz/declaration-indigenous-cinema/.

Smith, Linda Tuhiwai. *Decolonizing Methodologies: Research and Indigenous Peoples*. 2nd ed. London: Zed Books, 2012.

Sperschneider, Werner. "Landet bag isen: Grønland i 1920'erne og 30'ernes kulturfilm." *Kosmorama* 232 (2003): 113–24.

Stewart, Michelle. "Of Digital Selves and Digital Sovereignty: *of the North*." *Film Quarterly* 70, no. 4 (2017): 23–38. https://doi.org/10.1525/fq.2017.70.4.23.

St-Pierre, Marc. "The NFB Inuit Film Collection." National Film Board of Canada. Last modified August 15, 2017, http://onf-nfb.gc.ca/en/unikkausivut-sharing-our-stories/the-nfb-inuit-film-collection/#_ftn2.

Thornley, Davinia. "'An Instrument of Actual Change in the World': Engaging a New Collaborative Criticism Through Isuma/Arnait Productions' Film *Before Tomorrow*." In *Cinema, Cross-Cultural Collaboration, and Criticism: Filming on an Uneven Field*. London: Palgrave Pivot, 2014. 23–50.

Timar, Andrew. "Contesting Tradition: Inuk Vocalist Taya Tagaq." *Inuit Art Quarterly* 27, no. 3 (2014): 32–38.

Tompkins, Ann. "Dealer's Choice: Mosha Michael." *Inuit Art Quarterly* 15, no. 1 (2000): 38–40.

Turner, Mark David. "Nunatsiavut's Cinema." *Newfoundland Quarterly* 109, no. 1 (2016): 22–25.

———. "A Revolution (Briefly) Embodied." *Luma* 1, no. 2 (2015).

Varga, Darrell. "Claiming Space, Time and History in *The Journals of Knud Rasmussen*." In *Storytelling in World Cinemas, Volume 2: Contexts*, edited by Lina Khatib, 172–82. New York Chichester, West Sussex: Columbia University Press, 2013. https://doi.org/10.7312/khat16336-015.

Wachowich, Nancy. "With or Without the Camera Running: The Work of Inuit Film-Making." *The Journal of the Royal Anthropological Institute* 26, no. 1 (2020): 105–25. https://doi.org/10.1111/1467-9655.13181.

Webb Jekanowski, Rachel. "From Labrador to Leipzig: Film and Infrastructures Along the Fur Trail." *Canadian Journal of Communication* 46, no. 2 (2021): 291–314. https://doi.org/10.22230/cjc.2021v46n2a3809.

White, Jerry. *The Radio Eye: Cinema in the North Atlantic, 1958–1988*. Waterloo ON: Wilfrid Laurier University Press, 2009.

———. "Frozen but Always in Motion: Arctic Film, Video, and Broadcast." *Velvet Light Trap* 55, no. 1 (2005): 52–64. https://doi.org/10.1353/vlt.2005.0010.

Wilkinson, Douglas. *Land of the Long Day*. Toronto: Clarke, Irwin, 1955.

Williams, Lisa A. "Media, Identity, and International Relations: The Arctic and Inuit in Film and Canada's Arctic Foreign Policy." PhD diss., York University, 2012.

Winifield Norman, David. "Inuk Silis Høegh: Kalaaleq Filmmaker and Interdisciplinary Artist." *First American Art Magazine* 7 (Summer 2015), 62–67.

Winton, Ezra. "Curating the North: Documentary Screening Ethics and Inuit Representation in (Festival) Cinema," originally published on ArtThreat.net on December 17, 2015. http://ezrawinton.com/2015/12/22/curating-the-north-documentary-screening-ethics-and-inuit-representation-in-festival-cinema/.

"Zacharias Kunuk: Video Maker and Inuit Historian." *Inuit Art Quarterly* 6, no. 3 (1991): 24–28.

Zwick, Jim. *Inuit Entertainers in the United States: From the Chicago World's Fair Through the Birth of Hollywood*. West Conshohocken, PA: Infinity, 2006.

Index

This index is intended to help readers quickly find people, places, organizations, and basic concepts that are mentioned in the text. It was developed for English readers but, as in the body of the text, it preferences place names and titles in Inuit languages. Two examples: the entry on Greenland refers readers to Kalaallit Nunaat and *Healing Each Other*, the English language title for Fran Williams's 1999 film, will direct readers to *Saputjinik*.

Abel, Sarah, ix, xi, 6, 9, 152–165, 208
Aboriginal Peoples Television Network, 139, 140, 145, 155, 158, 160, 162, 175
Academy Awards, 173
acting, 47–55, 97
Adlon, Percy, 201
Aidt, Lene, 196
Akkitirq, Atuat, 43, 176
Akornatsinniitut – Tarratta Nunaanni (Among Us – In the Land of Our Shadows, 117, 221
Alaska, xiii, 9, 10, 122, 127, 170, 171, 172, 173, 174, 177
Alaska Native Heritage Film Project, 174, 177, 195, 196, 197, 200
Alaska-Siberia Expedition, The, 170
Alaskan Eskimo, The, 173
Alaskan-Siberian Motion Pictures, 170, 185
Alexandrovitsch, Annelise, 198
Algar, James, 173, 192
Allakariallak, 171
amauti, 33, 87, 90, 93

American Education Development Center, 173
American Mutoscope & Biograph Company, 170, 184
Ammaaq, Rosie Bonnie, 219
An Esquimaux Game, 170
Andersen, James Robert (Uncle Jim Andersen), 172, 205, 212, 214
Andersen, Lotte, 215
Angilirq, Paul Apak, 49, 176, 1994
Angimajuka Tinnagu – Notitausimanningi Inuit Labrador Tagganimiut (Without Consent – The Resettlement of Inuit of Northern Labrador), 144
Angotee – Story of an Eskimo Boy, 59, 172
Angry Inuk, 104
Angus, Michael, 217
Anik B satellite, 175
animation, 8, 27, 31, 90, 91, 96, 173, 177
Ánorâk Films, 178, 208, 209, 211, 212, 218, 219, 220, 222, 223
Antitube, 73

Aputik, Simon, 170
APTN. *See* Aboriginal Peoples Television Network
archives, 8, 90, 96–98, 100–102, 129–130
Archy, 179
Arctic, 9–11, 19, 33, 62, 102, 139, 149, 170, 172, 179
Arctic Hunters, 172
Arctic Indigenous Film Fund, 179
Arctic Saga, 172
Arke, Pia, 203
Arnait Video Productions, x, xiv, 6, 7 14–57, 66, 68, 176, 177, 201, 202, 203, 205, 208, 212, 214, 215, 216, 217, 218, 219, 222
Arnaktauyok (Germaine Arnattaujuq), 223
Arnaquq-Baril, Alethea, ix, 63, 70, 91, 177, 179, 215, 218, 219
Artcirq, 177, 212
Arviat, 175
Asagaroff, Georg, 187
Ashevak, Kenojuak, 169, 173
asinnajaq (Isabella Rose Weetaluktuk), ix, x, 6, 7, 8, 11, 12, 84–108, 220, 221
Asivaqtiin (The Hunters), 174
At Our Place. See *Nunatinni*
Atanarjuat – The Fast Runner, 43, 49, 51, 57, 68, 116, 122, 176
Atlantic Satellite Network, 144
Aubert, Robin, 220
August, Bille, 205
Auksaq, Allen, 217
Aung-Thwin, Mila, 211
Avery, Katie Doane, 220
Avid, 155–162
Avingaq, Susan, ix, 19, 29, 45, 176, 214, 218
Axtell, Tom, 137

Baffin Island. *See* Qikiqtaaluk
Balikci, Asen, 173
Ballard, Carroll, 199
Balling, Erik, 192
Bang, Jette, 189, 195

Bang, Kirsten, 205
Bartlett, Captain Robert (Bob), 187
Baulu, Kat, ix, x, 6, 84, 103–108
Bear Facts, The, 177
Beaudine Jr., William, 196
Beaudry, Danielle, 207
Bech, Torben, 178, 213
Beechey Island. *See* Iluvialuit
Before Tomorrow, 43, 176
Belhumeur, Alain, 210
Betacam, 155
Betbeder, Sébastien, 220
Birdsall, Alfred Ward, 185
Blais, Gilles, 195
Blaise, Aaron, 210
Bonnière, René, 193
Borker, Merete, 196
Borre, Katrine, 200
Boulton, Laura, 172, 190
Boye, Ulla, 210
Brachmayer, Scott, 218
Brault, Nicolas, 210
British Columbia Arts Council, 64
Brown, Quentin, 173, 194
Buck, Ken, 199
Buckley, Rhonda, 212
Budgell, Anne, 199
Bulbulian, Maurice, 199
By Dog Sled Through Alaska. See *Med Hundeslæde gennem Alaska*

camera, 11–12, 15, 17, 21, 23, 29, 43, 55, 59, 60, 61, 63, 65, 67, 69, 91, 97, 111, 116, 119, 120, 121, 138, 141, 144, 154, 155, 156, 162, 171
Canada, ix, xiii, 6, 8, 9, 10, 11, 62, 64, 72, 73, 79, 80, 84, 98, 122, 127, 133, 134, 137, 170, 172, 173, 174, 175, 179
Canada Council for the Arts, 19, 29, 64
Canada Manpower, 140, 150, 151
Canada Media Fund, 179
Canadian Broadcasting Corporation, 8, 21, 47, 149, 150, 151, 153

CBC North, 174
Cannes Film Festival, 176
Canadian Heritage, Department of, 140
Canadian Radio-Television and
    Telecommunications Commission, 175
Carnegie Museum Alaska-Siberian Expedition,
    The. See *Alaska-Siberia Expedition, The*
CBC. *See* Canadian Broadcasting Corporation
Chamberland, Manon, 221
Charcot, Jean-Baptiste, 187, 188
Chorale, xiv
Christina Parker Gallery, 90
Christopher, Neil, 222
Chukchi, xiii, 9
Chukotka, xiii, 9, 10, 170
Churchill, Jane, 211
cinema, x, xiv, xv, 3, 4, 6, 7, 9–12, 21, 103, 118,
    119, 127, 128, 169, 176
Cinéma du Parc, 71
Cinémathèque Québécoise, 73
cinematography, 110, 111, 171, 172, 174
Cohen, Ari A., 216
Cohn, Norman, 17, 176, 200, 203, 212, 218
Cohn-Cousineau, Samuel, 47
Collardey, Samuel, 222
Columbia, Nancy, 170
Communication Canada (Department of
    Communication), 150, 151, 175
Concordia University, 89
Connolly, Marcia, 212, 214
Conseil des Arts et des Lettres du Québec, 73
Cornellier, Bruno, 75
Cousineau, Marie-Hélène, ix, x, 6, 7, 8, 14–57,
    66, 68, 176, 205, 208, 212, 215, 218, 219,
    222
Coyle, John T., 188
Cross, Daniel, 211
Cuarón, Jonás, 216
Curley, Koomuatuk, 218

Dahl, Kai R., 187
Dalsheim, Friedrich, 171, 188

Dawn, Norman, 187, 191
de Pencier, Miranda, 216, 222
Decolonizing Methodologies: Research and
    Indigenous Peoples, 3
Demand, Thomas, 125–126
Denmark, 9, 10, 122, 170, 171, 172, 173
Dicker, Christine, 135
Dicker, Joan, xi, xv
Digital Indigenous Democracy Project, 176
Dignard, Martin J., 208
directing, 41–47, 55, 66, 69, 80, 110–112, 115
documentary (film), 7, 17, 37–39, 47, 51, 78, 84,
    115, 116, 119–120, 125, 129–130, 140, 150,
    159, 162
Documentary Educational Resources, 174, 194
Dorfmann, Jacques, 203
Drums of Winter. See *Uksuum Cauyai*
Dwan, Allan, 187

Eason, B. Reeves, 188
Eastman, Gordon, 196
Echalook, Bobby, 211
Elder, Sarah, 174, 196, 197, 200
Elder(s), 29, 35, 41–45, 47, 57, 140, 144, 145,
    147, 159, 163–165
Emil i Lönneberga (*Emil of Lönneberga*), 111
Encyclopedia of the Documentary Film, 172, 173
Eneutseak, Esther, 169, 170
Engstfeld, Axel, 211
Erlingsson, Gísli Snær, 207
Ernst, Franz, 198
Escabana, 170
Eskimo (W.S. Van Dyke), 172
Eskimo Artist – Kenojuak, 173
Eskimo Arts and Crafts, 172
Eskimo, Der, 172
Eskimo Summer, 172
Eskimobaby, Das, 170
Esquimaux Dance, 170
Esquimaux Game, An, 170
Esquimaux Game of Snap-the-Whip, 170
Esquimaux Leap-Frog, 170

Esquimaux Village, 170
Esquimaux Village, The, 170
ethics, 65–78, 79–83, 105–106, 179
Europe, xv, 11, 58, 121, 122, 170, 178
Exercise Piulitsinik, 157
Eye of the Storm, 160
Eyes of the People. *See* Inuiaat Issat

Facebook, 43, 93, 116, 120
Fafard, Marc, 217
Feeney, John, 173, 192, 193
Ferrand, Carlos, 211
Film.GL, 178, 179
Finnie, Richard, 188
First American Art Magazine, 128
First Peoples Cinema: 1500 Nations, One Tradition, 178
Fitzmaurice, George, 188
Flaherty, Louise, 223
Flaherty, Robert, 12, 171, 172, 173, 187
Fleischer, Ujarneq, 213
Flucht ins weiße, Die, 172
Folger, Edward, 174, 197
Folger, Mosha, 218, 220, 221
France, 72, 173
Franck, Arnold, 188
Frank, Ivalo, 214
Franklin, Harry S., 192
Freuchen, Peter, 172
Friedberg, Louise, 214

Gagnon, Dominic, 71, 179, 219
Galster, Julius, 189
Gavron, Sarah, 216
Gayet-Tancrèd, Paul. *See* Samivel
Gaylor, Brett, 211
Gear, Glenn, 220
Germany, 86
Gies, Daniel, 222
Gjerstad, Ole, 205, 207, 215, 219
Greene, David, 204
Greenland. *See* Kalaallit Nunaat

Greenland Eyes Film Festival, 178
Greenwald, Barry, 200
Grønland 1914 I–III, 170
Grønlykke, Jacob, 205
Gulking, Cathy, 204

Halpern, Elliott, 204
Hamilton-Brown, Alex, 205
Hansen, Aka, 219
Hansen, Laila, 209
Hansen, Leo, 171, 187, 188
Hansen, Paul, 187, 189, 190, 191
Hansen, William, 200, 201
Hargrave, George, 206
Harper, Ray, 201
Hart, Roger, 196
Hartkopf, Stig, 205
Hasselbalch, Hagen, 191, 192
Hastrup, Jannik, 208
Haulli, Bruce, 212
Haxthausen, Tørk, 199
Healing Each Other. See *Saputjinik*
Heath, Joel, 215
Heilmann, Karsten, 110
Hendel, Lorenzo, 211
Henning-Jensen, Astrid, 192
Henning-Jensen, Bjarne, 192
Henoche, Echo, ix, 5, 220
Here and Now, 149
Heritage of Adventure, 171
Hermansen, Claus, 198
Hettasch family, 155
Hubbard, Bernard, 188, 189, 193
HF (High Frequency), 151
Hjort, Mette, 11
Hoedeman, Co, 196, 202
Høegh, Inuk Silis, 7, 8, 109–131, 206, 208, 209, 211, 212, 218, 219
Hollywood, 117, 128, 171, 172
Hopedale, xi, 133, 136, 137, 142, 152, 159, 164, 174
Høst, Per, 193

Hot Docs, 91
Housberg, Daniel, 199
Houston, James, 59
Houston, John, 206, 209, 211, 215
How to Build an Igloo, 172
Howe, John, 192
Hudson's Bay Company, 170
    RMS *Nascopie*, 170
Hughes, Ivan, 219
Husain, Aeyliya, 222
Hyde, Laurence, 194

I Am But a Little Woman, 177
Ichac, Marcel, 192
Idlout, Sarah, 211
Igloliorte, Heather, x, 88
Igloolik, 7, 15, 17, 19, 21, 29, 45, 47, 55, 175, 176
Igloolik Isuma. *See* Isuma
Iluvialuit, 85
imagineNATIVE Film+Media Arts Festival, 91, 178
Indigenous, xiv, 3, 5, 6, 9, 10, 39, 55, 61, 64, 65, 66, 67, 70, 71, 72, 74, 75, 76, 77, 89, 98, 174, 177, 179
Ingemann, Ulannaq, 220
Innu, xii, 174
Innuksuk, Nyla, 217, 219, 223
International Sami Film Institute, 179
Inuganguaq, 49
Inuiaat Issat, 178
Inuinnaqtun, xiii
Inuit Art Quarterly, 3, 176, 179
iNuit Blanche, ix, x, 4, 90, 96
Inuit Broadcasting Corporation, 17, 21, 27, 49, 136, 137, 138, 139, 149, 173, 175, 177, 178
Inuit Circumpolar Council, 9, 10
Inuit Communications Systems Limited, 137
Inuit Nunaat, xiv, 10–11, 170, 172
Inuit Nunangat, xiii, 4, 9, 10, 59–61, 63, 65, 67, 69–70, 79–80, 82, 85, 92, 169, 170, 172. *See also* Inuvialuit Nunangat, Nunatsiavut, Nunavik, Nunavut

Inuit Studies Conference, ix, x, 4, 6, 75
Inuit Tapiriit Kanatami (Inuit Tapirisat of Canada), xiii, xiv, 10, 175
Inukjuak, 60, 85, 99, 102
Inuksuk Project, The, 47
Inuktitut, xiii, 19, 21, 43, 80, 85, 107, 133, 134, 139–142, 144, 147–151, 156, 162–163, 176
Inuktun, xiv
Inuktut, x, xiii, xiv, 6, 7, 15, 172
Inupiaq, xiii, xiv, 172
Iñupiaq, xiv
Inuttitut (Inuttut), ix, xi, xiv, xv, 8, 132, 174, 175
Inuugatta Inuktuuqta Conference, 128
Inuvialuit Nunangat, xiii, 9, 67
Inuvialuktun, xiii
Iqaluit, 63
Iqaluit, 29, 127, 128, 173, 175, 177, 178
Iqaluk, Laura, 211
Iqaluktuuttiaq, 175
Irniq, Peter, 212
Isaac, Alexie, 199, 200
Isaac, Elisapie, 210
Isuma (Igloolik Isuma Productions), 51, 58, 63, 68, 128, 176, 177, 179
IsumaTV, 6, 177, 179
Ivalu, Julie, 17
Ivalu, Madeline, 7, 14–57, 176, 212, 218, 222

Jacobovici, Simcha, 204
Jensen, Kaj Mogens, 195
Joint Task Force Atlantic, 157
Jørgensen, Pipaluk, 217, 221
Jørgensen, Teit, 199
Journals of Knud Rasmussen, The, 51, 104, 176
Julén, Staffan, 199, 212
Julén, Ylva, 199

Kaganovsky, Lilya, 11
Kalaallisut, xiii, xiv, 10
Kalaallit Nunaat, xiii, xiv, 7, 8, 9, 109, 170, 171, 172, 173, 178, 179. *See also* Nuuk, Qaqortoq

Kalaallit Nunaata Radioa, 117–119, 175
Kalleo (Holwell), Rosina, 135
Kalleo, William, 135
Kamerling, Leonard, 174, 195, 196, 197, 200
Kamerling, Norman, 195
Karetak, Elisapee, 207
Kasudluak, Linus, 211
katingavik inuit arts festival, ix, x, 4
Katznelson, David, 216
Kaufman, Philip, 196
Kaukai, Eva, 221
Keaton, Buster, 187
Kidd, Dorothy, 137
kinatuinamot illengajuk, 9, 135
Kinngait, 173, 177
Kirkeby, Per, 195, 196, 200
Kitikmeot Region, 173
Kjærulff-Schmidt, Palle, 199
Kleinschmidt, Frank E., 171, 185, 187
Kleist, Malik, 215, 218, 223
Knutzen, Jan, 197
Koperqualuk, Gabriel Nuraki, 222
Kotierk, Jessica, 217
Kreelak, Martin, 205
Kristensen, Birgitte, 216
Künheim, Paul, 188
Kunnuk, Carol, 176, 215
Kunuk, Mary, 31, 205, 208, 212
Kunuk, Zacharias, 17, 29, 63, 116–117, 122, 176, 200, 201, 203, 204, 206, 209, 211, 212, 213, 215, 218, 220, 221, 222, 223
Kurosawa, Akira, 196
Kuujjuaq, 84

Labrador Inuit Association, 153, 160
Labrador Land Use Conference, 174
Labrador Resources Advisory Council, 174
Labradorimiut, 138, 140, 141, 144, 152, 159, 160, 162, 163, 175
Laliberté, Morgane, 199
Land of the Long Day, 172
Languepin, Jean-Jacques, 191

Larsen, Berda, 223
Larsen, Sidse Torstholm, 222
Lau, Lasse, 221
Leaf, Caroline, 196
Lemieux, Hector, 192
Lemire, Jean, 210
Lennert-Sandgreen, Angayo, 213
Leo, Arvo, 218
Lepage, Marquise, 212
Leroux-Lévesques, Aude, 220
Liberman, Xavier, 219
Library of Congress (USA), 170, 175
Lichtenberg, Nic, 195
Lindgren, Astrid, 111
Littauer, Karen, 205, 209
Living Stone, The, 173
Living with Giants, 60–61
Lost in the Arctic, 170
Lougheed, Kendall, 137, 145
Lucky. See *Upinnaqusittik*
Lumaajuuq, 177
Lund-Sørensen, Sune, 195
Lynch, David, 115
Lynge, Aqqaluk, 195, 196

MacGillivray, William D., 211
MacKenzie, Scott, 11
Mackenzie, Shelagh, 200
MacLean, Andrew Okpeaha, 215
MacMillan, Commander Donald Baxter, 171, 186
Magidson, Mike, 211, 216, 219
Magny, Pierre, 203
Maillard, Yves, 217
Makkik, Blandina, x, 6, 7, 15–57, 169
Makkivik Corporation, 8
Makkovik, 133, 136, 137, 142, 172, 174
Mala, Ray (Wise), 171
Malaurie, Jean, 196
Maliglutit, 41, 51
Man: A Course of Study, 173
Mangaard, Annette, 215

Mannstaedt, Per Ingolf, 199
Markham, Nigel, 144, 199, 205, 208, 209, 216
Marton, Andrew, 188
Mary-Rousselière, Guy, 173
Mason, Bill, 196
Massot, Claude, 201, 203
Matter, Fred, 188
Mauro, Ian, 215
McIntyre, Lindsay, 207, 208, 209, 210, 211, 213, 214, 216, 219, 220, 221
McMahon, Kevin, 204
McNair-Landry, Sarah, 217
Med hundeslæde gennem Alaska, 171
Melting Barricades, 130
Memorial University, x, xi, 161
Extension Service, 174
Merkeratsuk, Beni, 154
Metro-Goldwyn-Mayer (MGM), 172
Michael, Mosha, 174, 196, 197
Michelin, Ossie, 223
Millar, David, 194
MiniDV, 155
Mitchell, Wayne, 195
Mittimatalik, 175
Mohawk, 105
Mong, William V., 170, 185
Montreal, x, xii, 8, 11, 17, 21, 23, 37, 39, 47, 58, 66, 71, 82, 83, 84, 86, 87, 89, 91, 92, 94, 95
Morton, Ella, 223
Moulins, Joe, 206

Nagle, Pat, 136, 137
Nain, xi, xv, 8, 109, 132, 133, 136, 137, 142, 147, 150, 152, 159, 160, 164, 171, 174
Nanook of the North, 12, 171, 173, 175, 178
Nascopie. See Hudson's Bay Company
National Aboriginal Communications Society, 139, 175
National Film Board of Canada, x, 6, 8, 17, 84, 144, 160, 172, 173, 174, 177
National Film Registry (USA), 175, 177

Native Communications Society of the NWR (Native Communications Society of the Western Northwest Territories), 175, 178
Natsik Hunting, 174
Neilsen, Astra, 170
Netsilik Eskimo Series, 173
Newfoundland Independent Filmmakers Co-operative, 161
Nguyen, Kim, 220
Nielsen, Jørn Kjær, 197
NIFCO. *See* Newfoundland Independent Filmmakers Co-operative
nikku, 95
Ningeok, Willia, 211
Ningiuk, Caroline, 211
Nirvana, 130
Noldan, Svend, 188
North, 8, 39, 59, 60, 61, 63, 65, 66, 76, 86, 94, 102, 111, 155, 156
Northern Native Broadcast Access Program, 140
Northwest Passage, 85
Norton, W. Kay, 191
NSCAD University, 84, 92
Nunalijjuaq, 72
Nunatinni, 176
Nunatsiakmiut, 173
Nunatsiavummiutut, xiii, xv, 8
Nunatsiavut xii, xiii, xiv, xv, 4, 5, 6, 7, 8, 9, 67, 109, 132, 133, 134, 137, 152, 160, 169, 170, 171, 172, 174, 175. *See also* Hopedale, Makkovik, Nain, Postville, Rigolet, Torngat Mountains, Voisey's Bay
Nunatsiavut Government, x, 4, 133, 137, 160
NunatuKavut, xii, 9
Nunavik, xiii, 6, 7, 9, 67, 84, 85, 87, 102, 116, 120, 171, 175. *See also* Inukjuak, Kuujjuaq
Nunavimmiutut, xiii
Nunavut xiii, 7, 9, 12, 47, 58, 63, 67, 116, 120, 169, 173, 174, 175, 176, 177, 178, 179. *See also* Arviat, Iluvialuit, Igloolik, Iqaluit, Iqaluktuuttiaq, Kinngait, Kitikmeot

Region, Mittimatalik, Pangnirtung, Qamani'tuaq, Qikiqtaaluk
Nunavut Animation Lab, 177
Nunavut Film Commission, 67, 177
Nunavut Film Development Corporation, 173, 177, 179
Nunavut Independent Television Network, 176, 177
Nunavut Media Arts Centre, 178
Nuuk, 8, 109, 127, 179
Nuuk International Film Festival, 122, 179
Nuummioq, 116, 178

Obed, Bonna, 154
Obed, Martin, 161
Obed, Sarah, 153, 154
Odsbjerg, Anders, 197
of the North, 71–75, 179
Oh, Gyu, 177, 215
Ohaituk, Dora, 211
Ohaituk, Rita-Lucy, 211
OKâlaKatiget Society, xi, 5, 8, 132–165, 174, 175
Okkumaluk, Rose, 21
Olsen, Erik Ole, 192
Olsen, Tupaarnaq Rosing, 216
Ommatimmiutagennaniattavut – IkKaumset Hebaronimit Notitausimanningit (Forever in Our Hearts – Memories of the Hebron Relocation), 144, 161

Packwood, Keith, 205
Pallesen, Per, 200
Palos Brudefærd (The Wedding of Palo), 115, 116, 171
Pangnirtung, 173
Pangnirtung, 177
Panorama of the Esquimaux Village, 170
Papatsie, Ame, 177, 215
Parbst, Karin, 205
Parks Canada, 158
Paskievich, John, 202
Paulmann, Friedrich, 187

Péronard, Emile Hertling, 220
Petrie, Duncan J., 11
Petroff, Boris, 192
Pevney, Joseph, 192
Piantanida, Thierry, 211
Pilon, Benoît, 212, 219
Pilskog, Sturla, 222
Piugattuq, Noah, 21
Platoú, Kunuk, 110, 207
Poisey, David, 201
Porter, Edwin S., 170, 184
Postville, 136, 137
Poulette, Michel, 216
printmaking, 60, 89
Productions Réalisations Indépendantes de Montréal, 73
Project Inukshuk, 175
pualok, 87, 93
Pulp Fiction, 115
Puskas, Stephen Agluvak, ix, 6, 7, 8, 11, 58–83, 179, 220

Qaggiavik, 27
Qaggiq, 138, 175
Qallunaat (Qallunaaq), xv, 25, 27, 49, 65, 68, 70, 84, 85, 93, 101, 103
Qallunaat! Why White People Are Funny, xv, 61
Qalluplluit, 31
Qalupalik, 177
Qamani'tuaq, 175
qamutiik, 101
Qaqortoq, 8, 109, 110, 121
qarmmaq, 49
Qikiqtaaluk, 85, 172
Quassa, Paul, 201
Quebec, xiii, 6, 11, 61, 62, 64, 67, 70–71, 72, 73–74, 134, 176, 179
Quebec Arts Council, 64
Qulaut, Elizabeth, x, 7
Qulitalik, Pauloosie, 176, 200, 203, 204, 209
qulliq, 33

Radford, Tom, 211, 213
radio, 8, 15, 72, 117, 119, 121, 132, 133, 134, 135, 136, 137, 138, 139, 140, 141, 142, 145, 146, 146, 148, 150, 151, 153, 154, 161, 165, 174, 176
Radio Eye: Cinema in the North Atlantic, 1958–1988, The, 11
Rasmussen, Kenneth, 110
Rasmussen, Knud, 115, 171
Ray, Nicholas, 193
Raymont, Peter, 211
Reed, Patrick, 211
Reeve, William, 208
Rencontres Internationales du Documentaire de Montréal, 76
Rendez-vous Québec Cinéma, 71
Rickard, Paul M., 211
Rietveld, Laura, 219
Rigolet, xiv, 136, 137
Riml, Walter, 188
Rist, Sébastien, 220
Ritzau, Tue, 199
Robertson, Jack, 187
Romance of the Far Fur Country, 171
Rondot, Guilhem, 220
Ronild, Peter, 200
Roos, Jørgen, 172, 193, 194, 195, 198, 199, 200, 201, 205
Roos, Lise, 200
Rosbach, Marc Fussing, 117, 221
Rosing, Jens, 195
Rosing, Otto, 178, 213
Rossman, Earl, 187
Roth, Lorna, 173, 175
Roy, Gabrielle, 27–29
Rydbacken, Andreas, 214

S. Lubin, 170
Saladin, Guillaume, 208
Salkow, Sidney, 189
Samivel, 190
Sanavallianiq Isumagijaujunut – Building for

Dreams (Inuit Broadcasting Corporation), 178
Sandiford, Mark, xv, 212
Sands, Ezna, 219
Sanguya, Joelie, 215
Saputjinik, 161
Sarin, Vic, 203
Saturviit Inuit Women's Association of Nunavik, 87
Savard, Nancy Florence, 217
Schall, Heinz, 170, 185
Schnedler-Sørensen, Eduard, 186
Schnéevoigt, George, 187
Schuurman, Hubert, 196
Scott, Cynthia, 196, 199
Scott, Ewing, 188, 191
sculpture, 109, 114, 121, 123–125
Searchers, The. See *Maliglutit*
Secretary of State (Canada), 134, 136, 140–141
Selig Polyscope Company, 170
Sermeq Fonden, 178
Sharpsteen, Ben, 192
Sherman, Vincent, 192
Siegstad, Mike, 198, 199
Silis, Ivars, 203, 205, 208
Sixth Thule Expedition, 171
Slade, David, 212
Smith, Charles Martin, 211
Smith, Linda Tuhiwai, 3
Smith, Stephen A. 216
Smithsonian Institution, 178
Snow, Sasha, 208
Société de développement des entreprises culturelles, 64
Sol, 43–45, 66–68
Sooq Akersuuttugut, 130
Sorento, Kenneth, 223
Sorge, Ernst, 188
St. John's, ix, 11, 90, 154, 161, 162, 172
Stæhr, Lene, 219
Star, Jerry, 154
Stavrides, Stavros, 199

Steen, Lennart, 198
Stenport, Anna Westerståhl, 11
Stocking, Barbara, 199
Storch, Inuuteq, 220
SUMÉ – Mumisitsinerup Nipaa (The Sound of a Revolution), 112, 114–118, 120–121, 125–128, 130–131, 178
Summerville, Slim, 187
Sundance Film Institute, 179
Super 8, 116, 129, 173, 178
Sweetnam, Randy, 137
Swerhone, Elise, 200
Szucs, Julia, 216

Tagaq, Tanya, 12, 88, 178
Taggamiut Nipingat, 149
Takuginai, 49
Tala, 172
Tamânevugut, 144–145, 152, 159
Taqramiut Nipingat, 139, 175
Tarriaksuit, 35, 45–47
Tassinari, Patricia, 204
Telefilm Canada, 144
Tester, Frank, ix, 220
Thalbitzer, William, 170, 185
The Rooms Provincial Art Gallery, 172
Thompson, Lorraine, 153
Thompson, Niobe, 213
Thomsen, Sven, 195
Three Thousand, x, 8, 84, 106
Thule Expeditions. *See* Fifth Thule Expedition, Sixth Thule Expedition
Tia and Piujuq, 15, 35, 37, 45, 55
Till We Meet Again – Moravian Music in Labrador, 160
Timuti, 90, 104
Torngat Mountains, 85
Torngat Mountains National Park, 157–158
Toronto International Film Festival, 178
Tougas, Anne-Marie, 216
Townley, Sarah, 143
Trading into Hudson's Bay, 171

Traditional Seal Hunt in Nunatsiavut, A, 162
Tulugarjuk, Lucy, 7, 8, 14–57, 222
Tumit Production, 118
Tunumiit oraasiat, xiv, 171
Turkey, 173
Two Lovers and a Bear, 63

Ukiuktaqtumi, 64, 67, 77–78
Uksuum Cauyai – Drums of Winter, 177
Umqiḷir, 171
Underwood, Caroline, 210
Ungalaaq, Natar, 122, 208, 220
Unitas Fratrum – The Moravians in Labrador, 160
University of Bristol, 109, 110–111
Upinnaqusittik, 96
Uvagut TV, 6, 179
Uvanga, 37–39

Vakhrushev, Aleksei, 215, 221
Van Raalte, Sharon, 200
Van Valin, William, 185
Venice Biennale, 179
VHF (Very High Frequency), 151
VHS (Video Home System), 17, 143–144
Vibe, Christian, 193
Vidéographe, 73
Villinger, Bernhard, 187
Voisey's Bay, 152
von Fritsch, Gunther, 195
von Gunten, Matthias, 218
VTR (video tape recorder), 174

Wadman, Malte, 197
Walker, John, 213
Walker, Robert, 210
Wangel, Gunnar, 192
Wapikoni Mobile, 61
Ward, Vincent, 202
Warhol, Andy, 92
Waters, Katrina, 200
Wawatay, 134
Way of the Eskimo, The, 170

Weetaluktuk, Isabella Rose. *See* asinnajaq
Weetaluktuk, Jobie, x, 6, 8, 84–103, 211, 213, 214, 216
Wegener, Alfred, 187
Wegener, Else, 188
Weiner, Gerry, 141, 150
Wera, Françoise, 199
Wharram, Douglas, xi, xv
Whelan, Dianne, 214
White, Jerry, 11
Why We Fight. See *Sooq Akersuuttugut*
Wilkinson, Douglas, 172, 191, 192
Williams, Fran, xi, 6, 9 133–151, 161, 206
Williams, Jennie, 223
Withers, Denise, 202
Wivel, Anne Regitze, 212
Woods, Mark Kenneth, 220

Wrangel Island. *See* Umqiḷir
Wright, Jonathan, 177, 215
Wulff, Thorild, 186
Wyckoff, Harold M., 186

Yerxa, Michael, 220
Young, Robert, 173, 194
Youth Fusion, 61
YouTube, 75–76, 93, 179
Yupik, xiii, 9

Zad, Zacharias, 170
Zelcer, David, 153
Zetterling, Mai, 198
Zinner, Tinne, 221
Zweig, Alan, 220